MONSTERS BY TRADE

MONSTERS BY TRADE

Slave Traffickers

in Modern Spanish Literature

and Culture

Lisa Surwillo

Stanford University Press

Stanford, California

Stanford University Press
Stanford, California

Printed in the United States of America on acid-free, archival-quality paper.

Library of Congress Cataloging-in-Publication Data

Surwillo, Lisa, author.
Monsters by trade : slave traffickers in modern Spanish culture / Lisa Surwillo.
pages cm
Includes bibliographical references and index.
ISBN 978-0-8047-8879-3 (cloth) | ISBN 978-1-5036-1364-5 (paper)
1. Spanish literature--19th century--History and criticism. 2. Spanish literature--20th century--History and criticism. 3. Slave trade in literature. 4. Slavery in literature. 5. Slave trade--Spain--History--19th century. 6. Slavery--Cuba--History--19th century. 7. Spain--Colonies--America--History--19th century. 8. Collective memory--Spain--History--20th century. I. Title.
PQ6073.S53S87 2014
860.9'3552--dc23

2014007325

ISBN 978-0-8047-9183-0 (electronic)

Typeset by Bruce Lundquist in 10.9/13 Adobe Garamond

Contents

Acknowledgments

While writing this book, I benefited from interactions with a number of treasured colleagues who encouraged me to think harder about the project. Their insights enriched this work beyond what I could ever have attained in solitude, and they assisted me in countless ways, from answering specific questions to engaging in sometimes seemingly interminable conversations about the minutiae of the nineteenth century. Special thanks are due to Hester Blum, Mary Coffey, Dru Dougherty, Bradley Epps, Tania Gentic, Sepp Gumbrecht, Tamar Herzog, Ruth Hill, Michael Iarocci, John Lipski, Ruth MacKay, Susan Martin-Márquez, Jenny Martinez, Michael Predmore, Ralph Rodriguez, Sherry Roush, Gabriella Safran, Carmen Sanjuan-Pastor, Priya Satia, Christopher Schmidt-Nowara, and Akiko Tsuchiya. I would also like to thank the participants of the "Treating the Trata" colloquium held at Stanford University who shared their new work and raised provocative questions about how we deal with the slave trade in Hispanic Studies. In addition, the arguments I propose in this book were strengthened immensely by the suggestions of an anonymous reader who reviewed the manuscript for Stanford University Press with real dedication and to whom I am sincerely grateful.

This book emerged from the archives, and my successful exploration of documents was carried out thanks to generous funding from a variety of sources. I gratefully note the support of the Gilder Lerman Institute; the Program for Cultural Cooperation between Spain's Ministry of Education, Culture and Sports and United States Universities; the Africana Research Center at the Pennsylvania State University; the Institute for Arts and Humanities at the Pennsylvania State University; and a Hewlett Faculty Grant. I am forever indebted to the staff at The Bancroft Library, where this project first began, and to Adán Griego of the Stanford Libraries, who sets a new standard for academic librarians.

I would also like to acknowledge several undergraduate and graduate research assistants, including Ruth Alonso, Mark Bajus, and Kelvin Smith, and especially Nicole Barraza with whom I shared great debates on nineteenth-century literature. I also thank the Unió General de Treballadors de Catalunya for providing me with correspondence from their archive and Iván Larra Plaza for sharing his work and his vision with me and for granting permission to include his art here.

This book has only become a material reality through the support of editors Norris Pope and Stacy Wagner at Stanford University Press. The interventions of Ann Gelder and Alice Avery made this book more readable than it otherwise would have been.

I also am grateful to the Stanford University Work Life Office where a dedicated staff efficiently implements the university's progressive policies for untenured faculty with young children. Finally, this book never would have been written without the limitless patience and support of my husband and daughters.

A Note on Translation

Quotations from Spanish or Catalan maintain original spelling, punctuation, and grammar. Unless otherwise attributed in parenthetical citations, all translations were undertaken by Nicole Barraza and Lisa Surwillo.

MONSTERS BY TRADE

Introduction

Blanco White and Monsters of Coloniality

Books on nineteenth-century Spanish literature and culture have often begun by reciting the familiar debates: whether Spain underwent a liberal revolution; if the nation witnessed the rise of an authentic bourgeoisie; and why (or if) Spain's modernization remained "uneven." This book will not rehash these debates. Rather, it seeks to shift their terms by analyzing roles played by literature, art, and, more recently, leisure in exploring anxieties or cultivating silences around the fact that the modern, liberal nation of Spain, as well as several of its constituent parts, were a product (economic, political, cultural) of the particular nature of its post-1824 empire. That is, how might we tell the story of Spanish literature if an awareness of *coloniality* rather than a search for *modernity* were the privileged terms of analysis? Twentieth-century criticism has theorized how metropolitan Europe, more generally, was shaped by its colonies (consider the work of Hall, Said, and Fanon). Yet this framework has only recently come to bear on Spain in a systematic way, in no small part due to Franco's long dictatorship and the resulting contentious nature of the discourses over the Spanish nation(s) throughout the twentieth century.

Inspired by Walter Mignolo's theorization of the linkage of modernity and coloniality, this book follows the premise that a study of the culture and literature of modern Spain requires reading coloniality as inherent in their creation. Mignolo proposes a reading of coloniality that considers it "quite simply, the reverse and unavoidable side of 'modernity'—its darker side, like the part of the moon we do not see when we observe it from the earth" (22). Moreover, Mignolo notes that while histories of any number of European metropolises elide mention of their colonies, a history of Algeria, for example, "cannot avoid France" (51). Studies of

Cuba, following this logic, cannot (and do not) fail to refer to Spain; yet the reverse has not been equally true, especially in the realm of culture. The implications of this framework of occlusion are particularly grave for the nineteenth century, when Spain's claims to modernity were tenuous, in spite of its thriving Caribbean empire. This book analyzes Spanish literary, architectural, and artistic works that addressed unease over the means by which Cuba remained profitable and Spanish culture and Spain continued on a path to modernization. I intend to contribute to a more rounded understanding of modern Spain by recovering a nineteenth-century understanding of these interlocking systems of coloniality and peninsular modernity with slavery as their key. Indeed, the case of nineteenth-century Spain is unique among Atlantic powers in that although the empire was fundamental to the rise of early modern Spain, the arrangement was reformulated and the slave trade proved most influential in shaping Spanish modernity after it was declared illegal. I therefore return to the debates and tensions over the price of modernity as they were articulated in literary works of the nineteenth and early twentieth centuries, when modernity/coloniality had not yet been fully decoupled into the categories of "domestic" and "foreign."

From the Spanish perspective, the nineteenth century is bracketed by two major imperial disasters: the independence of mainland North, Central, and South America and the Spanish-American War of 1898. Until 1898 Spain retained the most profitable real estate in the world: the slave economy of the sugar-producing, "ever-faithful" isle of Cuba. Slavery in Cuba is among the most important phenomena of the nineteenth century, influencing various dimensions of human life—cultural, social, political, economic, psychological, and moral, as well as its fundamental biological conditions—in the metropolis as well as in the colonies. According to historian Enriqueta Vila Vilar, "La cuestión esclavista en la España del siglo XIX, íntimamente unida a la situación colonial, es uno de los temas más espinosos, controvertidos y densos de todo el panorama político de la segunda mitad de esta centuria y difícilmente podrá encontrarse un acontecimiento externo o interno que de forma directa o indirecta no esté afectado por este hecho." (Vila Vilar and Vila Vilar, 11; The issue of slavery in nineteenth-century Spain, intimately tied to the colonial situation, is one of the thorniest, most controversial, and dense subjects across the political landscape of the second half of this century and one will hardly be able to find an external or internal event that was not affected by this fact directly or indirectly.) Vila Vilar wrote of the institution of slavery, but the same observations hold true for the even more controversial issue of the transatlantic slave trade.

Because of geopolitical divides in academic specializations, slavery and the slave trade have been studied, quite rightly, in the contexts of Cuban, Puerto Rican, and North American literature, but they have not been considered in relation to peninsular society, culture, and literature. The slave trade is, in fact, among the most overlooked topics in cultural and literary studies of the Spanish nineteenth century. What is peculiar about colonial Cuba is not the institution of slavery—which lasted until 1863 in the Dutch colonies, 1865 in the United States, and 1888 in Brazil, for example—but the simultaneously illegal and lucrative transatlantic slave trade that fed it. The transatlantic slave trade was carried out by *negreros*—slave ship captains—but this same word was also used to describe the capitalists who financed and masterminded slaving expeditions to Africa and then managed the smuggling of contraband men and women onto the island. These businessmen created huge fortunes and vast networks of influence that extended across insular (Cuba) and peninsular Spain. The traffic in Black Africans primarily provided labor for the island's sugar plantations. It was also a means for the imperial government to manipulate the racial composition of the colonial population and foster a sense of need, among White Cubans who feared a repetition of the Haitian Revolution, for the presence of the Spanish military.

The nineteenth-century transatlantic slave trade is unique for several reasons. First, it was newly illegal in this period, and much of the North Atlantic world—excepting Spain and, to a lesser degree, the United States—was united in working toward its suppression. In *Slave Trade and the Origins of International Human Rights Law*, Jenny Martinez recently argued that the birth of modern human rights tribunals dates from the international mixed courts that tried alleged slave traders. Second, the slave trade was incredibly successful. In spite of international treaties, mixed courts and active British interception of slave ships, between the late eighteenth century and 1867, 780,000 enslaved Africans reached Cuban shores, equivalent to the numbers that had arrived in all of Spanish America during the previous two centuries.[1] Third, the commerce was extremely lucrative: Luis Alonso has calculated that profits from the transatlantic slave trade to Cuba came to more than $58 million between 1821 and 1867, using the value of the dollar in 1821–25.

The nation-state of modern Spain was literally nourished by its slave economy and by the protected markets this economy entailed: Spain saw profits from the island directly, and metropolitan producers in all regions benefited from the captive markets guaranteed by protectionism. Indeed, positions on the markets and abolition crossed lines of allegiances. Christopher Schmidt-Nowara has demonstrated how debates over slavery were inseparable from those dividing camps between protectionism and free-trade in Spain (*Empire and Antislavery*, 57). Historically, Spain was by no means unique in its economic dependence on Antillean sugar. Before the Haitian Revolution, more than one-fifth of the metropolitan bourgeoisie and one-third of the French population were engaged in commercial activity related to the slave economy.[2] But in spite of imperial Spain's long and complex relationship with its American territories, the sugar and slave economy of the nineteenth century marked a new chapter in transatlantic relations—most importantly because it was built upon a decidedly illegal trade in human cargo.

Three major treaties between Spain and England changed the nature but not the fact of the slave trade: the treaty of September 23, 1817, abolished the trade north of the equator; that of May 30, 1820, abolished the trade south of the equator; and that of June 28, 1835, reiterated laws that Spain had no intention of honoring. Spain continued to transport Africans to its Antillean colonies (mostly Cuba) averaging about ten thousand people per year (totaling six hundred thousand between 1816 and 1867). Many in Spain rejected the idea that the trade was anything but legitimate, holding that Great Britain had coerced Spain into signing the treaties, or that Spain had only acceded to them as part of a long-term plan to recover its prominent position in the Atlantic. Some Spanish attitudes regarding British pressures on slave policies in the Caribbean, informed by a centuries-old rivalry, viewed the abolition of the slave trade as a ploy on the part of England to continue a Caribbean conquest (starting with Jamaica in 1655 and followed by Havana in 1762). In the words of Juan Bernardo O'Gavan, the treaty was "arrancado á nuestra debilidad" (seized because of our weakness), and as a result, Spain was subjected to a foreign tribunal who would "nos fiscalice, nos *inquisicione*, y nos condene dentro de nuestro propio territorio, á pesar de estar declarado *libre é independiente*" (10–11, original emphasis; try us, *inquisition* us, and condemn us within our own territory, in spite of it having been declared *free and independent*). King Fernando VII of Spain used the indemnity of four hundred thousand British pounds sterling paid to him by Britain for agreeing to suppress the slave trade to purchase warships from Czar Alexander of Russia as part of a plan to resume control of the former American colonies, rather than to modernize Cuban agriculture.[3] What might have happened had these ships not arrived with rotting hulls is one of the great "what-ifs" in the history of the Western Hemisphere. Even without the Russian fleet, however, the Spanish king intended to expand colonial wars. For example, the Spanish continued to attempt the Reconquest of Mexico in 1821–29, even after officers dispatched to the Americas, led by Rafael de Riego, rebelled in Andalucía in 1820. In other words, abolition of the trade in 1817 was but a strategic step in the Spanish monarchy's much larger struggle for control over the Atlantic world.

Reformers on the side of the law supported the treaties with England against unofficial (but protected) corruption. For example, Wenceslao Ayguals de Izco (who is the subject of Chapter 1 in this study) denounced María Cristina (wife of Fernando VII and mother of Isabel II) and her vast network of corruption in *Palacio de los crímenes: ó el pueblo y sus opresores* (1855), comparing the government's oppression of peninsular citizens with various colonial practices, including human trafficking. The queen mother was, in fact, "the head of an influential and wealthy 'slave-trafficking society' [*sociedad negrera*] based in Madrid with partners and agents in Cuba" (La Verdad, 5; qtd. in Quiroz, 487). Both literature and the daily press discussed the vitality of the outlawed trade. Spaniards living in the Peninsula were thus not ignorant of the trade and its role in maintaining Cuban slavery, increasing sugar production, fortifying the royal treasury, and stimulating peninsular trade (especially because of the trade restrictions on the Caribbean). As a structural principle of the empire in general, the slave trade influenced how Spaniards in the metropolis understood their cities, societies, and culture. To that end, this book focuses much less on 1898 than on works that explore ambiguity over the practices of empire and the fear of a colonial control of Spain, as well as a persistent disavowal that has had real implications for understanding the various nations that comprise Spain. Much has been written explaining how a national consciousness was formed in the early nineteenth century and the cultural implications of such a transformation, both for Spain as a whole as well as for stateless nations within Spanish borders, such as Catalonia. Yet from traditional studies of Spanish culture, so rooted in "nationist" traditions, one might have believed that peninsular literature drew neat lines between home and abroad and that this organizing principle of modern Spanish finance and society was of marginal concern, at best.

Studies in the field of "New Imperial History," Edward Said's *Culture and Imperialism*, and Christopher Miller's *The French Atlantic Triangle* provide models for such integrative work on former empires that are currently reassessing their pasts. In *The Conquest of History*, Schmidt-Nowara has analyzed the development of a particular narrative in Spanish historiography that naturalized the understanding of Spain-as-empire and Spain-as-nation. Literature is vital to this project because, while facts can be and are recovered, literature as a space of fantasy provides a locus for imagining what was generally known but officially unacknowledged. Only five years ago Alda Blanco noted:

> In spite of the fact that Spain's nineteenth- and early twentieth-century literary landscape is dotted with colonial artifacts (places, commodities from its overseas colonies, literary characters in narratives and plays that take place in the Americas or Africa), critics and scholars rarely perceive the underlying imperial texts or, put another way, the inscriptions of empire in the cultural production of a nation that continued to be, in spite of its clearly diminished stature and size, the metropolis of an empire. ("Spain at the Crossroads," 5)

Concerns regarding this oversight have been voiced by others, too. More than a decade ago, Silvia Bermúdez noted that "while Paul Gilroy's *The Black Atlantic* evaluated the British empire's role in the slave trade, no such study can be found within Spanish Cultural Studies. This is a very telling void since there is a multitude of cultural artifacts—the musical form of the 'Habaneras' comes to mind—that would allow us to access that repressed historical memory of Spain's Atlantic imperialist past" (178). There has been a sea change in the approach to the nineteenth-century empire in Spanish literary and cultural studies in recent years. Michael Iarocci broke new ground in this line of thinking with his reading of *Don Álvaro*, arguing that "rather than separating modernity and coloniality [the play] represents them as two sides of the same coin. . . . [Alvaro] is a reminder of modernity's roots in empire and colonialism" (134). Victor Sánchez, Brad Epps, as well as Alda Blanco herself, among others, have worked extensively in this direction.[4] In her most recent work, Blanco specifically tackles the disjuncture between current analyses of nineteenth-century Spain as a nation without an imperial identity and nineteenth-century Spain's understanding of itself as an empire (*Cultura y conciencia*, 20).

The nineteenth-century colonial project had a very real economic and cultural impact on Spain's development and place, in both the Atlantic and European worlds. Nevertheless, when the empire has been read into modern Spanish culture, it is usually within a discourse of decline, loss, or, most importantly, disaster. In particular, reflections on empire in nineteenth-century Spain tend to gravitate toward the "disaster" of the Spanish-American War of 1898. Angel Loureiro specifies that, in fact, it is in the second half of the nineteenth century when the view of Spanish history as a decidedly downward trajectory becomes commonplace ("Spanish Nationalism," 66). As this perspective gained traction, it obscured—and has continued to obscure—the other roles empire played in Spanish literature. Loureiro sees the loss of the colonies as a constant presence in modern Spain: "A nation beset with problems of self-understanding and self-esteem, Spain has been haunted for two centuries by the specter of its former colonies" ("Spanish Nationalism," 65). In spite of (and, indeed, to a great extent, because of) this haunting, Spain remained committed to its imperial agenda throughout the nineteenth century, as its campaigns in Santo Domingo, Africa, and the Guerra del Pacífico demonstrate. Cuba and other territories were not simply part of a culture framed in decadence but also constitutive of modernity and the nation as it evolved in the nineteenth century. As well as a legacy of the past, the colony was a source of power.

However, the discourse of decadence was not a product of the collapse of the nineteenth-century empire. Critiques of colonialism began centuries before; as Ricardo Padrón has written, many Spaniards felt that expansion into the New World and "acquiring its gold and silver represented nothing less than the downfall of their national culture, its disastrous surrender to monstrous avarice" (13). In Spain, as in France and Britain, eighteenth-century theorists identified Spanish degeneration as a result of coloniality, emphasizing a corrupting addiction to precious metals, the destruction of native American peoples, and inefficient systems of commerce as the sources behind the Iberians' decadence (see Pagden). In other words, the idea that the process of colonization had somehow infected metropolitan Spain and jeopardized its economic and political development (if not exactly modernization) was more than a century old by the time Cuba assumed a central role in modern Spain. Neither imperial malfeasance nor fear of coloniality were nineteenth-century inventions, although they were reshaped in the later century.

Both political conservatives and economic liberals exploited the Cuban system. For example, Juan Álvarez Mendizábal, one of the statesmen most responsible for the liberalization of the Spanish economy, was accused in 1837 of shady dealings in the Cuban economy (Fradera, *Colonias para después*, 163).[5] The colonial project—of which *negreros* were crucial members—was central not only to the liberal regime in a political sense but also to capitalism itself. A study of Spanish literature that fails to take this aspect of modern, liberal Spain into account is one-sided and, in viewing the Americas as separate, too strongly determined by the consequences of the wars of independence. By contrast, my work aims to account for the place of empire and the practices of its retention, in everyday peninsular life, both past and present.

This study begins in the second decade of the nineteenth century when the Napoleonic occupation of Spain made it a veritable colony of France and the Cádiz Congresses undertook to redefine the terms of empire, Spanishness, citizenship, and nation.[6] The American colonies began to secure their independence (Venezuela in 1819, Mexico in 1821, and Bolivia in 1825). These years also witnessed a profound transfer of wealth, knowledge, and technology from the former Saint-Domingue to Cuba, following the Haitian Revolution, resulting in the latter's refashioning into the most lucrative land on the globe. This is also the period, of course, of the gradual legal abolition of the transatlantic slave trade.

The slave trader addressed in this book differs in representation, if not in kind, from earlier periods. There had always been an illegal contraband trade in all sorts of commodities (including men and women) to the Americas. While only specific Spanish towns and merchants were allowed to import a variety of goods to the Americas (papers, shoes, wheat, and so forth), numerous renegade merchants pirated these items, circumventing the payment of either taxes or privileges. In this sense, an illegal slave trade always existed, as such merchants introduced Africans on the American marketplace without the authorization of the Spanish crown (Quiroz, 480). That is, the illegal slave trade grew out of a culture that had previously accommodated—in its structure and processes of consumption—piracy and contraband, corruption, and bribery.

In 1765, as will be discussed later in Chapter 4, the Spanish crown extended the right to trade with the colonies to all peninsular Spaniards. In 1789, Carlos III liberalized imperial policies further, transforming the slave trade into a free-market enterprise: no longer did merchants have to acquire an "asiento," or permit. Such changes in policy established new practices that characterized the trade for the subsequent century. Josep Fradera notes that two hundred thousand enslaved Africans were legally imported between 1790 and 1820: this influx solidified a trend that set into motion dramatic changes to the social, racial, and labor relations for the Caribbean islands under Spanish control (*Colonias*, 89).[7] The subsequent (il)legitimate trade was—even for those who defended it—profoundly ambiguous, as the slave trade kept Cuba Spanish (through its racial policy) and a number of influential Spaniards wealthy. In literature the figure of the slave trader embodied this ambivalence toward modernity and the conditions that forged modern Spain. He was, simultaneously, a symbol of Spanish defiance of the British maritime ascendency, a conduit of wealth for the empire, the occult force behind the government, and an outlaw, in many ways beyond the control of Cubans or the Spanish government. By studying this figure, I attempt to accomplish two goals: first, to understand how the slave trade was debated; second, to think beyond "Spain as nation" in the nineteenth century. That is, by reconsidering the nineteenth-century empire as it was carried out in the name of the nation, I hope to contribute to a reevaluation of the extent to which the empire made the nation. This process was not only economic and political (as has been amply documented) but also a means by which the nation became constructed through the discourses of "home" and domesticity to shore up the boundary between empire and colony, at a time when wealthy, influential Cuba was, arguably, of greater geopolitical importance than the Peninsula.

Indeed, Fradera identifies the "imperial debacle" of the early nineteenth century as the starting point for modern nation building around the concept of Spain. In other words, for this historian, it was not the occupation of the Peninsula by a foreign (that is, French imperial) army and resistance to that army, but rather the victory of the American republics that sparked the project of modern Spain. "It is precisely the imperial ideal's continuing validity that explains the lack of a recognizably nationalist or proto-nationalist movement in Spain before the nineteenth century" ("After Spain," 166). But the transition from empire to nation was not a swift, clean break with the past. "Spain" was shaped by its nineteenth-century empire—not just as a modern economic unit or political system (a liberalism paid for, in part, by the colonial system) but also as a cultural field. Yet since the reformulation of Europe in the second half of the twentieth century, analyses of Spanish culture have privileged a perspective that emphasized Spain's place within the European community. In recent years historians and literary critics have begun to crack this monolithic story; for example, Susan Martin-Márquez, in *Disorientations*, analyzed the Spanish recovery of its Andalusi past and demonstrated the influence that this cultural project had in the contemporary colonialist projects in Africa. However, the slave trade has remained at the margins of

Spanish culture, even as the empire is slowly recentered. Unlike England, or even France, Spain has no claim to humanitarian magnanimity: its unapologetic adherence to the trade confirmed its Black Legend reputation even as this adherence made modern Spain politically viable. The grand narrative of nation building is complicated when we reconsider the nineteenth-century empire; the role of literature in both constructing and questioning the national narrative is similarly complex. In nineteenth-century fiction, the slave trader often embodied this complexity, representing the monstrous form of the state: an imperiled empire, complicit with Black Legend stereotypes, but within the capitalist framework that enabled the empire to flourish.

In reconsidering modern Spain's roots in its nineteenth-century imperial practices, I first examine how the slave trade was discussed and debated in literature during the nineteenth century. I then analyze the ways these issues have resurfaced and been transformed through literary and cultural practices in the late twentieth and twenty-first centuries. Fernando VII may have decreed in 1817, that slavery "lejos de ser perjudicial para los negros transportados de Africa a América, les proporcionaba el beneficio de ser instruidos en el conocimiento del Dios verdadero y de la única religión" (Real Cédula, 19 diciembre 1817; far from being detrimental for Blacks transported from Africa to America, provided them the benefit of being instructed in the knowledge of the true God and the only religion). But in literary works the immorality of the slave trade was rarely in doubt. In fiction, the trade presented an economic puzzle, based on the assumption that the *trata* was the sole means to guarantee Spain's control over the colonies, in particular the "pearl of the Antilles," Cuba.

As Stuart Hall has written, "colonization was never simply external to the societies of the imperial metropolis. It was always inscribed deeply within them" (246). Literature is one place where this phenomenon is manifested, and the colonizing experience in modern Spain's cultural origins is revisited. The slave trader and the deeply emotional responses and anxieties he evoked in the public imagination are represented with surprising complexity in numerous literary works from the nineteenth century through today. The colonizing experience was much more than a simple binary between metropolis and colony (Hall, 247), and the Spanish treatment of the slave trader illuminates the degree to which metropolitans understood that complexity. Slave traders were many different things: they were monsters by trade according to Blanco White, or vile criminals who flaunted international law, but later some came to be seen as influential men either whose business acumen fueled the metropolitan economy or whose aggressive politics subjected the metropolis to the colony. More recently, they are remembered in contemporary depictions as pioneers of the American Dream. If empire was unthinkable without slavery, it was the *negrero* who kept the empire afloat in the literature of the nineteenth century and drew together geopolitical fantasy and ethical anxieties.

The common understanding of slavery and the slave trade as a Cuban issue is also part of the cultivation of a European, domestic frame for Spain-as-nation. Slaves were not foreign to Spanish domesticity in the sixteenth or the nineteenth centuries; thus it is not of merely anecdotal importance to note African figures (including Juan Parejo) in the work of Diego Velázquez or the picaresque landscape of *Lazarillo de Tormes*. By the nineteenth century, slavery and Afro-Spaniards were seen as an importation from the colonies, associated with men who had made their fortunes abroad, even as slaves—or Afro-Hispanic servants—represented the absorption of the colonial into the metropolitan "home." Christopher Miller notes that for the same period in France, "the colonies and its slaves were out of sight and out of mind" (xi), a truth that cannot, however, be applied to Spain where the iron-fisted hold on the Antilles was consciously maintained by manipulation of race, slavery, and the power of slave traders. (For Spain, the American Dream was thriving until well into the twentieth century.) The slave trade and the corrupt avenues for wealth that it created added a particular incentive to the hemisphere of opportunity. A position in the notoriously corrupt Cuban customs house was the bureaucrat's dream, and countless novels capitalize on that fantasy.

Literature gave space to imagine the best and worst of the slave trader and his domain, but it existed alongside very explicit descriptions of reality. For example, in 1858, Dionisio Alcalá Galiano, a member of the conservative pro-Spanish party in Cuba, wrote the following description of the island in order to clarify colonial conditions for a peninsular readership:

> Hé aquí la ocasión de soltar otra de esas verdades que escuecen, pero que conviene oir, porque no es dable ni el desmentirlas ni aun siquiera el disimularlas. El pais es negrero. Todo lo que se diga en contra es una farsa, como antes ya he insinuado; y salvo algunas pocas individualidades sinceras (entre cuyo número he de incluirme) no hay casi un habitante de Cuba que no sea cómplice moral en este género de contrabando. Si unos son sus agentes; otras son sus instigadores; y los demas aplauden desde afuera cuando

> propone el aumento de brazos. Entre criollo y peninsular no existe aquí [in this issue] la menor diferencia, escepto la del oficio á cada cual corresponde su suerte. (112)
>
> (Here is the occasion to release another of those truths that sting, but that should be heard, because it is not feasible to refute or to even conceal them. The country is *negrero*. Everything said to the contrary is a farce, as I have hinted before; and except for a few sincere individuals [among whose number I include myself] there is hardly an inhabitant of Cuba that is not a moral accomplice to this kind of smuggling. If some are their agents; others are their instigators; and the rest applaud from the outside when the increase of laboring hands is proposed. Between Creole and peninsular there does not exist here the smallest difference, except that of the trade that corresponds to each of their fates.)

One way literary authors expressed opposition to the path that the Spanish empire had taken in the nineteenth century was by denouncing the outlawed slave trade and the unchecked power of the *negreros*. Nevertheless it would be misleading to simply define these positions as "abolitionist," given the strong Anglo-American model of what such a movement could become. That said, Spaniards opposed to the trade initially shaped their arguments based first on British and then on American models. After the trade had effectively ended, as I show in Chapter 3, Spanish writers began to depict the *negrero* story as fundamentally Spanish.

Vila Vilar claims to find a "silencio casi enfermizo que se produce sobre esta cuestión en los altos medios científicos y literarios [in the nineteenth century]. Salvo algunas notables excepciones . . . es raro encontrar escritos que tomen postura o que se refieran abiertamente al tema esclavista fuera del ámbito propagandístico de la Sociedad Abolicionista . . ." (Vila Vilar and Vila Vilar, 11; . . . an almost sickening silence occurs on this issue in the high scientific and literary circles [in the nineteenth century]. Excluding some notable exceptions . . . it is rare to find writings that take a stance or that refer openly to the subject of slavery outside the confines of the Abolitionist Society's propaganda.) While the range and intensity of Spanish texts do not match those produced in, say England, I argue that we must read for more than open and direct treatment of slavery on the Anglo-American model. Some of the nineteenth-century works examined here were indeed abolitionist, even though not every aspect of these works was sympathetic to slaves: to many Spaniards in the nineteenth century, abolition was a political move, and its imagined consequences were framed by a very real fear of race rebellion in the Antilles, a loss of the last remnants of the empire for Spain, and the potential for economic disaster on a personal level. Further, various groups were abolitionist for reasons that were not at all humanitarian: Spain rightly feared that England might seize Cuba or the United States might annex it. In other corners, racist fears fueled a concern over an "Africanization" and consequent destabilization of Spain's most valuable real estate.

The less overt calls for abolition in Spanish texts, as compared to their Anglo-American counterparts, can be traced to the relative awareness of slavery and the slave trade on the Peninsula. In spite of an anxiety of ignorance about the empire on the part of the intelligentsia (Blanco, *Cultura y conciencia*, 113) and the fact that precise and profound knowledge of the Spanish possessions was rare, mention of the slave trade and intercepted slavers was a regular occurrence in Spanish newspapers, reported as part of daily events. My analysis of literature demonstrates that nineteenth-century Spaniards not only read about the illegal trade but also acknowledged and remembered it. Indeed, many of the most penetrating works on Spanish *negreros* were created retrospectively as men and money from the islands transformed the Peninsula—in some cases long after the final suppression of the trade. In addition to the pieces discussed in this book (and a considerable number of others not addressed here), even the most canonical realist novelists wove slavery and the slave trade into their works seamlessly, without complicated introductions or weighty ideological pronouncements: such polemics were unnecessary, as the presence and relevance of slavery and the slave trade in the late nineteenth century were amply understood by contemporary readers. In short, Ultramar (as the overseas provinces—colonies—were called) and Spain's policies toward it were everywhere in the nineteenth century, tightly woven into both fictional and journalistic representations of daily life.

For example, Galdós, who is the subject of Chapter 3, offered some of the keenest observations on the transformations of metropolitan life resulting from coloniality. In several works he underscores how Cuba, construed as a "safety valve," compromised peninsular morality. In his historical novel *O'Donnell* (1904), an *episodio nacional* (written after the historical loss of Cuba but set in the early 1850s), Galdós explicitly reviews and modifies the overseas options for bankrupt Spanish aristocrats. Early in the novel, the Marqués of Beramendi speaks with Guillermo Aransis, a fellow aristocrat who is about to lose the last of his meager funds. Beramendi recognizes that the common route of financial recovery would be for Aransis to go to Cuba and either accept bribes in the customs house or trade in slaves, but he instead counsels his friend to marry well. After conceding that few eligible heiresses are to be found in Spain, he suggests that Aransis find one in Cuba. Given that Beramendi has just explained from where Cuban wealth derives, Aransis's financial salvation would very likely not be morally pure, but he would not be considered personally involved:

> Ya sabes que en España tenemos un medio seguro de aliviar la desgracia de los que por su mala cabeza, por sus vicios o por otra causa, pierden su hacienda. Se les manda a la isla de Cuba con un buen destino, y allá se arreglan para recobrar lo que aquí se les fue entre los dedos. España goza de esta ventaja sobre los demás países: posee un heroico bálsamo ultramarino para los males de la patria europea. . . . No te sulfures, ten calma, y óyeme hasta el fin. Ya sé que consideraras denigrante el tomar un empleo en Cuba; ya sé que tú, si lo tomaras, no irías allá con el fin bajo de ensuciarte las manos en la Aduana, o de especular con los desembarcos fradulentos de carne negra. . . . No . . . , ya sé que no harás esto, y que, si vas pobre, volverás puro con los ahorros de tu sueldo, y nada más. . . . el casamiento redentor que aquí no encontraríamos fácilmente, allí *te saldría* en cuanto llegaras, por la vitud sola de tu esplendorosa persona, por tu elegancia y nobleza, y la fama que has de llevar por delante. El género de ricas herederas abunda en aquella venturosa isla. (77–78)

> (You know that in Spain we have an assured means of alleviating the misfortune of those who because of their wrongheadedness, their vices, or another cause, lose their estate. They are sent to the island of Cuba with a good position, and over there they manage to recoup what they lost here. Spain enjoys this advantage over other countries: it has a heroic overseas balm for the ills of the European homeland. Don't be riled, be calm, and hear me until the end. I know you would consider it demeaning to take a job in Cuba; and I know that if you took it, you would not go there with the despicable purpose of getting your hands dirty in Customs, or to speculate with the fraudulent landing of Black flesh. . . . No . . . , I know you will not do this, and that if you go poor, you will return pure with the savings of your salary, and nothing more. . . . the redeeming marriage that we would not easily find here, there will jump out at you as soon as you arrive, on the sole virtue of your splendor, your elegance and nobility, and the reputation that will proceed you. The stock of rich heiresses abounds in that fortunate island.)

Marriage to an Antillean heiress is a much less distasteful alternative to entering the slave trade directly. (Surprisingly, in this novel Galdós does not allude to the well-known fact that General Leopoldo O'Donnell himself became scandalously wealthy through collusion and corruption with *negreros* while serving as Capitán General in Cuba in the 1840s.)[8] Beramendi's account depicts a Spanish fantasy: namely, that Cuba considered the metropolis as its superior even as Spaniards themselves saw the island as little more than a "heroico bálsamo ultramarino" to cure their self-inflicted financial disease. The metropolitan arrogance that provides the logic of the imperial family imagines Cuban heiresses as rich simpletons, immediately conquered at the appearance of the dashing European. Beramendi's fairy tale of a loveless affair is a version of the standard conquest narrative that posits that the (in this case, Creole) natives deserve their subjugation, given that they are so foolish as to be taken in by the splendor, elegance, and nobility that they believe they see in the decadent person of Guillermo Aransis and his kind. As discussed in depth in Chapter 3, Galdós plays with the gendering of the relationship between Cuba and the metropolis in complex and unexpected ways. He reconfigures the paradigm of metropolis and colonial daughters as one of marriage, in which the Cuban wife becomes the locus of conflicting moralities, a victim of Spanish rapaciousness, yet also the site of Spanish, masculinized fears of unfaithfulness and the secrets of private life.

Although I focus in this book on the nineteenth and twentieth centuries, earlier writers had of course censured slavery and slave trading: modern abolitionist literature neither sprang from a void nor was a wholly imported language from the Anglo-American world.[9] The highly ironic letters about the slave trade in José Cadalso's *Cartas Marruecas* (1793) are an example from the Spanish tradition, contemporary with, but markedly different from, the British campaign of Thomas Clarkson. Abolition of the slave trade and slavery in Spain and its colonies did not take place until the nineteenth century, but philosophical discussions regarding these issues and imperial principles began as soon as the trade did. Bartolomé de las Casas is the best-known voice; others included Tomás de Mercado, Alonso de Sandoval, and Bartolomé de Alboronoz.[10] Although an analysis of early modern Spanish literature that critiqued the empire is beyond the scope of this study, it is important to recognize that modern abolitionist literature had notable precedents, with *Don Quijote* as the most canonical example. Agustín Redondo reads the references to slave trading in chapter 29 of part I as a denunciation of the *trata*. In this episode, Dorotea, disguised as the Princess Micomicona from beyond the seas (Redondo places the kingdom of Micomicón in Guinea), leads Sancho to believe that his master will become the new king of Micomicón and he a lord over thousands of Black vassals. Sancho considers the benefits offered to him by his new vassals and effortlessly assumes the perspective of a slave trader: "¿Qué se me da a mí que mis vasallos sean negros? Habrá más que cargar con ellos y traerlos a España, donde los podré vender, y adonde me los pagarán de contado, de cuyo dinero podré comprar algún título o algún oficio con que vivir descansado todos los días de mi vida?" (340; What difference does it make to me if my vassals are Blacks? All I have to do is put them on a ship and bring them to Spain, where I can sell them, and I'll be paid for them in cash, and with that money I'll be able to buy some title or office and live on that for the rest of my life?) While Sancho refers to slave markets in Spain rather than in the colonies, the two commercial enterprises were fundamentally interconnected. The systems of human trafficking, *asientos*, and contraband in both continents were the same; in fact, the first years of the seventeenth century marked the peak of African slavery in Spanish cities (Redondo, 134–35). Rather than exhibiting a noble desire to protect his vassals, Sancho dehumanizes and commodifies them. In his avid desire to become a wealthy man of leisure, Redondo argues, Sancho serves to provide a clear example and criticism "de las práctias al uso a pesar de que no ha llegado aún el tiempo de la puesta en tela de juicio fundamental del principio mismo de la trata" (of the practices used although the time had not yet come to call into question the fundamental principle of the slave trade). In Redondo's reading, *Don Quijote* presents an "antiesclavista" voice avant la lettre (139) and foreshadows the practices of the ennobled *negreros* of the nineteenth century.

The first work to urge the abolition of the slave trade that I address here was a memorial to the victims of Spanish greed: a call to remember the Africans transported across the Atlantic by Spaniards and for Hispano-Cuban economy.[11] Blanco White's characterization of Spanish slave traders as *monstruos por oficio* casts the fledgling debate over the transatlantic slave trader in the racial, biological, and commercial terms that would mark the contours of nineteenth-century European nationalisms. During the Napoleonic occupation of Iberia, representatives from Spanish territories across the globe met in Cádiz to draft a constitution for a reconfigured nation based on popular sovereignty. During these sessions, which dismantled the ancien régime and reshaped the transatlantic nation, the legality of the transatlantic slave trade was debated, and on April 2, 1811, Spain did, in fact, debate the trade (without overt British coercion). However, the Havana planters' vigorous denunciation of the measure ("Representación de la Ciudad de la Habana"; see Gomáriz) caused the Cádiz deputies to retract on this initial abolition; from exile,

Joseph Blanco White advocated for its renewal. His plea did not produce the desired effect, of course, but echoes of his text's presentation of the *negrero* as a self-made monster reappeared throughout the century.

Blanco introduced a discourse of abolition of the slave trade on an unabashedly English model. His *Bosquexo del comercio en esclavos* (Sketch of the commerce in slaves; 1814) written in England for a Spanish public,[12] is clearly inspired by and indebted to William Wilberforce's *Letter on the Abolition of the Slave Trade* as well as British abolitionism more generally. Yet, Blanco expressly tailored his arguments to Spanish realities. In particular, he presented the issue of the slave trade not only as a moral concern in terms of universal human rights, but also as a reworking of the early modern Black Legend, for Spanish immorality in the nineteenth century was being proven in the Atlantic, embodied by cruel slave traders who had become monsters—not because of religious fanaticism but rather the greed of commerce. He also recasts peninsular Spain's relationship with Africa in terms of its War of Independence (1808–14). The abolition of the slave trade would be a way to cast off the legacy of the ancien régime as well as to avoid reenacting the nightmare of the Napoleonic invasion and instead forge a new Spanish nation.

Blanco White presents himself as a translator, or informant, bringing Spaniards to information (or information to Spaniards) but insists that he is not a pioneer in turning to English debates. He relates that slave owners in Havana had recently adopted the rhetoric and argumentation used for decades by English colonists in the West Indies, with a great deal of success. However, according to Blanco, the slave trade in Havana is much less important than it had been for the British West Indies (at the time it had not yet reached its gargantuan proportions), so the comparisons made by the colonists on economic and imperial terms are simply not valid. The author's protestations aside, he was decidedly influenced by British abolitionism. Joselyn Alemeida has argued that this uniquely bicultural writer must be read in a global frame, with reference to Spanish, British, and Latin American contexts (437). "Rather than reading Blanco's construction of identity as a choice between the Anglo or Hispanic worlds, Blanco's sense of self, mind and writing . . . point to how hybrid identities found a voice within British Romanticism, mirroring in their texts nascent global networks of culture and politics" (440). Blanco's position in the *Bosquexo* is, in this same way, solidly Anglo-Hispanic, drawing together various political and economic narratives for understanding the human capacity for human cruelty.

The essayist was a logical spokesman for the antitrade movement. Born into a Hispano-Irish family in Seville in 1775, he became a Catholic priest whose lifestyle, faith, and political consciousness were incompatible with church dictates for the clergy. (He is perhaps best known for his essays and autobiography in which he harshly criticizes Spain and, in particular, the Catholic Church for its oppression of the Spanish people.) He moved to England in 1810, when the French invaded Andalucía. Shortly after his arrival, Blanco founded the newspaper *El Español*, a publication that censured the Spanish government during the Napoleonic occupation and—congruent with his anti-institutional outlook—denounced the suffering that Spanish Americans had endured under Spanish imperialism.[13] Not surprisingly, the Spanish regency prohibited *El Español* from circulating in Spain (Menéndez y Pelayo, 666).

Of concern to us here is Blanco's work on the abolition of the slave trade in the *Bosquexo*. But before he wrote the longer piece, Blanco had addressed the trade in several articles in *El Español*, including No. XXIV (April 30, 1812) in moral terms, and announced he would "appeal" to the Spanish nation in an attempt to "recurrir a su humanidad" (call upon their humanity) (248). In this earlier publication, Blanco reduces the slave trade to a single political question:

> ¿Debe el Gobierno de España quejarse en nombre de la nación que lo ha constituido a su frente, de que hay quien incomode a sus vasallos que se emplean en robar hombres, mujeres y niños, para venderlos a gentes que los hacen trabajar toda la vida, apropiándose el fruto de este trabajo, y hasta los hijos que produzcan en esta miserable esclavitud? El hecho, presentado de este modo, parece una paradoja inconcebible. (249)

> (Should the government of Spain complain on behalf of the nation that has constituted it as its head, that there are some people who inconvenience vassals who make their living by stealing men, women and children, to sell them to people that make them work all their lives, taking the fruit of this work, and even the children that they produce in this miserable slavery? The fact, presented in this way, seems like an inconceivable paradox.)

What is at stake is not only the fate of tens of thousands of Africans, but also the nature of the new modern nation that has actively chosen to pursue the *trata* and cast its lot with the agenda of the Havana planter class. Blanco emphasizes that in retracting this law, Spain has handed over power to a minority in Cuba, in spite of maneuvers to maintain hegemony in the Peninsula (one reason for the constitution's manipulation of racialized citizenship). Blanco White draws attention to the wider paradigmatic racism built into the new articulation of transatlantic Spain that permits pro-*trata* positions. The slave trade, race, and humanity are undeniably linked, but in the most basic terms, the modern state has chosen to protect businessmen who claim to need these slaves in Cuba, rather than uphold the principles that informed many of the other, radically liberal, laws of the new nation. "¡Sólo por atender a las quejas de media docena de especuladores irá España a manchar sus manos en esta abominación!" (250; Spain will stain her hands in this abomination merely in order to heed the complaints of half a dozen speculators!)

The *Bosquexo* is primarily a political essay responding to a specific historical moment. But its value is not simply documentary. Blanco states that his essay "está lexos de ser una obra literaria: es un Memorial dirigido á cada Español en nombre de las victimas que la codicia de algunos de sus paisanos está arrancando todos los dias de la costa de Africa" (iv; far from being a literary work: it is a Memorial dedicated to every Spaniard, in the name of the victims who are being torn every day from the African shore by the greed of some Spanish countrymen). The author's claims notwithstanding, stylistically, the strength of the text comes from its literariness. Blanco borrows heavily—and quite successfully—from the tradition of the *comédie larmoyant*, a genre popular in Spain in the 1780s and into the 1790s that explicitly proposed to make the public cry through its sentimental and pedagogical bent. Its topics were contemporary and the characters recognizably bourgeois. Most often, moral triumph resolved tragic situations. Within the *Bosquexo*, the fate of Spaniards at the mercy of Napoleon's troops, Africans at the hands of monstrous *negreros*, and the political or ethical agenda of the Spanish nation in the clutches of Cuban speculators constitute a layered version of such a story. Blanco instructs his readers exactly how to approach his political lesson in order to effect change: "La historia que va empezar [*sic*], aunque desaliñada y diminuta, no se podra leer sin lagrimas, á no ser por los comerciantes de esclavos. Pero la humanidad las exige:—la noticia de estos horrores es lo que unicamente puede acabarles de poner remedio." (48, original accentuation; The story that will begin, although disordered and tiny, cannot be read without tears, except by slave traders. But humanity demands tears:—the news of these horrors is the only thing that can remedy them.) Significantly, the *negreros*, bereft of human emotion, cannot read correctly. This difference in the sentiment, reason, and humanity of the slave trader frames Blanco's larger argument.

It is thus that the *negrero* comes to life in chapter IV, "Caracter general de los Capitanes de Buques Negreros, y de los Conductors de Esclavos: Miserias del Pasage á las Colonias" (57–58; General Character of Slave Ship Captains and of Slave Drivers: Miseries of the Passage to the Colonies). In an age when emotion and the capacity for compassion defined humanity, Blanco draws upon a larger philosophical tradition of compassion extending back to Montaigne, Shaftesbury, and Rousseau. The Common Sense philosophers insisted that compassion and pity exist by nature, but habit can denaturalize people such that they no longer respond to cruelty: "All of these thinkers considered denaturing habits to be among the greatest evil for humankind" (Levine, 215). Slave traders are, for Blanco, the supreme example of an entire group of people whose nature has been transformed, with the authorization of the nation's laws. "Debemos, pues, sentar como cosa indudable que no puede haber ningun capitan ni gefe de barco negrero, que sea compasivo y humano por naturaleza." (58; We must, then, take as a given that there can be no head of a slave ship that is compassionate or human by nature.) Blanco continues to describe the process of brutalization, by which a *negrero* loses his human essence (compassion) and passes to barbarity, one of the traditional justifications for natural slavery (infused with race in the modern age). That is, if the *negrero* becomes, by nature, neither humane nor compassionate, then one might follow an Aristotelian-inspired binary and suppose he becomes a beast. The following long quotation draws together Blanco's points on the dehumanization catalyzed by the slave trade:

> El que por sus malos pasos se halla reo de ciertos delitos y forzado por las circunstancias á echarse, por exemplo, a bandolero; se desnuda por precision de todos los sentimientos de humanidad hasta tal punto, que la lengua castellana lo expresa con la verdadera y filosófica expresión de, *echarse el alma atras*.
>
> No hay hombre que no pueda *echarse el alma atras*: y unos con mas facilidad que otros.—De esta clase debe ser todo capitan ó gefe de expedicion que va por esclavos; porque, como queda probado, debe ser cruel é insensible por naturaleza. Todo hombre pierde la sensibilidad compasiva por la costumbre de ver objetos dolorosos:—el capitan del buque negrero no ve otra cosa durante su viage. Todo hombre ahoga su sensibilidad quando no tiene otro recurso para acallarla:—el capitan del buque negrero, y quantos le acompañan y ayudan en su expedicion, serían, moral y fisicamente, victimas de su compasion si, teniendola por naturaleza, no se empeñáran con el mayor esfuerzo en ahogarla. Si la disposicion natural, la costumbre, y la necesidad se combinan para despojar á una clase de personas de todo sentimiento humano ¿que seran

> sino verdaderas fieras?—Asi es que todo el que se emplea activamente en la conduccion de negros es un monstruo, por oficio. (58–59)
>
> (He who because of his missteps finds himself the culprit of certain crimes and forced by circumstance to become, for example, a bandit; necessarily strips himself of all human sentiments to such a point, a point that the Spanish language expresses with the true and philosophical expression of "*echarse el alma atras*" [ignoring one's conscience].
>
> There is not a man alive who is not able to *echarse el alma atras*; and some more easily than others. All slave captains or heads of slave expeditions must come from this sort; because, as proven, he must be cruel and insensitive, by nature. Every man loses his compassionate sensitivity from the habit of seeing painful things: the captain of a slave ship doesn't see anything else during his voyage. Every man drowns his sensitivity when he has no other means of silencing it:—the captain of a slave ship and all those who accompany him and help in his expedition would be, morally and physically, victims of their own compassion if, having it by nature, they didn't endeavor with the greatest effort to stifle it. If a man's natural disposition, habit and need combine to strip an entire class of people of all human feeling, what will they be other than veritable beasts? Thus it is that everyone who is actively engaged in the traffic of Blacks is a monster, by trade.)

Thoroughly brutalized by their experience of brutalizing Africans, reduced to the level of beasts (*fieras*), slave-ship captains in Blanco's narrative do not become slaves by nature, but rather monsters by their trade. In other words, trade, or profession, overrides *naturaleza* and creates this third, human-driven definition of behavior in the slave trade, one in which Africans are recognized as equals to Europeans and *negreros* can be rehumanized. Ultimately, Blanco treats the slave traders with compassion, explaining that while they are cruel and insensitive by nature (that is, flawed in their constitution and more likely than others to have stunted emotional intelligence), their lack of compassion is necessary for their self-preservation. More than a century later, Aimé Césaire would famously write that in order to understand the colonizing process we first have to "study how colonization works to *decivilize* the colonizer, to *brutalize* him in the true sense of the word, to degrade him, to awaken him to buried instincts to covetousness, violence, race hatred and moral relativism" (13). With a different political agenda, Blanco White asked some of these same questions. He revived the Black Legend unease over the depraved behavior of agents of imperial Spain and recast them according to contemporary concerns regarding commerce and nascent bourgeois identity. He conceded that some Spaniards were monsters, not as a condition of their nationality, but rather as a result of performing their legally authorized trade. These men created their own identities, but the ultimate responsibility for their existence lay with Spanish lawmakers.

While attacking the racist logic behind Article 22 of the Constitution of 1812 in *El Español*, in his "Sexta Carta de Juan Sintierra" (202), Blanco White delves into the concepts of monstrosity and nature as they pertain to the rights of Afro-Hispanics stripped of the opportunity to partake of the sovereignty of the nation.[14] Quoting the Mexican representative José Miguel Gordoa, Blanco White invites his readers to share the view of the American

> sobre la monstruosidad . . . que me presentan las Américas por el aspecto que toman en este artículo por el que aparecen gozando el dulce título de ciudadanos todos los de las clases precisamente consumidoras, mientras que los de las productoras, es decir, las más dignas o con más justicia (hablo de la justicia y dignidad relativas al objeto y al fundamento) para obtener este título, se ven despojadas de él. (207)

> (on the monstrosity . . . that the Americas show me by the appearance they have in this article, in which precisely all of the consumer classes enjoy the sweet title of citizens, while, the producer classes, that is to say, the most worthy or with more justice [I speak of justice and dignity relative to the object and principle] to hold this title, are divested of it.)

Gordoa introduces the idea of the monstrosity of the exclusion of laborers from citizenship. Because Spain does not have (or has assimilated) a population with African ascendency, America alone becomes the site of this monstrous inversion of justice. As elsewhere in continental Europe in the age of revolutions, monstrosity here is employed to depict a perversion of ordered government; for Gordoa and Blanco it represents a racialized citizenship designed to maintain a majority of votes (and, consequently, parliamentary power) in European Spain.[15]

In the broadest sense, monsters in the Western tradition are quite simply those whom we wish to exclude from our community for physical, moral, or political reasons. As José Miguel G. Cortés has written, every society has a monster, and whatever its form, it corresponds to anything that challenges society's understanding of its ideal self: "Las criaturas monstruosas vendrían a ser manifestaciones de todo aquello que está reprimido por los esquemas de la cultura dominante. Serían todo aquello que ha sido silenciado, hecho invisble. Lo monstruoso hace que salga a la luz lo que se quiere ocultar o negar." (19; The monstrous creatures would be manifestations of all that is repressed by the structures of the dominant culture. They would be everything that has been silenced, made invisible. The monstrous brings to light that which we wish to hide or deny.) The *negrero* in the *Bosquexo* is such an "other" within the body politic that threatens its destruction.

Aristotle posited that some men are naturally slaves ("from the hour of their birth, some are marked out for subjection, others for rule" ["Politics," 1132]), although it is not always possible to perceive the difference between natural slaves and natural masters based on physical traits. The distinction lies, rather, in the ability of self-rule, or having rational principle (Aristotle, "Politics," book I, sections 3–8). In contrast, Aristotle's monster is a mistake of nature, a creature that failed to attain its natural end (Aristotle, "Physics," 250). Over time, monstrosity in Europe became grounded in the belief that people are what they look like, that physical deformity (Aristotelian monstrosity) is a mark of evil that merits poor treatment.[16] The *Liber Monstrorum*, written between 900 and 1000, presented the idea that God permits monsters to exist as a way of instructing about good and evil (Gilmore, 55). During the Renaissance, "type thinking"—the idea that personality is determined by what one looks like—took hold (Hannaford, 137). Aristotle's "slave by nature" was transformed over the same period as the beliefs in a correlation between exterior traits and interior character gained ground and, simultaneously, the idea that the mark of Ham designated a flawed humanity solidified the racialization of slavery that reigned during the age of the European expansion in the Atlantic.

Throughout the *Bosquexo*, *negreros* are not fantastical creatures of the imagination, but all too real, the consequence of a specific logic harming humanity—a humanity extended to Africans through extensive argumentation. Monsters and slaves are set in opposition over the course of the treatise. In contrast to the colonialists in Cuba who insist that Africans are barbaric subhumans and the trade a sort of philanthropic civilizing force, Blanco White underscores Africans' humanity, sentiment, and reason (Pons, "Blanco White abolicionista, II," 37). If Africans are "semi-brutos," according to the *Bosquexo*, it is a result of the treatment they received at the hands of *negreros* (25). Blanco White acknowledges Aristotle's concept of slaves by nature as implicitly engaged by the pro-*trata* faction, and he points out that many people consider that "Negros" were "formados por la mano de Dios, inferiores á ellos, y destinados á servirlos como las bestias del campo" (25; formed by the hand of God, inferior to them and destined to serve them like domesticated beasts). In contrast, Blanco White's "monstruos por oficio" are not marked: they are not monsters by nature or race but by choice of their trade (in the *trata*). Departing from Aristotle, Blanco White's monster results from a flaw in the social or emotional character of a man: the institution of trade and the conditions of oceanic commerce pervert human behavior and change a man into a monster. Blanco White's monsters of trade demonstrate the idea that one could choose to create one's identity through *oficio*, through labor, rather than being assigned it through caste and station—a solidly nineteenth-century concept of identity. But while *negreros* became monsters through their own choices, they could be redeemed by legal abolition of the slave trade.

Blanco White inverts the characteristics of monstrosity and, correspondingly, race and the justification of the trade in Africans. By severing the idea of physical appearance from monstrosity, he undercuts the fundamental belief in racial thought: that external physical traits reveal something about the individual person's character, spirit, soul, or essence. He tells us, fundamentally, that you cannot trust what you see—a characteristically radical position to take at a time when modern race recast these old beliefs in scientific terms.

While an advocate for Africans, Blanco is keenly concerned that a *negrero* mind-set from colonialists in Cuba has undermined the liberal principles that informed much of the new constitution. Quite dramatically, Blanco proclaims that all Spanish lands, save Cuba, had been unanimous in their enlightened desire to outlaw the slave trade in the Cortes de Cádiz: "Las unicas reclamaciones que hicieron cejar de su noble propósito á los legisladores de España" (71; The only claims that made the legislators of Spain relent in their noble purpose) were the Memorial that the Chapter, Patriotic Society, and Body Landowners of Havana presented to the Courts. His distinction between this one island and the rest of the imperial system oversimplifies the situation, ignoring Spanish interests in maintaining the slave trade, as well as supposing the Cádiz deputies to be representative of the population as a whole. But Blanco's argument is important because it will be repeated throughout the rest of the century: *negrero* policy in Cuba overrides Spanish will, reason, and law. Pitting the humanitarian against the economic as the ultimate bottom line, Blanco White asks Spaniards to consider the supposed "males mayores" (greater evils) that Havana slave owners claim would result from abolition, as compared to the human crimes for which Spaniards are responsible, through permissive national laws: "las crueldades, robos, incendios y desolaciones que causan sus barcos en el Africa" (140; the cruelties, thefts, fires, and desolation that their boats cause in Africa).

Finally, Blanco White also Hispanizes the English discourse on abolition through reference to Napoleon and, like twentieth- and twenty-first-century writers, decenters Spain in order to delegitimize a *negrero* logic. While ostensibly describing Africa, the *Bosquexo* is replete with mentions of famine, war, and invasion that evoke the recent events in Spain. The people of European Spain have suffered immensely from the same calamities as Africans ("hambre" [hunger], "insolvencia" [insolvency], and the fact that "ninguno goza seguridad personal" [13; no one enjoys personal security]), a situation caused not by the slave trade, but rather by European wars played out on Spanish soil. The battle between French and English control over the future of Europe impacted Spaniards' lives in ways very similar to what Wilberforce and Clarkson had shown that the slave trade had done to Africa.

Blanco White first refers to victims of the trade as "esos pobres Africanos a quienes en vuestro nombres se martiriza" (these poor Africans who are martyred in your name) and then compares them to Spaniards, who themselves have only recently been liberated "del yugo de vuestros opresores: acordaos que tambien vosotros habeis visto a extrangeros asolar vuestra patria; dexad pues, en paz a la agena; dexad a esos infelices africanos" (143; from the yoke of your oppressors: remember that you, too, have seen foreigners destroy your homeland, leave in peace that of others; leave these unhappy Africans alone). It is not only the slaves who are martyrs, but also those Spaniards who, unlike Blanco White himself, remained in Spain after 1810 and have been martyrized through their heroism and patriotism in the face of the Napoleonic invasion: "¡Martyres del patriotism español! vosotros los que habeis perdido las prendas mas queridas de vuestras entrañas, sacrificadas á la ambicion de un extrangero que quiso esclavizar vuestra patria! . . ." (144; Martyrs of Spanish patriotism! You who have lost the most beloved tokens of your wombs, sacrificed to the ambition of a foreigner who wanted to enslave your country! . . .) At the conclusion of the *Bosquexo*, Blanco clearly lays out the parallel that he has been slowly hinting at: he harnesses patriotism to call on Spain (as the new Spanish nation) to greatness, by emulating England, its ally against Napoleon and the leading abolitionist nation in Europe. Spaniards have lived firsthand the penuries of war, famine, invasion, and plagues caused by Napoleon. That is, they lived what Blanco equates with a regular

"African" existence, and they now should understand experientially and emotionally why abolition of the trade is necessary. He ends by insisting upon Spain's potential for moral excellence, building on a national consciousness stemming from its collective memory of the recent War of Independence. Now that they have been informed of the evils of the slave trade, Blanco White sees no reason why they should not make a nationalistic decision to outlaw the *trata* and the actions of the Spanish monsters. He concludes, "por vuestro dolor, y amargura, no permitais que *Españoles* vayan, de hoy mas, á la costa de Africa á exceder en crueldad é injusticia á esos mismos Franceses que os han destrozado el alma. Dexad al padre sus hijos, al marido su esposa, vosotros que sabeis lo que es verlos arrancar de sus hogares, por un invasor extrangero!" (144; For the sake of your pain, and bitterness, do not allow Spaniards to go, hereafter, to the coast of Africa to exceed in cruelty and injustice those same French who have shattered your souls. Leave the children with their father, the wife with her husband, you, who know what it is like to see them torn from their homes, by a foreign invader!) But Havana is leading Spain along Napoleon's model.

Because the monumental issues that this book attempts to address had a direct bearing on nearly every aspect of nineteenth-century Spanish cultural, political, literary, and social histories, it has been necessary to limit the project's parameters at several junctures, namely in terms of texts and chronology. As I trace the arc of discourses around the slave trade from apathy to knowledge to ignorance, through the nineteenth and twentieth centuries, I do not attempt to provide a compendium of all of the pieces published or written in Spain that mention slavery or the slave trade.[17] It is also important to note that alongside the false *negrero* memoires and false family confessions are a few false runaway narratives. Very few enslaved or free Afro-Cubans published in Spain (Juan Gualberto Gómez is, of course, a major exception to this rule) and the general silence of this population in and for Spain is an issue I return to in Chapter 4. In 1818, even the Spanish consul in Havana noted the discursive limitations on understanding slavery, given the obligatory silence imposed on the enslaved. In an astonishing admission of the will and humanity of Africans, the pro-slavery party wished that they could solicit the wishes of the enslaved: "Quisieramos que los mismos africanos tuviesen voz y esperiencia, y pudiesen decir á los gabinetes de Europa, si de continuar la trata de esclavos, prefieren serlo de portugueses ó de españoles. ¿Si les convendria y esperarian ser mejor tratados por la una que por la otra Nacion? Si querrán mejor ser llevados al Brasil que á la isla de Cuba?" (Havana, "Representación"; We wish Africans could have a voice and experience, and were able to state to the cabinets of Europe, if the slave trade were to continue, whether they would prefer to be slaves of the Portuguese or the Spanish. If it would suit them, and if they would expect to be treated better by one nation or the other? If they would rather be taken to Brazil than to the island of Cuba?) The wishes of the enslaved constitute a separate line of inquiry; this book, instead, draws out the *negrero* and his legacy in Spanish culture and nations. I hope that, as a consequence of my checks on this vast topic, others will revisit these questions, beyond what I have been able to do here. Chapters follow a chronological order, but not every year or even decade is discussed, and the works range across genres and regions.

In the first chapter, I analyze the trilogy of novels by Wenceslao Ayguals de Izco (1801–75), who introduced a large, new public to contemporary social issues during the 1840s and 1850s (the first two decades after the Spanish treaties outlawing the slave trade). Through his serial novel *María, la hija de un jornalero*, among the most successful popular novels of the nineteenth century, Ayguals presented a gallery of enduring characters who personified the socialist goals of the first half of the nineteenth century (anticlericalism, abolition of the death penalty), including a fugitive African slave, el Negro Tomás ("Black Thomas"). The bulk of this chapter addresses how Ayguals used this character to argue for a true abolition of the transatlantic slave trade, to emphasize Spain's civilizing mission and to understand how national, domestic governance was inseparable from imperial governance. Beyond his presence in *María* and its two sequels, el Negro Tomás created a preface for the more famous American Tom whose translation into Spanish, and massive advertising, Ayguals would carry out a few years later. *Uncle Tom's Cabin* became the master narrative for discussing slavery in American terms, but it remained in dialogue with the already famous Tomás. This chapter first presents a close reading of the Spanish Negro Tomás and, second, analyzes the theatrical adaptations of Stowe's novel for the Spanish stage, arguing that in drama, Spanish slave traders became the new villains imperiling not slaves' well-being, but the Spanish hold on Cuba.

After the slave trade ended several decades later, massive amounts of capital and peninsular men linked to the slave economy flooded the metropolis. Chapter 2, "The Colony in the Capital," analyzes the initial rewriting of the empire's slave trading just as its Cuban phase concluded and Spain began to incorporate the *negrero* legacy into the fiber of domestic politics and culture, not as a story shaped by England or the United States, but by a Spanish empire turning on itself. This chapter is structured around a close reading of two novels by the leading realist novelist Benito Pérez Galdós in which he narrates the invasion of Madrid by this colonial lobby and its *negrero* politics—politics that had won the Ten Years' War in Cuba (a failed war of Cuban independence) and swept in the Bourbon Restoration. This chapter examines how Galdós pushes the discourse of realism in imagining the destruction of Spain by the "Havana colony" that ruled in Madrid. I argue that Galdós transforms the novel, a genre of consolidation—of property, nation, and marriages—into a genre of dissolution, where divorce is imagined as a means of narrating the destruction of the Spanish empire and of Spain itself by its overseas practices.

Whereas Galdós depicts Restoration Spain as the *negreros*' creation, Pío Baroja casts *negreros* as crucial Basque agents, creating the Spanish empire on the high seas through their wild, individual pursuit of profit and adventure. Chapter 3, "Baroja's Atlantic, Beyond Slavery," examines maritime novels of the early twentieth century as an explicit attempt to commit the past to paper, so that a Spain that was beyond slavery, beyond empire, and beyond the concerns of the nineteenth century might not completely condemn its past to oblivion. The narrative of these works is propelled by an archivist's desire to preserve history before its records self-destruct and illustrates the impossible documentary task—or readers' expectations of finding truth therein—of historical fiction. Firsthand memories of the slave trade had all but disappeared by the first decades of the twentieth century, and Baroja's novels present a highly self-conscious attempt to use fiction to reverse a growing social amnesia and retain knowledge of what the novels deem to be a crucial aspect of Basque culture. Although usually grouped with the writers in the Generation of '98, Baroja's prose does much more than examine Spain's nature for fatal flaws that prompted the imperial disaster of the Spanish-American War. His maritime novels revisit one of the murkier chapters of Spanish imperial history and narrate the lives of fictional Basque mariners who transported Africans across the Middle Passage to Cuba after the trade had been outlawed.

In spite of the multifaceted engagement with the complexities of imperialism and modernity, examined by a range of authors, including those discussed here, the lettered Spanish public slowly has forgotten its nation's historical role in Atlantic slavery. By the middle of the twentieth century, with reinventions and revisions of the history of the nation-as-empire, the transatlantic slave trade had vanished from cultural memory. Most importantly, as the nineteenth century (as a historical period) changed meaning, slavery disappeared from twentieth-century understandings of the nation's modern past.

Contradictory processes of commemoration complicate the memory and oblivion of Spain's *negrero* past in Spain today, where the Cuban "adventure" is cast as a means of overcoming economic and cultural stagnation. Chapter 4, "Postimperial Detours and Retours," shifts the book's focus from the early twentieth century, when the memory of living slave traders disappeared, to the reconstructed memory of the traders as colonial entrepreneurs today. This chapter proposes a cultural history of the legacy of the *indiano* (Spaniards who made their fortunes in the Americas and returned to Spain in triumph) in northern Spain since 1992, the quincentenary of Spain's Atlantic empire. While thousands of Spaniards crossed the ocean to find their fortune in the Americas during the nineteenth century, the *negrero*'s fabulous rags-to-riches story provides the narrative arc for a reconsideration of a period of profound imperial and state failure to retain control of the American territories as one of resounding financial and imperial successes. In this chapter, I situate the ostentatious mansions built by Spaniards who had made their fortunes in the colonies in the cultural and political contexts of the nineteenth century. I then analyze three points on new tourists routes in Asturias and Cantabria dedicated to narrating the *indiano* "adventure." The story of imperial success that structures these sites intersects with both local concerns and the nostalgia for the age of the "self-made man." The result, I argue, is a new complex history of the monsters of empire created by and for Spanish tourists. The current cultural tourist product commemorating the *indiano* reassembles a nineteenth-century narrative to suit present concerns about Spain's place in the Atlantic world (Connerton, *How Societies Remember*). My discussion of contemporary tourism also points to several questions latent in Asturian and Cantabrian regional identity regarding the place of the slave economy in some of northern Spain's architectural, cultural, and social legacies: How does the story of Antillean wealth (transformed into hospitals and schools by generous *indianos*) link Spain's most disadvantaged classes with colonial slaves? Does civic benevolence sanction general absolution? But was there even guilt in the first place? Indeed, how can we resolve contemporary ethical positions with commonplace (albeit illegal) business practices? More specifically, how did the sugarhouses (such as the Azucarera Montañesa founded in Torrelavega, Cantabria, in 1898), tobacco factories and mines run by *indianos* import this history, and how was it lived by those who worked there?

The *negrero* has returned to once again shape Spanish understanding of the region's place in the Atlantic world. Chapter 5, "Family Ties and Narrative Confessions in Catalonia," addresses the revival of the character of the slave trader in recent Catalan literature. Catalonia, among the areas of Spain most integrated into the finances of the nineteenth-century empire, yet tenuously attached to the Spanish state today, is the site of a literary subgenre that narrates Catalan ties to the slave-trading past in the guise of confessional family tales. Literature is currently playing a pivotal role in the recovery of the area's consciousness of its colonial debts and the integration of the Antilles into the capital city's contemporary reinvention of itself.

In concluding this book, I examine the reformulations of nation and the idealization of modernity in the constructions of nation and state today. Moving from Catalonia to Spain more generally, this section also examines the artistic response to the rebirth of the slave trader in recent years. The book ends with an examination of the journalistic treatment of present-day *negreros* who traffic in African laborers destined for Spain and, ultimately, France or England. I argue that the current immigration disaster created by the new *negreros* of the last fifteen years may succeed in causing all of Western Europe, but especially Spain, to reconsider the contemporary implications of its former imperial policies. *Negreros* are a point of entry into the racial politics, exploitation, and trafficking carried out in modern Spain (both nineteenth century and present) under imperialist capitalism, in the name of "the nation."

§1 Negro Tomás and the Trader

Blanco White deemed *negreros* "monsters by trade" in the highly charged moment following the Napoleonic occupation of Spain. His political tract responded to a specific document presented by the Havana contingency at the Cortes of Cádiz and attempted to influence policy during a moment of great political change. Thirty years later, Spain's geopolitical situation was radically different. No longer sovereign in the Atlantic, the vanquished empire capitulated to British demands and legislated anti-*trata* laws. In spite of antitrade laws and a dynamic slave-based economy, local Capitán Generals (colonial governors) colluded with slave traders and sugar producers, while the Spanish government enacted policies based on a belief that their hold on the "ever-faithful isle" depended on an unceasing entry of slaves into Cuba and a booming slave-based labor economy, even as metropolitan debates responded to the changing Atlantic world. As a result, the prices for enslaved Africans fluctuated during the century in response to supply and demand following the surge in slaving in the 1820s and 1830s, technological advances in the agricultural sector, and the trade in Asian coolie laborers; prices then skyrocketed in the 1850s as sugar eclipsed coffee cultivation, sugar prices rose, and the slave trade to Brazil ended (Bergad, Iglesias García, and Barcia, 57).

In this context, literary abolitionism took flight in Spain around two characters: el Negro Tomás ("Black Thomas") and the slave trader. The axis of the conversation shifted from Blanco White's English discourse to a romantic melodrama in dialogue with Harriet Beecher Stowe's sentimentalism. However, this chapter argues that Spanish abolition was not simply derivative of the major imported discourses of the age, but rather took shape to respond to the specific concerns of the Spanish empire, specifically the slave trader.

This discussion considers a number of literary works written during the central decades of the century. Wenceslao Ayguals de Izco's trilogy of installment novels (*María, la hija de un jornalero* [1845–46]; *La marquesa de Bellaflor* [1846–47]; and *El palacio de los crímenes* [1855]) introduced a Spanish readership to the sympathetic character Negro Tomás. Aygual's novel *María* was Spain's first best seller in the modern sense (Martí-López, 41). Its unparalleled popularity not only guaranteed that subscriptions sold out quickly, but even led to crime! According to the author, "Muchas de las entregas de la lujosa obra *María la hija de un jornalero* han sido robadas sin llegar por consiguiente á manos de los suscritores. Otras han llegado manchadas y estropeadas." (Ayguals de Izco, "¡Escándalo!", 203; Many of the installments of the luxurious work *María la hija de un jornalero* have been stolen without, consequently, reaching the hands of the subscribers. Others have arrived stained and damaged.) Ayguals de Izco claimed that a conspiracy aimed to sabotage the success of the novel based on its social message. His concern over ideological warfare was not unfounded; in 1852, at the height of debates over the slave trade, *María* was placed on the *Index* of prohibited books and in 1855, all three novels in the trilogy were prohibited in Cuba.[1]

Ayguals also translated and promoted *Uncle Tom's Cabin* in Spain and thus diffused an abolitionist text with a different abolitionist message than his initial *María* novels. Stowe's novel inspired a number of plays about slave traders that linked the Spanish empire with the outlawed *negrero*. I will discuss two such works from 1853: *La cabaña del tío Tom* by Ramón de Valladares and *Haley, ó, el traficante de negros* by Angel María de Luna and Rafael Leopoldo de Palomino.[2] The pieces awaken empathy for slaves by means of their victimization, but at the same time, slave traders (that is, ships captains, slave-market traders, and, more generally, those Spaniards who profited from the slave trade) are treated with relative complexity compared to their Anglo-American counterparts.

The plays by Valladares and Luna and Palomino were adaptations of Stowe's *Uncle Tom's Cabin*, performed within a year of the initial publication of the novel in Spain. The two plays, as well as the various editions and translations of the "original" novel, differed from each other artistically and ideologically: the cultural power of the American tale was transformed to satisfy opposing political agendas. *Haley*, staged in Cádiz, responded to international attention to the Spanish involvement in the transatlantic slave trade; *Cabaña*, which premiered in Madrid, was an adaptation of an earlier French theatrical adaptation and repeated pro-slavery arguments. Both plays, and *Uncle Tom's Cabin* itself, were in turn part of a larger "Black Tom" phenomenon in Spanish social literature of the midcentury that began with *María, la hija de un jornalero.*

By the 1850s, *negreros* were understood to represent, paradoxically, both a means to control the island and threats to Spanish hold of it. The redeemed slave trader was particular to midcentury literature when the focus on Cuban (American) slavery crystallized around the *negrero* and interest shifted from Tomás to his traffickers. In Spanish works preceding *Uncle Tom's Cabin*, the *negrero* had much less depth and certainly held out little promise for redemption. In works such as the *costumbrista* novel *El marinero africano* (1844),[3] the trafficker was an oddity of Spanish society, belonging to a world that mainstream readers knew existed but did not understand. The depiction of the life story of this "type" in *El marinero africano* is infused with technical descriptions and the jargon of maritime life, and it illustrates the most exotic aspects of the least discussed subculture of the seas. But the novel refuses to grant the *negrero* any appeal of adventure; rather, he is a subversive character who threatens the integrity of society: "Nunca hace caso del *qué dirán*, y como hasta cierto punto su brusca carrera le hace vivir fuera de las convenciones sociales, en diciendo 'poco ze me dá á mí' lo tapa todo, queda muy satisfecho, y con la cabeza erguida se presenta en público al medio de la luz del día, dando el brazo á una prostituta, riendo, conversando . . . " (69–70; He never heeds *what people say*, and up to a point his rough career makes him live outside social conventions, simply by saying 'I couldn't care less' he puts a lid on everything, is very satisfied, and with his head held high he presents himself in public in broad daylight giving his arm to a prostitute, laughing, talking . . .) In the literature of the age of Negro Tomás, the renegade trader is redeemed and condemned.

Ayguals de Izco

Stowe's first Spanish translator was the author, editor, and publisher Wenceslao Ayguals de Izco, who produced Spanish editions of numerous French novels (see works by Elisa Martí-López and Jesús Martínez Martín). Although his *La choza del Negro Tomás* was an independent publication, Ayguals intertwined it into his "María" trilogy. His three original novels portray the history of Spain over twenty years (1835–55) through the life of a single family in Madrid. The plot and characters of Ayguals's triple-decker, like any serial novel of the time, are numerous.[4] Necessarily setting aside important themes and subplots, one strand of the story is as follows. *María la hija de un jornalero* recounts the life of the poor, but virtuous María, as she survives attempts on her honor by the lascivious friar Patricio and triumphs in marriage to the aristocratic and morally upright Luis, son of the Marqués de Bellaflor. In the second novel, María is now a *marquesa,* and the plot is driven by Luis's suspicions of María's infidelity—stemming from her philanthropic protection of a young unwed mother and her child. Not surprisingly, Luis's mistrust is encouraged by the machinations of immoral men with designs on his wife. In the first two novels, María is saved from both sexual abuse and death by an unusual protector: a runaway Cuban slave named "el Negro Tomás."

The two characters meet early in the first novel. The Marquesa de Turbias-Aguas (Marquise of Murky Waters), a "false" aristocrat in the service of Fray Patricio, imprisons María in her palace and whips the girl in order to beat her into submission and acceptance of the friar's sexual advances. During her enslavement, Turbias-Aguas charges her servant Tomás with the task of cutting away the medallion that the girl wears around her neck—a symbol of her chaste love for the nobleman Luis. Subjected to abuse, María literally loses her mind, becomes an animal (biting those who whip her, for example), and all but loses her humanity during her imprisonment. In other words, María embodies the very behavior and lack of reason ascribed to Africans by apologists of slavery, but her descent from humanity counters that same argument by demonstrating that savagery is a result of a "civilization" based on imprisonment and enslavement, rather than the essence of these people themselves. Indeed, María's imprisonment and potential sexual enslavement preludes a lengthy discussion of colonial slavery and introduces images that are more often associated with the overseas territories than the relationship between domestic servants and their aristocratic employers in the metropolis.

A great deal of the first novel's dramatic tension arises from the possibility that María will be raped or otherwise abused by Patricio. But, during the period of María's imprisonment by Turbias-Aguas, Tomás, rather than the friar, is expected to capture her medallion. Wood-block illustrations depict his entrance into her room at night with a dagger just before he tears open the bed curtains. But suddenly, the plot changes course and perspective: Tomás speaks. Rather than witness María's rape or murder, readers hear Tomás recount the crimes of the slave trade and a universal message of abolition. The violence endured by Tomás's family and hundreds of thousands of other Africans just like him dwarfs the suffering that readers expected María to experience. By means of this disorientation, Ayguals harnesses readers' raced and gendered fears of a perverse attack in the middle of the night by a Black man in a White Spanish woman's bedroom as a way to illustrate the magnitude of the crimes of slavery.

Tomás originally had intended to kill María, not because of the orders given by Turbias-Aguas and Patricio, but rather to carry out his personal vengeance against all White Spaniards complicit, by definition, with colonial slavery and the slave trade. Touched by María's pain and belief that her father had died, they share the same mattress (although not at the same time), she accepts the gift of his dagger, and they exchange stories of loss and suffering. After a long description of his life in Africa, capture, and enslavement by *negreros*, details of the transatlantic voyage, slave life in Cuba, and his escape to Europe, Tomás convinces María of the righteousness of his quest for vengeance:

> Estuve algunos meses en Cádiz, donde tuve proporción de dar pasaporte para el otro mundo á otros varios blancos; pero aun no está satisfecho mi deseo, porque un padre vale mucho, señorita, y todo hijo que tenga sangre en las venas, debe tomarse cumplida venganza cuando han asesinado bárbaramente á su padre.
>
> —Tienes razon, negro, tienes razon . . . —esclamó María abriendo compulsivamente sus grandes ojos que parecían querer saltarse de sus órbitas.
>
> —Vine á Madrid, y hace un año que estoy en esta casa buscando ocasiones de matar blancos. Entré aquí con intencion de matar á usted, señorita; pero al saber que tambien han asesinado á su padre, me declaro protector de usted, y me encargo de buscar á los asesinos . . . Me uniré á usted, señorita, para buscarles . . .
>
> —Sí, negro, les buscaremos . . . y les hallaremos . . . ¿no es verdad que les hallaremos? ¡Oh! . . . sí! . . . morirán! . . .
>
> —Así lo confio. Ahora, acuéstese usted, y . . . reserva sobre todo . . . si quiere que sea completa nuestra venganza.
>
> El negro Tomás desapareció con las luces, cerrando la puerta.
>
> María se tendió en la cama con el puñal en una mano y el medallon en la otra.
>
> Cansados su imaginacion y su espíritu, durmiose la infeliz por fin repitiendo:
>
> —¡Venganza! ¡Venganza! . . . ¡Ven..gan . . . za! (292–93)

(I was in Cádiz for a few months, where I had the means to send several other Whites to the other world; but my desire is not yet satisfied, because a father is worth a lot, miss, and every son that has blood in his veins, should take revenge when they have brutally murdered his father.

"You are right, '*Negro*,' you are right . . . "—exclaimed María compulsively opening her big eyes that seemed to want to pop out from their sockets.

"I came to Madrid, and it's been a year since I have been in this house seeking opportunities to kill Whites. I came in here with the intention to kill you, miss; but knowing that your father also has been murdered, I declare myself your protector, and I will look for the murderers . . . I will join you, miss, in looking for them."

"Yes, '*Negro*,' we will look for them, and we will find them . . . isn't it true that we will find them? Oh! . . . yes! . . . they will die!"

"I trust that it will be so. Now, go to bed, and . . . above all be discrete . . . if you want our vengeance to be complete."

Black Tomás disappeared with the lights, closing the door.

María reclined on the bed with the dagger in one hand and the medallion in the other. Her imagination and her spirit tired, at last the wretched girl fell asleep repeating:

"Vengeance! Vengeance! Ven-geance!!")

Tomás may leave the room holding the light this time, but María will recover her reason and does not succumb to Tomás's call for revenge. Rather—and quite significantly—it is Tomás who is reformed: for virtue is more powerful than anger in Ayguals's moral landscape. María, as a model of piety and true civilization, subdues and domesticates el Negro Tomás. Her character demonstrates that virtue can amend for the past crimes of Spanish colonialism and convert Tomás from a vengeful savage to a "subject" and "product" of Spanish civilization. Indeed, the final lines of *La marquesa de Bellaflor* retitle the second novel in the trilogy as "la venganza de un negro" (the vengeance of a Black), for this is how Tomás characterizes his reasoned, sensitive response to the attempts made on his life and his honor.

Tomás's story is appealing. Although she ultimately convinces Tomás to abandon his plans for revenge, María, the personification of *castiza* Spain, clearly comprehends the logic of his rage. Unlike the equally wronged title character of *Atar-Gull* or Lugarto in *Mathilde*, Tomás articulates the pain that Ayguals imagines that Africans feel and justifies rebellion, revolution, and armed uprising among *bozales* and other enslaved Cubans in terms that any humane Spaniard should understand. But neither of Eugène Sue's vengeful slaves met their match, as Tomás did, with María.

Indeed, Tomás's reasoned vengeance is the opposite of the violence undertaken by Atar-Gull.

Ayguals braids the characters of María and Tomás tightly together, and as much as María's empathy for Tomás models abolitionist sentiment toward slaves, her own story early in the first novel denaturalizes the justifications for enslavement, destruction of the family, imprisonment, and sexual violence that colonialism is built upon. Tomás and María develop a spiritual relationship beyond the bounds of race, built on a fraternity of orphanhood. Their behavior is emphatically similar, alternately fierce, passive, infantile, or wise, according to how they are treated. María and Tomás are twinned as indigent and slave, bereft of personal rights, self-protection, or recourse to the boons of Spanish *moderado*-style liberalism. At the end of *Palacio de los crímenes* the two characters die within pages of each other. Ayguals was primarily concerned with metropolitan Spain and the fate of its working class. Nevertheless the slave/worker analogy that binds Tomás to María functions as more than metaphor: Ayguals was wary not only of the promises of free market discourses but also of a central government transformed by its wealthy colonies.

After 1852, Ayguals became more conventionally abolitionist, and, as Rubén Benítez points out, Ayguals consistently connected his abolitionist work with Stowe's novel.[5] Two years after he translated *Uncle Tom's Cabin*, and eight years after he supposedly concluded María's story (the prospectus for *Marquesa* described the forthcoming novel as the "continuation and conclusion" of *María*), Ayguals incorporated characterization and action from *Uncle Tom's Cabin* in a new novel: *El palacio de los crímenes o el pueblo y sus opresores*. This third novel should be read in conjunction with both *María* and *Marquesa* and *Uncle Tom's Cabin*. From a different angle, Russell Sebold emphasizes the stylistic distinctions between the first two novels and *Palacio*: *María* and *Marquesa* were, he argues, conceived and written as a unit, whereas the third novel has a different narrative tone and is even more politically charged (15).

Trilogies such as Ayguals's maintained cohesion through the technique of recurring characters, pioneered by Balzac in the early 1840s. Raymond Bach has argued that their presence

> produces at certain moments a radical collapse of difference between the individual texts. The reader who stumbles across a name from another novel can indeed sense '*la transparence du temps*,' for the boundaries that normally separate these texts within the reader's memory give way: which text is he

> reading? When and where is he reading it? . . . He senses that the connections between the works are not fortuitous, that they fit together into '*une unité secrète*,' yet he also suffers moments of extreme disorientation in which he is no longer capable of disentangling the stories he has read from one another, in which the identities of the various narrators and characters lose their clear delineation and blur together in a strange, unsettling fashion. (178)

Ayguals projects such a disorienting unity with the character of Tomás in his novels. In name "el Negro Tomás" prefigures Stowe's title character and Ayguals underscored the connection in his translation. Specifically, Juan José Lanero has identified two of the Spanish translations of *Uncle Tom's Cabin* as the work of Ayguals (110). The title of one of these made the connection between Stowe's Uncle Tom and *María*'s *Negro* Tomás explicit: *La choza del Negro Tomás*. Because Ayguals introduces el Negro Tomás as a Cuban slave, the first two novels of the trilogy set the groundwork for readers of *Uncle Tom's Cabin* to find equivalences between the struggles of the two American slaves named Tomás and, later, to recast Stowe's US story onto Spanish Cuba.

In *Palacio de los crímenes*, Ayguals develops the plot and characters of the previous two original novels and further aligns colonial slaves and metropolitan citizens through their shared oppression by a central government that abuses its population with the worst practices from its imperial playbook. Tomás becomes an armed rebel against the government in Madrid 1854, fighting in the barricades during the popular uprisings. But, as a result, he and other rebels, including María's father and brother, are sentenced to exile to the Philippines. During the description of these events, Ayguals de Izco not only creates an analogy between slave traffickers and sectors of the Spanish government that treat liberals as slaves to be transported across the Middle Passage, but also he employs the images and themes of *Uncle Tom's Cabin* to indict the Spanish government's tyranny within Iberia and show the conservative *moderado* regime's complicity with human traffic. Ayguals justifies his analogy thus:

> Se ha escrito un libro contra los traficantes de esclavos, un libro que ha dado la vuelta al mundo entre el aplauso universal, por la valentía con que anatematiza los feroces instintos del negrero que maltrata á su esclavos. ¿Y hemos de callar, y no hemos de escribir nada, y hemos de contemplar con paciencia que aún se rindan inciensos á los asesinos de los hombres libres? (199)

> (A book has been written against the slave traffickers, a book that has traveled around the world amidst universal applause, for the courage with which it

anathematizes the ferocious instincts of the slaver who abuses his slaves. And must we be silent; must we not write anything, must we contemplate with patience that they still surrender to the murderers of free men?)

Whereas *Uncle Tom's Cabin* is the novel denouncing the American slave trade, *Palacio* is the novel that denounces the enslavement of peninsular Spaniards and, at the same time, the Spanish involvement in the outlawed slave trade (a topic that could only be discussed obliquely). María's brother and father (along with other prisoners) are placed in shackles, marched to prison, and, ultimately, placed in a ship that is compared—on numerous occasions—to the *negreros* that transported contraband African slaves to the Spanish colonies. "Setenta y dos ciudadanos españoles fueron amarrados como amarran los negreros á sus ecclavos [*sic*] de Africa; operacion repugnante que duró hasta la una y media." (342; Seventy-two Spanish citizens were tied up like the *negreros* tie their slaves from Africa; a disgusting operation that lasted until half past one.)

These men were legally free, but their personhood had a price, for their liberty was for sale on the black market: family members of the incarcerated could pay ladies of Queen María Cristina's *camarilla* to emancipate their loved ones. This sale of prisoners is yet another scheme to enrich the queen mother that is never entered in official registers. Of course, political exile is significantly different from the sale of enslaved Africans, but the two branches of contraband commerce appear as elements of a single system of "infame tráfico" (402). Madrid is infected with an imperialist mind-set; the royal family and its *camarilla* have become traders and adopted *negrero* views of humanity. In sum, María Cristina and her *camarilla* govern the Peninsula the way they govern the Antilles.

At the conclusion of *Palacio de los crímenes*, Negro Tomás becomes part of the urban landscape: "Pocos serán los habitantes de Madrid que no recuerden haber visto entre los grupos de los defensores de la libertad la decision de un negro que alentaba con su arrojo á los demás valientes, si es que no á todos les sobraba el invencible denuedo de los libres." (368; Few inhabitants of Madrid will not remember having seen among the groups of defenders of freedom the decision of a Black man whose boldness encouraged other brave men, if everyone was not already overrun with the invincible courage of free men.) Tomás leaves the page to become "real," part of the public consciousness as a freedom fighter, an armed Black man (with Aygual's emphasis on his skin color) fighting for political liberty, not in Cuba, but in Spain, in the heart of the metropolitan government. In this sense, Tomás completes his initial purpose of traveling to Spain: combating a racial and economic system that enslaved his family and killed his father.

Uncle Tom in Spain

While translations of foreign novels were generally popular in nineteenth-century Spain, in 1853 *Uncle Tom's Cabin* appeared in more editions in a single year than any other imported novel heretofore in that century. Many novels by Dumas and Sue held trans-Pyrenean appeal, and Chateaubriand's *Atala* enjoyed sustained publication in Spain (Montesinos, 186), but Stowe's explosive best seller was unequalled in its rate of diffusion.[6] Strictly in terms of number of readers, the impact of this text was phenomenal. Within six weeks of the initial offering of the first edition in December 1852, readers had purchased all four thousand copies of Wenceslao Ayguals de Izco's translation, much of the second edition, and an equal number of at least six other translations. In addition, if they had not encountered the novel as an installment by Ayguals or other editors, readers had likely seen at least a section of it serialized in *La Época, Las Novedades, La Nación,* or *El Clamor Público*, daily political papers of a liberal ideology that inundated the capital and provincial cities with independent translations of *Uncle Tom's Cabin* in early 1853. These four periodicals were among the eight newspapers with the largest subscription rates in Spain (Cabrera et al., 103). It is difficult to ascertain the absolute number of issues printed; however, based on postal records—about half of all issues were sent to subscribers outside the capital city (Sánchez Aranda and Barrera, 142)—*Las Novedades* had an estimated daily circulation of fifteen thousand and *El Clamor Público* about four thousand (Cabrera et al., 117). Even casual readers, not committed to following the entire story, had ample opportunity to see one or two fragments of the famous work and become familiar with the main characters and themes.

Discussing the installment novel phenomenon generally in Spain during the second half of the nineteenth century, Jean-François Botrel has emphasized the massive impact that the fragmented format had on the development of readership. Basing his calculations on the rates of twelve to fifteen thousand copies per newspaper or installment edition and 3.5 readers per copy, Botrel estimates that each serialized work had between forty-two and fifty-five thousand readers—a sizeable segment of the national population (132). However, *Uncle Tom's Cabin* had not one publication but at least sixteen within one year: ten in Madrid, three in Barcelona, one in Cádiz, one in Valencia, and one in Paris (in Spanish). Employing conservative rates of diffusion (editions of four to fifteen thousand copies), the estimated number of readers of *Uncle Tom's Cabin* in Spain in 1853 was anywhere between 210,000 and 787,500. With a literate population in Spain in 1860 of 3,835,000, this novel therefore reached approximately 5 to 20 percent of all potential readers, or 1 to 5 percent of the entire national population of 15,673,000.[7] The number of illiterate persons who became familiar with the work from having heard it read aloud constitute yet another layer of readership. By means of this massive diffusion of the text, the American Uncle Tom was wholly transformed almost immediately into Tío Tom: a veritable celebrity among the dramatis personae of Spanish literature. Within months, the character and the novel were frequently referred to in the periodical press, even in magazines that never fully discussed the work.

The clamorous reception of *Uncle Tom's Cabin* was unique, and even more surprisingly, it was first published in Spain during a period of intense censorship of fiction and commentary about the overseas provinces and the slaves that lived there. In a period when politics were reported as creatively as novels were written, works of fiction were as vigilantly censored as political articles. Indeed, by the Royal Order of 23 April 1852, the two genres were to be read, analyzed, and censored indistinguishably. The same censor appointed by the crown to assess novels was also charged to read "todos los artículos y escritos relativos á Ultramar, observándose para estos casos las mismas formalidades y disposiciones que prescriben los anteriores artículos respecto de las novelas" (Article 8; all articles and writings related to the Overseas Provinces, observing for these pieces the same formalities and dispositions that the previous articles [of this royal order] prescribe for the censorship of novels). As novelists continued to frustrate the royal censors' efforts to suppress all criticism of the government or social mores, the Minister of Government (Ministro de la Gobernación) discharged a direct blow to literature with the October 1852 prohibition of popular novels by socially conscious foreign writers such as Sue, Sand, Soulié, Scribe, and Dumas.[8]

The effects of these measures were deplored by the Madrid daily *El Heraldo*: "En cuanto á la censura de novelas y de noticias de Ultramar, es increible lo que hemos padecido." (As far as censorship of novels and news about the overseas provinces are concerned, what we have suffered is incredible.) This paper (led by the future Conde de San Luis) claimed it had a "treasure" of news about the Philippines and Cuba that was simply prohibited by the government.[9] Given that journalists could not anticipate censors' reactions to their columns, *El Heraldo* claimed that it had to resort to writing in

> parabolas y apólogos con la esperanza de que llegasen á comprenderlos, en medio de la oscuridad en que los envolvimos . . . jugando al escondite en nuestras columnas; disfrazando unas veces nuestro pensamiento bajo el velo de la política estranjera; discutiendo otras en serio una cuestion ridícula; refugiándonos algunas veces para hablar de política hasta al terreno de los anuncios. ("Parte Política")
>
> (parables and apologues, hoping that they would be understood in the midst of the darkness in which we wrapped them . . . playing hide-and-seek in our columns, sometimes masking our thoughts behind the veil of foreign politics, seriously discussing a ridiculous point other times; at times even taking shelter in the realm of advertisements in order to talk about politics.)

For a readership accustomed to such rhetorical acrobatics in order to decipher the daily news, the American fictional landscape of *Tío Tom* offered rich and fertile ground for a transplanted consideration of the urgent affairs of Spain's own slave traffic, precarious imperial unity, and concerns regarding abolition. Indeed, one translator described his procedure as a triple translation from American English to Cuban Spanish to European Spanish, noting:

> Para la mejor comprension empleamos en el trascurso de esta novela las voces *tío* y *tía*, en vez de la palabra *táita*, que es la verdadera que corresponde á la que ha escrito la autora. *Táita* es un nombre tomado de los mismos negros que se da vulgarmente en nuestras colonias á los negros de cierta edad, y que por sus buenas cualidades se hace acreedores á este epíteto, considerado por ellos como de deferencia. Tambien empleamos la palabra *choza* por ser mas conocida entre nosotros que la de *bohio*, nombre verdadero de las habitaciones que se da á los negros del campo.[10]
>
> (For ease of understanding we use in the course of this novel the words *tío* and *tía* [for 'uncle' and 'aunt'], instead of the word *táita*, which is the one that truly corresponds to the one the author has written. *Táita* is a name, taken from the same Blacks, which is commonly given in our colonies to Blacks of a certain age, who because of their good qualities become entitled to this epithet, regarded by them as one of deference. We also use the word *choza* [for 'hut'] because it is more well known among us than *bohio*, the real name of the rooms that are given to Blacks in the fields.)

This unnamed translator provided such notes in order to explain the novel as an American novel about Cuban life.

Given the grim status endured by literature during these months, the government approval of *Uncle Tom's Cabin* is extraordinary. There are no accessible extant records of the government censor's comments regarding *Uncle Tom's Cabin*; however, the copy deposited at the National Library in Madrid records that the translator and editor Wenceslao Ayguals de Izco, responsible for the novel's initial introduction in Spain, finalized the censorship process and acquired the copyright for his editions on January 17, 1853.[11] It is significant that a foreign and translated novel was used as a frame for criticism of the government's slave policies when a vibrant literary circle within Cuba was engaging with this issue. Indeed the evolution of the Cuban novel was conditioned by the cultural tensions inherent in the issues of slavery and empire (Schulman, 356). Throughout the midcentury, the Del Monte circle created a series of texts with an antislavery (or antitrade) discourse, including *Francisco* (1835, published in 1875). While these were important works of literature markedly in favor of celebrating the African element of Cuban nationalism, their accessibility to Spanish readers was limited until later in the century (Naranjo Orovio and Puig-Samper, 795). Quite simply, the Cuban texts were too critical for Spanish censors. For example, Gertrudis Gómez de Avellaneda's radical abolitionist and feminist *Sab* (1841), written only eleven years before *Uncle Tom's Cabin*, was (like *María* and its sequels) prohibited in Cuba and initially had a restricted circulation in Spain. In contrast, Stowe's novel condemning the social and political policies of Spain's political adversary, the United States, was allowed to circulate freely. As a result, while not every Spanish citizen read *Uncle Tom's Cabin*, its high degree of availability and familiarity situated its characters and the explosive themes of slavery and the slave trade—both exotically North American and familiarly Hispano-Cuban—squarely within the national cultural imagination.

Mellado

Each edition of *Uncle Tom's Cabin* framed its abolitionist message differently and shaped the degree to which the novel was to be read as an explicit commentary of the politics of Spanish colonial slavery. Marketing, of course, mattered, too. One paper reported that "Miss Stowe, autora de la novela negra Unel-Tom [*sic*], es la heroina del dia. Es señora de mucho despejo, y que se interesa por los adelantos de España." ("El periodismo," 2; Miss Stowe, author of the Black novel *Uncle Tom's Cabin,* is the heroine of the day. She is a lady of great self-confidence and is interested in Spain's progress.) That is, the newspaper suggested Stowe's novel was not simply a foreign novel, adapted, read, and interpreted by Spaniards but actually somehow about Spain. Singularly from among the numerous translations and editions, the 1853 copy published by Francisco de Paula Mellado was relatively faithful to the American version in its translation, while the prologue clearly voices the views of Cuban slaveholders.

Francisco de Paula Mellado was, like his business rival Ayguals, a successful publishing entrepreneur who edited numerous literary publications (Martínez Martín, 40). But unlike Ayguals, ideology seemed to motivate him less than profits.[12] Shortly before the publication of Mellado's edition, the same translator (identified rather mysteriously only as "B***") began to shape the public's expectations of the forthcoming book. In the *El Universo Pintoresco* ("Mistress," 1–2), B*** introduces "Mistress Enriqueta Beecher-Stowe" as a gifted writer. But significantly, this article is followed by a brief essay by Luis M. de Larra, "La poetisa," in which the son of the famous Mariano José de Larra argues against female authorship: beautiful women are written about whereas women who write are "fea" (ugly). The antibluestocking opinion is not remarkable for its commonplace sexism, but its placement paratextually undercuts the glowing review of Stowe that precedes it. The attack on Stowe's work becomes explicit in the prologue to the Mellado edition, also written by "B***." After reprinting the biographical sketch published in *El Universo Pintoresco,* the prologuist argues that while, of course, everyone is opposed to slavery in theory, abolition wouldn't improve anyone's life, especially not that of the enslaved. Repeating an established pro-slavery position, B*** argues that slaves simply aren't ready for freedom.

As Ayguals will do in *Palacio,* this edition casts Stowe's novel as a work about the slave trade. However, unlike Ayguals's condemnation of the effects of human trafficking on the enslaved, the colonies, and the citizens of the metropolis, here, the same novel becomes evidence for the philanthropy that traders have executed: "Los encantadores negros de mistress Stowe, admitiéndolos tales como ella los pinta, si no hubieran sido traidos del Congo ó de la Guinea por negros filántropos sin saberlo, no leerían tan piadosamente la Biblia, y bailarían una horrorosa danza en derredor de una hoguera asando cadáveres enemigos." (v; Had the charming Blacks of Mistress Stowe, accepting them such as she paints them, not been brought from the Congo or Guinea by unknowing philanthropists, they would not so piously read the Bible, rather they would dance around a bonfire roasting enemy corpses.) The message is disturbing, but the choice of terms is significant. B***, who has positioned himself as the ideological adversary of Ayguals, doesn't simply reject the concept of literature as a means of social change, he parodies one of Ayguals's great values: philanthropy. In the evolving landscape of nineteenth-century charity, humanitarianism, or philanthropy, included the development of civic and commercial enterprises that fostered prosperity and a sense of cooperation (Valis, 108–12). Considering *negreros* as philanthropists ridicules not only abolitionism but also the larger message of progressive politics and association that provided the ideological framework for Ayguals's literary projects.

The novel has been misread, according to this prologuist, as a depiction of life as it is in the United States, rather than as a work of fantasy. *Choza*, argues the prologuist, actually demonstrates the necessity of slavery by presenting scenes of utter fiction. Voicing the arguments of Cuban slave owners, B*** advocates for gradual abolition through a process of apprenticeship. Neither of these positions is particularly original. But then Mellado's edition appropriates the cultural power of *Uncle Tom's Cabin* to deliver a characteristically Spanish solution to the question of Afro-Hispanics in the Americas. Contemporary with the campaigns for *blanqueamiento* (whitening) of the Antillean population and repatriation schemes of the United States and Great Britain, the prologuist to Mellado's edition proposes aggressive miscegenation in order to enact a wholesale whitening or "Torna atrás" (as the phenomenon had been known in the famous *Casta* paintings; see Katzew). Slavery is, in this framing, not a problem of economics, empire, or agriculture. It is a problem of race and civilization.

In this particular version of the "White man's burden," Africa is left to destroy itself while Whites in Europe and America must absorb all races into a master White race, a process already begun in Saxon-Norman England, the Latin/Gallic world, and Arabic Spain.

> En resúmen, la esclavitud de los negros desaparecerá enteramente con los negros. . . . La raza inferior ó degenerada desaparecerá; en Africa por el aislameinto y el esterminio, resultado de su propia barbarie; en América y en Europa, por la absorcion de la sangre de los negros en la sangre de los blancos, como las tinieblas de la noche se absorben en la luz de día. Y el mundo civilizado no tendrá entonces mas que una raza blanca, verdadera raza humana, en medio de la cual los últimos negros se perderán con los restos de la

servidumbre, como las sombras del crepúsculo en los valles. Pero esto no será la obra de una novela, ni de una sociedad bíblica, ni de una sesión legislativa. (vii)

(To summarize, the enslavement of Blacks will disappear entirely with Blacks themselves. . . . The inferior or degenerate race will disappear; in Africa, due to isolation and extermination, resulting from their own barbarism; in America and Europe, due to the assimilation of the blood of Blacks into the blood of Whites, as the darkness of the night is absorbed by the light of day. And the civilized world will then have only one White race, a true human race, in the midst of which the last Blacks will be lost along with the remnants of servitude, like the shadows of twilight in the valleys. But this will not be the work of a novel, or of a biblical society, or of a legislative session.)

The *mestizaje* acknowledged in colonial governance becomes a vehicle for racial annihilation. The issue of interracial marriage in colonial policy was hardly new, but in the nineteenth century, various new theories considered how to stabilize racial relations. For example in the French context, the Abbé Grégoire argued in 1823 that Christian intermarriage would produce a race stronger than either Black or White and concludes that it is important in its aim to undermine racial hierarchy (Andrews, "D'Eichthal," 244). But the proposal here denies any value to mulattos as anything other than a confirmation of the power of the White race to absorb. Indeed, it represents one strain of "whitening" strategies proposed by various Cubans, including Francisco Arango y Parreño, José Antonio Saco, and Gaspar Betancourt Cisneros (Silverstein, 108).

Joshua Goode has argued that midcentury racial thinkers in Spain saw the uniqueness of Spanishness in its "supposed history of racial mixture," a characteristic of Iberia that was understood to be responsible for Spain's former imperial successes (33). But this prologue from 1853 takes such ideas to radically different ends, suggesting that the United States abandon its racial purity, embrace a Spanish theory of fusion, and annihilate Blackness around the world as a means to abolish slavery. Violent racism in the abolition debates in Spain notwithstanding, this prologue is a parody of what were seen to be serious Spanish racial theories (see Goode), Saco's plan of *blanqueamiento*, Stowe's fear of the enslavement of Whites through miscegenation, and Ayguals's promotion of literature as a means to change the society.[13] By denying any importance to literature, philosophy, law, or economics, Mellado's edition does not simply recast Stowe's novel as fantasy, but also it excuses Spain and Spaniards from any responsibility for the human (and diplomatic) disaster taking place on the Atlantic.

Thus, B*** concludes in the vocative, speaking directly to Stowe, lauding her virtue and intelligence.

> Quereis y preparais sinceramente la salvacion de los esclavos negros. Pues bien, haced con este fin admirable alguna cosa mas eficaz y mas decisiva que la *Choza de Tomás* y sus millares de ejemplares regados con lágrimas. Teneis cuatro ó cinco hijos que heredarán vuestras virtudes, vuestro desinterés y vuestra mision; casadlos con otros tantos negros ó negras libres, ó al menos mulatos y mulatas, escogidos de entre los puros y las mas nobles víctimas de la preocupacion americana. Decid á todos los abolicionistas: *"Aquellos que realmente amen los negros sigan mi ejemplo"* y habreis dado, señora, la verdadera *llave de la casa de Tomás*, que tan pomposamente anuncian vuestros editores. Y habreis hecho por la rehabilitacion de los negros, y vos misma y por vuestra posteridad, mas que todos los predicadores, que todos los legisladores, que todos los escritores, y que todos los panegiristas y propagadores de vuestra obra.

> (You want and sincerely prepare for the salvation of Black slaves. Well then, do with this admirable purpose something more effective and more decisive than *Uncle Tom's Cabin* and its thousands of copies showered with tears. You have four or five children that will inherit your virtues, your selflessness and your mission; marry them to an equal number of free Black men and women, or at least mulattos, chosen from among the pure and most noble victims of American concern. Tell all the abolitionists: "Those of you who really love Blacks follow my example" and you will have given, Madame, the true *A Key to Uncle Tom's Cabin*, that your editors so pompously announce. And you will have done more for the rehabilitation of Blacks, and yourself and for your posterity, than all the preachers, all the legislators, all the writers, all the panegyrists and propagators of your work.)

Haley

Mellado's racist ravings refused to concede any place for literature in the debate over the transatlantic slave trade or slavery in the Atlantic world. But in theater, Stowe's novel was adapted to argue all manner of positions for and against slavery and against the slave trade. In Cádiz, a major port city with close cultural and commercial ties to Cuba, but removed from the literary elite in Madrid (and Havana), Ángel María de Luna and Rafael Leopoldo Palomino adapted *Uncle Tom's Cabin* as a new play, *Haley*, in order to interrogate the slave trade, its threat to Spain's colonial power in the face of British and American interests, and a growing Afro-Cuban population. *Haley* did more than incite pity for slaves and draw a parallel between those in the Southern United States and Cuba. It refocused its criticism on Spain's overseas policies, as the illicit slave trade had helped the Cuban slave economy to thrive and thus make Cuba so attractive to US expansionists.

Haley was written in early 1853, approved by government censors in April, and first staged in Cádiz in October of the same year. By midcentury, Spain was nearly bankrupt and its control over its wealthiest colony was precarious. Several years earlier, Spain had essentially mortgaged the island: British interests held legitimate financial claims to seize Cuba after Spain defaulted on its loans, but England instead allied with France in an attempt to prevent Cuba's annexation by the United States. Meanwhile, the United States unofficially urged Cubans to separate from Spain and transfer allegiances to Washington. Moreover, they unofficially tolerated the armed invasion of Cuba by private citizens, or *filibusteros*, while secretly authorizing Pierre Soulé, the French-born American ambassador to Spain, to purchase the island for $130,000,000 (Rauch, 281). While less rich in detail, the version of the political crisis available to the general reading public was, nevertheless, quite alarming. The overseas provinces' fate was discussed in the Spanish papers nearly every day between October 1852 and December 1853, and the various attempts by the United States to annex Cuba kept the nation's focus on "the ever-faithful isle."

For reasons of commerce and imperial pride, the Cuban crisis instigated a general mobilization in Spain. In October 1852, the Spanish public read that the government had begun sending reinforcements to Cuba on October 29. A few weeks later, driven by a sense of patriotism for the "conservacion de nuestra preciosa Antilla" ("Variedades," 1; conservation of our precious Antille), volunteers from the province of León requested authorization to embark for Cuba. Spaniards were keenly aware that the United States, far from sated after the annexation of Texas, was eager to invade Cuba. The Spanish newspapers defined Presidents Fillmore and Pierce as men of state according to the degree to which they treated the filibuster invasions as "American piracy" ("Correo Estrangero"). Perhaps most importantly, the press did not hide the world's opinion of the Spanish slave trade, and at the height of the Tío Tom fervor, Spaniards read of the uses made by the United States of Spain's continued transatlantic trade in order to justify its foreign policy of Manifest Destiny expansionism in Cuba.

The editors of *El Clamor Público* commented upon the American refusal to join France and England in guaranteeing Spanish possession of Cuba. They reported that the US government was unable to renounce hopes for the future annexation of Cuba, an event that would be prompted by an agreement with Spain, an appeal by Cuba's inhabitants, "o bien por una *guerra legítima*" (or by a *legitimate war*; original emphasis). The concept of just war was, of course, a traditional justification for colonization, reformulated by Francisco de Vitoria, among others (Martinez, 118). Digesting the official American stance for readers, the editors sadly predicted an invented war for economic gain: "La anexion á mano armada: hé aquí la última palabra de la política americana. Muy pronto hemos de ver los suterfugios [*sic*] de que se valen los oradores americanos para justificarla." ("Correo Estrangero"; Annexation by force: this is the last word of American politics. Very soon we will see the subterfuges that American orators will employ to justify it.) The United States had economic, political, and military superiority over Spain, which feared, but indeed expected, the seizure of their wealthiest province.

Near the end of the Fillmore administration, *El Heraldo* (among several other Spanish papers) published US Secretary of State Edward Everett's long discourse on American policy regarding Cuba. True to the racist ideology of Manifest Destiny, Everett justified geographic expansionism by a fear of African "barbarism":

> No haré sino aludir á un mal de primera magnitud, á saber, el comercio de esclavos africanos, cuya supresion interesa tan vivamente á la Francia é Inglaterra; un mal que forma hoy todavia el mayor baldón contra la civilizacion cristiana y perpetúa la barbarie del Africa, y para el cual es de temer que no puede haber esperanza de completo remedio, mientras Cuba continúe siendo una colonia española. ("Parte Política," February 22, 1853)
>
> (I must not fail to mention an evil of the greatest degree, that is, the commerce in African slaves, whose suppression is of vital interest to France and England; an evil that today constitutes the greatest harm to Christian civilization and perpetuates the barbarism of Africa, and for which we fear there cannot be a complete cure as long as Cuba continues to be a Spanish colony.)

Everett's concern was not the plight of the enslaved either while in transit or upon arrival in Cuba; his alarm at the continued transatlantic slave trade came from his perception of its racial and cultural effects on Cubans and, potentially, the nearby Southern United States. In the eyes of the relatively noninterventionist Fillmore administration, a Spanish Cuba was detrimental to the American definition of civilization and grounds for seizure of the island by the United States. But whereas Fillmore was vocally against an armed invasion of Cuba, his successor, Franklin Pierce, was correctly seen in Spain as actively pro-annexationist. Spaniards read Pierce's arrogant threats of annexation in his March 4, 1853, inaugural speech (placed just above a chapter of *Uncle Tom's Cabin*) on the front page of *Las Novedades*. "No debemos disimularnos que nuestra actitud como nación y nuestra posición en el globo, hacen en estremo importante para nuestra protección la adquisición de ciertas posesiones que no dependen de nosotros . . . " ("Novedades"; It is not to be disguised that our attitude as a nation and our position on the globe render the acquisition of certain possessions not within our jurisdiction eminently important for our protection . . .) When he assumed the presidency of the United States on March 4, 1853, Spanish fears of the impending loss of Cuba escalated.

From Tío Tom to Haley

A basic, nearly indisputable, principle of Spain's overseas "second slavery" policy was the assumption that the traditional plantation slave economy ensured the fiscal health and imperial conservation of Cuba (Corwin, 22; Tomich). Officially, these slaves were to come from within the Americas. However, Spaniards read about the slave traders in the Atlantic and knew exactly how the slave economy and conservation of the island were secured. Poetic traditions aside, they were fully aware that traffickers were characters far more complex than romanticized, free-spirited pirates and, moreover, that the political consequences of their exploits were grave. In addition, many feared that a continued "Africanization" of Cuba through the transatlantic trade would lead to a massive slave rebellion such as that of Haiti. Brief updates on the contraband trade were published in the periodical press (sometimes simultaneously with the serialization of *Uncle Tom's Cabin*). For example, in its front-page review of the state of affairs in Cuba in January 1853, *El Heraldo* reported that "la fragata inglesa la Vesta habia capturado en las aguas de la isla tres buques negreros" ("12 de enero 1853"; the English frigate the Vesta had captured three slave traders' ships in the waters of the island). *La nación* reported the parliamentary debates over piracy laws for slave traders in Italy ("Correo Estranjero," 2). A few months later, the Cádiz newspaper *El Nacional* reported the capture of a Spanish trafficker in May 1853, with a tone that suggested familiarity with the accused: "El bergatín inglés Buzard ha aprendido y conducido a la Habana al español Cora a quien se acusa de emplearse en tráfico negrero." (May 28, 1853; The English brigantine Buzard has apprehended and taken to Havana the Spaniard Cora who is accused of carrying on slave traffic.)

With *Haley, ó el traficante de negros*, Luna and Palomino brought their public close to the story by replacing the slave Tom with the trader Haley as the titular character and dramatized the slave trade through the fictional *negrero* in order to attack the idea that a tolerance of human traffic was necessary for the good of the nation, property, and the preservation of family honor. Specifically, Luna and Palomino used well-loved characters and a familiar plot line to present the swift and sudden death of traffic as the means of securing those ideals. They blended Spanish politics and contemporary history with American fiction to create sharp political propaganda.

Structurally, this piece built on previous knowledge of Stowe's story although neither its title nor its author appear on the title page. The play follows the slave trader Haley in his attempts to capture the runaway slaves Elisa (Eliza), Jorge (George), and their young son, Enrique (Harry/Henry), whom he had purchased from Arturo (Arthur) Shelby. The first two acts of this adaptation closely match episodes from the novel in characterization, dialogue, and action, while the second two acts radically invert character development, offer new dialogue, and redirect the plot. The differences between the two pieces are key to analyzing the uses made of *Uncle Tom's Cabin* as a tool to criticize Spain's handling of the immediate political crisis, while eluding the censors.

The first real change that pointedly implicates the Spanish audience occurs at the end of the first act. Elisa breaks the theater's fourth wall and addresses the audience as she prepares to flee with Enrique. Her speech actualizes her situation for the Spanish public and draws her out of the fictional "Kentuki" into their historical present. An American story becomes a Spanish moral issue through Elisa's direct appeal to maternal love and duty in all of the actual "*madres*" in the theater. In doing so, Elisa obliges the merchant class of Cádiz to consider her plight according to Spanish social mores and to imagine her as a member of their community.

Only after a familiar retelling of Jorge and Elisa's story during the first two acts does substantial transculturation of Stowe's novel occur in the form of topographical adaptation. Act III places Wilson—resting after a failed search for Elisa—at an inn on the shores of the Ohio River. However, in the altered dramatic landscape, the inn is not patronized by Stowe's stereotypical Kentuckian hunters, but rather by sailors, stereotypical inhabitants of the port city of Cádiz. These are the harshest critics of the slave trade in the play. Not only do they cheer when a poster about the runaway Jorge is defaced, but their spokesman, the innkeeper Samuel, unequivocally also denounces the trade: "¡Verguenza es para nuestro pais . . . que se tolere semejante tráfico!" (Act III, scene 10; It is to our country's shame that such a trade is tolerated!) After seeing this play, the spectators in Cádiz might have joined their on-stage representatives and call shame onto Spain for tolerating such commerce.

Following dialogue and action taken directly from the novel, in act IV the plot begins to establish a new path and ideological purpose, and it further adapts the story of American slavery into a Hispanic consideration of the slave trade. Haley's assistant, Loker, catches Elisa, and the frame of the piece shifts. The larger philosophical concerns underpinning the work no longer come from Stowe's novel. Jorge and Elisa begin to lose agency, and their quest for freedom is eclipsed by the future damnation or salvation of Haley's soul. A significant amount of dialogue is dedicated to the slave trader's defense of *la trata*, and the entire cast of characters (initially divided into supporters and opponents of the trade) becomes aware of the evils of human traffic. Lest the moral agenda of *Haley* remains unclear, the dramatists indicate that the entire cast is to be reintroduced in front of a slave ship during the final scenes of the play.

The action in act IV begins with a passage that echoes a famous scene in the contemporary play *Don Juan Tenorio*. Loker and Haley pause to brag of their feats as heartless traffickers and successes at separating mothers from their children, shocking the audience much as the shameless charmer Don Juan and his rival Luis Mejías entertain and scandalize them in a strikingly similar recitation of the statistics of their crimes against women. Moreover, each character transgresses social mores, plays the fate of his soul, and is saved while expiring his last breath; however, the specter of Don Juan in the Haley character is important because it develops the cultural adaptation by suggesting a parallel between the nineteenth-century *traficante* and a famous literary figure born in and representative of the Spanish Golden Age and the height of the Spanish empire. As a monstrous sinner and a stereotype of Spanish masculine sexuality, Don Juan embodied Spain's international cultural identity from its glorious past, while the *traficante* symbolized Spain's troubles in contemporary international politics.

Beside the traffickers, the entire Shelby/Wilson clan then unites on stage while a distraught Elisa cries at her separation from not only Enrique but also, remarkably, her owner Emilia Shelby. Haley's other slaves march onto the steamship in the background and the physical and emotional realities of human traffic are fully represented before the Cádiz public. Senator Wilson, who has served as the on-stage spectator for the audience, pronounces a long lament on the woes of Africa, but urges the continent to rise and assume its appointed role in human civilization, predicting for it a future of "splendors." Both Africa and "legitimate" slave society at either end of the Middle Passage suffer at the hands of the trader.

Finally, disguised as a Spanish Creole landowner, Jorge arrives at the last minute to purchase Enrique from Haley, thus reuniting father and son, guaranteeing the Shelby family honor, and returning a slave (Elisa) to her benevolent mistress and her prescribed place in society. However, Jorge has a dual nature. As a Spanish landowner he conforms to "good" slave law, but when unmasked as a runaway slave, he becomes a volatile element to be subdued. Jorge reveals his true identity to all and draws his pistols to ensure his own escape. Loker promptly attempts to disarm him. In a classic deus ex machina, however, one of the guns accidentally discharges and Haley falls fatally wounded. Jorge's armed revolt against his legal owner stages the rampant Spanish fears of a "Haitian" race war in Cuba. The threat of further slave rebellion and Haley's deathbed morality bring about the final resolution to the play. Immediately after the gunshot, the sound of the lifting anchor fills the stage: Haley's boat of slaves is about to depart and—figuratively—so is his soul. Seizing the opportunity to repent, Haley frees all slaves aboard and thus gains eternal salvation by turning away from the trade at the last possible moment. Haley expires and the ideological message of the play is again delivered rather heavy-handedly in the final scenes, with the death of personified "traffic" as the means to the reconstitution of the traditional family-based (and slave-holding) society.

The final tableau poses a group of emancipated slaves, including Jorge (no longer symbolizing the threat of a race war after the death of traffic), Elisa, and the Shelbys on their knees around the dead body of Haley. Senator Wilson, the representative of the state, remains standing and closes the play with the call "¡Justicia del cielo!" (Heaven's justice!) It is under this guidance between the powers of Heaven and Earth that disorder is resolved.

In terms of scenery, the introduction of the *buque negrero* (slave ship) in the final act brilliantly stages the focus of international crisis. Haley's ship is a Mississippi steamship, but it is also a scenographic adaptation of Stowe's analogy of the horrors of the American slave trade with the

Middle Passage (Stowe, chap. 31). Moreover, ships were a veritable symbol of the commerce upon which the wealth of Cádiz had been built, including the commerce in slaves during the eighteenth century (see Torres Ramírez). In revealing the nightmarish truth of the slaver, the stage scenery capsized the merchant's vessel's respectability and perhaps provoked guilt in the public. As an element of a textual adaptation across that space, the ship in act IV performs the symbolic function of Uncle Tom's cabin in the final section of the novel, invoking the memory of the effects of the trade in all spectators.

(Up)-staging *Uncle Tom's Cabin*

Haley delivers a shocking and unexpected ending—a coup that represents an important Spanish interpretation of the Tío Tom story. *Haley* is not an abolitionist play but rather a reformist play regarding the effects of the *negrero* on society. Haley's self-redemption only frees those slaves who are *in transit*, who are being trafficked; Elisa, for example, remains enslaved and is apparently content to return to her mistress, Emilia Shelby (who had called her husband a "monster" for trading Elisa in the first place). Nevertheless, the success of the denouement was predicated on a residual sentimentality among the public from the experience of reading the abolitionist novel and their surprise at differences between the two pieces. Specific references and instances of abridgement continually draw the public from the play to the novel and back again, into a comfortable hybrid space of *déjà-lu* and *déjà-vu*. One means by which Luna and Palomino achieved this intertextuality, and thereby fortified the impact of their *drama*, was by staging several of Stowe's crucial narrative or descriptive passages. In one form or another, *Haley* includes Eliza's escape across the Ohio River, Lucy's suicide, and Tom's death.

The play's focus on Haley, Jorge, and Elisa, and the omission of other prominent characters from subplots of the long novel does not detract from the unity of the play as a whole. However, Tom's absence from the cast of characters in *Haley* is remarkable. He, along with Eva, was the novel's most celebrated character, featured on the cover of the illustrated edition in Madrid. Whereas in the novel, George and Tom each represented opposing (but effective) paths to liberty, in the play, no voice of passivity counters Jorge and Elisa's active quest for freedom. Indeed, in *Haley*, the only victim of slave policies to be saved is society itself. Yet Uncle Tom's presence resonates throughout in the play's final scenes.

Specifically, the dramatic Haley appropriates Tom's redemptive power. Once fatally wounded, the trader begins to consider the state of his soul.

> Hal. ¡Ay!
> Lok. ¡Cielos!
> Hal. ¡Me he muerto!
> Wil. ¡Socorrámosle!
> Hal. No, dejadme. Mi herida está aquí . . . en el alma . . . Dios es el que me ha herido.

> (Haley: Ah!
> Loker: Good Heavens!
> Haley: I am dying!
> Wilson: Let's help him!
> Haley: No, leave me. My wound is here . . . in my soul . . . it is God who has wounded me.)

The trafficker interprets his own death as the resolution of a divine social order. Before the eyes of a higher justice (and out of concern for his own salvation), Haley reverses his treatment of slaves. The sound of the slave ship's lifting anchor unexpectedly prompts him to send Loker to the barge. "Sujetad ese buque . . . id, desembarcar los negros, sean todos libres!" (Stop that boat . . . go, disembark the Blacks [slaves], let them all be free!) Haley's order enacts precisely the part of the international treaties pertinent to the real Spanish contraband *negreros*. Captured slavers were to be brought before judges and the slaves aboard their ships set free (*Tratado*, art. 13). By translating their message into a scenographic language, Luna and Palomino further elude censorship of their sharp criticism of Spain's breach of the treaty.

Haley does indeed free the slaves, to the astonishment of all. In his protracted death scene Haley is an inversion of the moribund Uncle Tom. Like him, Haley brings the witnesses of his death to Christ. Chiefly, he saves his own soul by ordering Jorge to become Christian. Gasping, he commands, "Jorge . . . ya eres libre . . . hazte cristiano." (Jorge . . . now you are free . . . become a Christian.) In addition to the overt religious meaning, to a Spanish audience this command also carries a political and cultural charge. Spaniards traditionally referred to themselves as "cristianos" (Christians) and their language as "cristiano" (Christian); the term also implies speaking clearly and sensibly. Therefore, by directing Jorge to "become Christian," Haley essentially orders him to "be Spanish," both culturally and politically, and to return to the traditional norms of behavior. Jorge's assent is visually confirmed in his kneeling submission to a Christian God and an earthly political system represented by Wilson, in the final tableau that closes the piece. But it also implies that Jorge and Elisa do not reunite because of their own strengths, but rather that the abolitionist spirit of the slave trader is the sole means to securing the stability of the national family.

Jorge's tirades about independence, national identity, and separatism in acts I and III are married to religion (for example, he declared "yo no soy cristiano" [I am not Christian] just as he was about to run away) and, consequently, nationality. In addition to his rebellion, evoking fears of violent ethnic and cultural consequences from the protracted traffic to Cuba, Jorge points to the real political instability in a province that was beginning to reexamine its identification as "Spanish."[14] Historically, a reevaluation of race, culture, and nationality as different from those of Iberia at midcentury framed the political debate regarding Cuba's sovereignty and relationship to Spain, and the various contemporary attitudes toward slavery and trade (Naranjo Orovio and Puig-Samper, 791). In *Haley* a suppression of the trade guaranteed the subjugation and reincorporation of Jorge's troublesome Spanish identity back into the imperial family (under the control of the *madre patria*).

Jorge's Spanishness is first questioned in act III, when he arrives at the inn where Wilson is relaxing and talking with sailors. In the equivalent passage from Stowe's novel, the runaway George *appears* Spanish, but introduces himself with an American name and later explains that he had darkened his skin and hair. In contrast, Haley's Jorge completes the transformation, presenting himself as "López de Mendoza," a Spanish businessman from New Orleans, one of the cities where Spanish Creoles negotiated invasion and annexation with the United States. The Spanish press harshly condemned these separatists as pompous traitors and ridiculed their cause: *Salvadores de Cuba* (Cuba's Saviors), "como si esta isla, rica y feliz bajo la bandera española, pudiese querer la salvacion de manos de la gente más perdida de los Estados de la Union, de la escoria que la Europa envia diariamente al nuevo mundo" (*El mensajero*, April 12, 1853; as if this island, rich and happy under the Spanish flag, could want salvation from the hands of the most vile people of the United States, from the scourge that Europe sends off daily to the New World). Although both George and Jorge fled slavery in a Spanish disguise, the mask had a different cultural valance in Spain than it did in the United States. Jorge is not simply blurring ethnic lines between European and African, his representation as a dark-skinned Spanish Creole had further nationalist and political implications. Indeed, among contemporary concerns was the question of whether Cubans were being "Africanized" by the trade to such a degree that they were no longer Spanish, much as the American statesmen Edward Everett had claimed. Jorge, the false Spaniard of act III, will be told to become *cristiano*, for according to Luna and Palomino, the rightful place of both slaves and Spanish Creole Cubans was under the control of the Spanish state.

Politics of *Haley*

Ángel María de Luna and Rafael Leopoldo de Palomino are, at best, marginal figures in the annals of Spanish theater. The total number of plays attributed to Palomino is a mere eight titles, and Luna has no other known plays (Rogers, 329). In the cultural history of mid-nineteenth-century Cádiz, however, they were prominent *hommes des lettres* and vociferous social critics. The dossier on their activities as editors of the newspaper *La Palma*, currently stored in the provincial archive, documents a melodramatic tale of their challenges to censorship and prison evasion. Like Ayguals de Izco, they saw the potential of *Uncle Tom's Cabin* as a powerful tool for social criticism; however, they tailored it to address the domestic issue of Spain's tolerance of the transatlantic trade. *Haley* was their first foray into drama, and their social earnestness is supported by almost schoolboyish basic elements of Aristotelian tragedy.

Luna and Palomino did not set their play in Cuba, nor did they explicitly codify Haley as Spanish. Nevertheless, *Haley* represented an attempt by these authors to avoid direct government censorship while broaching the question of the transatlantic slave trade. Spanish theater of the previous fifty years was replete with examples of allegorical works transparently transposed onto the past or to distant lands, and the geographical relocation in this piece was merely perfunctory. In a "Note to Readers" included in the printed edition of the play, Luna and Palomino explain their markedly nonliterary reasons for recasting the story of American slavery as a play: theater, not the novel, is the most expedient means of instilling a new moral understanding in the public.

Haley was not government propaganda but rather a popular theater piece directed at a bourgeois public that, at best, enjoyed indirect access to the powers of the imperial administration. Nevertheless, the play coincided with more than one strain of reformist policies. In December 1852, the president of the council of ministers, Bravo Murillo, was unseated and the ensuing political upheaval brought about a new administration headed by the Count of San Luis (whose newspapers had serialized *La cabaña del tío Tom*). His colonial strategy was informed by a desire to pacify Great Britain and gain international support for Spanish control of Cuba (Cayuela Fernández, 12). Most importantly, he appointed the famously antislavery military officer Juan de la Pezuela as Captain General of Cuba, reversing a tradition (since 1834) of institutionalized bribery and semiofficial tolerance of the illegal trade. Pezuela implemented further changes that could have prevented future traffic, aided the illegally imported Africans already in Cuba, and made the island significantly less appealing to the United States. Not surprisingly, Cuban slave owners, who claimed that favorable treatment of free and enslaved Blacks would lead to race warfare (Cayuela Fernández, 12), resisted these measures. Pezuela was ultimately forced to compromise: the trade continued, slavery was abolished only in 1880, and Cuba remained a Spanish province until the Spanish-American War of 1898.

Valladares

The theatrical adaptation of Stowe's novel performed in Madrid presented a markedly different message from that of *Haley* and appealed to a different audience than the bourgeoisie of the port city of Cádiz. Ramón de Valladares y Saavedra was a prolific dramatist with nearly two hundred titles to his name, in addition to an acting manual (Gies, 55n35). He was particularly known for arranging, adapting, and translating French plays on bourgeois family life. In early 1853, his *La cabaña de Tom; o, La esclavitud de los negros* premiered at the Teatro del Instituto in Madrid and was subsequently published in at least four editions during the following sixty years. Pere Gifra Adroher reports that the play was performed in at least six theaters in the capital, at least twenty times in the Odeón in Barcelona, and in various cities along the Mediterranean coast (222). The same critic proposes that the play's sustained popularity throughout the 1860s and 1870s contributed to the Spanish public's understanding of their own nation's slave policy during those years (224).[15] Unlike *Haley*, adapted from Ayguals de Izco's translation of the novel from the original English, Valladares acknowledged that his was a "drama de espectáculo en seis cuadros escrito con presencia de la novela y de los dramas franceses" (spectacular play in six acts written alongside the novel and the French plays). Indeed, as Gifra Adroher has verified, Valladares drew heavily from the French *Le case de l'oncle Tom* by Dumanoir and D'Ennery. Also unlike *Haley* or Stowe's *Uncle Tom's Cabin*, Valladares's *Cabaña* argues against abolition.

Valladares's innovation is his treatment of the character Ricardo Harris. Alone among a host of benevolent (and White) slave owners and the redeemed Haley, the mulatto Harris personifies the evils of slavery in the play. Elisa summarizes this cruel, vicious, and wealthy mulatto: "Ve con gusto correr la sangre, que es la sangre de su madre." (10; He watches blood run with pleasure, the blood of his mother.) Harris illustrates the position popular among a significant sector of the European population that slaves should not be freed for they were unfit for self-governance. "Pobres ovejas, si algún día se convertiese en pastor una de ellas" (7; Poor sheep, if someday one of them should become the shepherd), remarks St. Clair. The danger is not a wolf among the fold, but the "unnatural" promotion of a sheep to shepherd. Indeed, the slave trader, who would be such a wolf, becomes humanized over the course of the play. This is in contrast to Stowe's novel, where slave traders and owners remain committed to their trades: as Hazel Waters notes, the trader Simon Legree "has the potential for redemption, but it is a potential on which he resolutely turns his back" (32). Here, as in other Spanish *negrero* plays, Haley is "conmovido" by Shelby's attachment to his slave Tom (Valladares, 16) and ultimately becomes an active abolitionist: "Me despido de mi oficio" (Valladares, 59; I'm quitting my profession), he announces. Free Blacks, not slave traders or slave owners are the greatest threat to society in Valladares's vision of America.

Even Tom's wife, Cloé, laments that freed men's "nueva condicion" (31; new station) makes them forget their social ties to the Black community. The well-spoken, serious, and cruel Harris is balanced in character by the buffoon Bengalí, an emancipated slave, who similarly dramatizes—but through humor—the position that Blacks are fundamentally unprepared for society after slavery. In a word, freedom transforms Bengalí into a beast. But because he never gains power, he slowly recovers compassion for his enslaved friends. Bengalí initially proclaims: "¡Oh! Yo queded [quered; quiero] la esclavitud cuando sed [soy] amo y no escavo" (Oh! I want slavery when I am a master and not a slave),[16] to which Senator Bird remarks, "Ahí tienes lo que es el negro libre." (39; Such is the free Black man.) Bengalí later sells his enslaved friend and sets fire to Harris's sugar mill in order to save Elisa: the antiabolitionist public thus witnesses the savagery of warfare among free Blacks.

Valladares adapted his play from the same Dumanoir who had written *Le Docteur noir* (with Auguste Anicet-Bourgeois) a play with a successful run starting on July 30, 1846, at the Théâtre de la Porte Saint-Martin, a venue where numerous social plays with Black protagonists were performed (Cooper, 84). *Le Docteur noir* presented a colonial Black doctor from the Île Reunion banished to the Bastille for marrying a White, socially superior woman. A meandering melodrama, the play nevertheless questioned colonialism, race, class, and ranks of citizenship within the French empire. As Barbara Cooper argues, it is a political work and the authors present a work with a humanitarian thesis that directly attacks the legitimacy of slavery (84). *Le Docteur noir* questioned the limits of citizenship by pointing to the geographic, class, and racial hierarchies at play in its false universality. The character of Harris in *Cabaña* raises these same questions of citizenship, highly relevant for Spain. Were the mulattos and free Blacks of Cuba, especially in the wake of the Escalera conspiracy, to be allies of Spain? Or partisans of an independent Cuba?

Valladares's play was an ideological counterweight to the work of the radical Ayguals, but it made *Uncle Tom's Cabin* palatable to a public that might have refused abolitionist works. Notably, while translations of Stowe's novel generally enjoyed great success, Valladares's play had lukewarm reviews, at best. The following selection of reviews reflects the overall critical reception. *El Clamor Público*, ideologically aligned with Ayguals, criticizes the staging, acting, and text of the play on its opening night, suggesting that after one act the public "se marchase durante alguno de los intermedios á pasar un rato á cualquier tertulia aunque estuviese en un estremo de Madrid" ("Crónica de teatros," 4; depart during one of the intermissions to go spend time in some salon, even if it is on the other side of Madrid).[17] The *Diario Español* of Madrid, allied to the "Unión Liberal," usually published robust reviews, commenting on the script, authorship, and actors, but it was uncharacteristically brief here, primarily noting the public's cold reception of the play. "*La choza de Tom*, estrenada en el Instituto, no ha correspondido en la escena á la asombrosa popularidad de la novela anglo-americana de donde la ha tomado el Sr. Valladares; y el público, que se muestra poco *negrófilo* en materias de literatura dramática, ha recibido con frialdad la filosofía humanitaria del seudo Tom, y los chistes en *bozal* de los negritos Benjamin y Filemon." ("Folletín. Revista de Teatros," 1; *La choza de Tom*, premiered at the Instituto Theater, did not hold up on stage to the astonishing popularity of the Anglo-American novel from which Valladares took his story; the public, showing itself to be not very *negrophile* in questions of dramatic literature, gave a cold reception to the humanitarian philosophy of the pseudo Tom and the jokes in *bozal* [the spoken Spanish characteristic of African-born slaves] by Benjamin and Filemon.) The observation that the public was neither negrophile nor interested in humanitarianism suggests that either the audience in the Instituto was different from the public who read the novel or they disapproved of the play's pro-slavery message.[18]

In contrast, the pro-government paper *El Heraldo* exuberantly reported on April 2, 1853, that not only was the play a great success, but also, as an indicator of the play's merits, the queen mother attended this adaptation of Stowe's work:

> Sigue atrayendo concurrencia al teatro del Instituto el drama *La choza de Tom*, cada vez mas aplaudido. La ejecucion se ha perfeccionado, los entre actos son ya cortos y se sale del teatro mucho antes de las doce. Parece que el martes próximo se representará el drama á beneficio del autor, y que la empresa y los actores piensan esmerarse. Si es así esto hace el elogio de los unos y de la otra.
>
> Anoche asistieron á la representacion S. M. la reina madre con su esposo el duque de Riansares y sus hijas, siendo la concurrencia numerosa y escogida. ("Teatros," 4)

> (The drama *Uncle Tom's Cabin* continues to attract attendance to the Institute's theater, each performance more applauded than the one before. The performance has been perfected, intermissions are now short and one leaves the theater long before twelve. It seems that next Tuesday the drama will be performed in benefit of the author, and the company and the actors will do their utmost. If so, they are all worthy of praise.
>
> Last night Her Majesty the Queen Mother attended the performance with her husband, the Duke of Riansares, and their daughters, the attendance being large and select.)

The royal family often attended the theater in Madrid. The same *El Heraldo* reported on March 29, 1853, that Queen Isabel, her husband King Francisco de Asis, the queen mother, her consort, and their daughters had attended *Roberto el Diablo* in the *Teatro Real* two days before ("Gacetilla de la capital," 4).[19] That is, it was not rare for the queen mother to attend Madrid theaters, but it was remarkable that the leading Spanish beneficiary of the illegal slave trade attended a play whose title was all but synonymous with abolitionism. Given the reviews of the play, it seems unlikely that María Cristina would have attended because of the play's dramatic qualities, but perhaps because Valladares's play offered an acceptable version of the popular work, with a vision that coincided with her personal investments, her attendance provided a metatheatrical means to demonstrate her antiabolitionist positions. María Cristina invested extensively in the slave trade to Cuba. Her affairs were managed through the mediation of Claudio Martínez de Pinillos, Conde de Villanueva, the treasury intendant general in Cuba (an official implicated in all manner of corruption schemes). Pinillos, in turn, served as the legal representative of Agustín Muñoz Sánchez (Duke of Riansares), and partnered with Antonio Parejo, an established slave trader (Quiroz, 487). In other words, the Duke and Duchess of Riansares were not occasional participants in the slave trade; rather, it formed a cornerstone of their vast commercial portfolio.[20] One wonders if the queen mother noted the irony of the actions of the antiabolitionist character Senator Bird. Fresh from voting for the a pro-slave trade bill (the Fugitive Slave Law, although the play doesn't specify), Bird exclaims his dismay at finding himself breaking said law each time he aids in the illegal transportation of the slaves Elisa and Enrique toward freedom in Canada (51–52). Elisa describes Bird: "Aprobando con los labios esa ley bárbara de los hombres, practicais en el corazón la santa ley de Dios." (52; Approving with your lips that barbaric law of men, you exercise God's holy law in your heart.) Bird is all but the inverse of María Cristina, the signatory of the 1835 abolition treaty with Great Britain and beneficiary of a slave-powered sugar industry.

Conclusion

Haley proposed the abolition of the slave trade as a means to ensure Spanish control of a Cuba with slavery, but in Spanish literature of the midcentury, the *trata* and slavery were commonly fused into one single crime. The play *Romper cadenas* (Breaking the chains), which premiered at the Novedades Theater in Madrid on January 14, 1873, marked the conclusion of plays about *negreros* during the age of the trade. Dedicated to the Spanish Sociedad Abolicionista, the drama celebrates 1873, the date of the abolition of slavery in Puerto Rico (but not Cuba), as the end of the reign of the corrupt *negrero* who had sewn vice in both the Peninsula and Cuba through his trafficking. That is, even in a play about the abolition of slavery, the antagonist is a transatlantic slave trader. Here, the slave trader is not redeemed; rather, he is killed off. The very simple plot revolves around Alfredo, the abolitionist son of a plantation owner and investor in the transatlantic slave trade and an abolitionist mother; his beloved, Adela; the *negrero*, Roberto; and Pedro, Alfredo's slave. Roberto wins over Alfredo's father and sister to his side after a successful clandestine landing of enslaved Africans including six hundred adults and ninety-two children, while the island's population turns against Alfredo, and Adela disappears. Roberto and his kind appear invincible, boasting of their feats in song:

> Chocad, chocad, amigos,
> las copas del licor,
> brindemos por la caza
> de gente de color.
> A salud de las olas
> y de Don Tomás,
> que mueran los cruceros
> y viva el capitán. (26)

> (Clink, clink, friends,
> your glasses of liquor,
> let us toast to the hunt
> of colored people.
> To the health of the waves
> and of Don Tomás.
> Death to the British cruisers,
> and long live the Capitán.)

But the Cuban slaves do not submit to the *negrero* willingly. One of Alfredo's slaves, Juana, asks Alfredo and his mother to arm her, "un cuchillo dadme" (63; give me a knife), in order to hunt down Roberto and an overseer. Although her attempts at armed resistance do not come to fruition, those of another enslaved person do change the course of the action in the play and, symbolically, in Cuba. When all hope of justice seems lost, Pedro, who has been following everyone's actions over the course of the play, restores order through both intelligence and violence. Unlike the Jorge of *Haley* whose gun goes off accidentally or the Jorge and Tom of Valladares's play who intend to fight but are pushed aside by a zealous Senator Bird, the actions of this hero are unequivocally those of a rebellious slave.

After fending off Alfredo's enemies and tracking down Roberto, at the play's conclusion, Pedro shoots two men: Roberto, Cuba's last slave trader, and Justo, a corrupt overseer. That is, simultaneous with the law emanating from Madrid (but before it has been announced), this Black character takes down the *trata* and the slave system single-handedly. Moreover, he saves the play's virtuous Spanish heroine, Adela, from rape by these same men. Significantly, Adela's fiery abolitionist, but ineffective, beloved, Alfredo, does not save her, nor does the slave trader undergo a moral transformation before his death. In what must be one of the most triumphant images of a reasoned, justified, and armed rebellious slave, Pedro enters the stage "con Adela en los brazos y la escopeta en la mano" (with Adela in his arms and the rifle in his hand) after freeing the plantation's slaves from their cruel overseer and Cuba from the unbridled control of the *negrero*. He then announces, "Pero á esos cobardes les quité la presa, / y al querer matarme, / fui yo mas ligero, / y desde ahora á nadie / le harán mas infamias. / *Resquiescat in pace*." (63–64; But I took away the prey of those cowards, / as they wanted to kill me, / I was quicker, / and from now on to no one / will they inflict any more infamies / *Resquiescat in pace*.) To which Alfredo responds, "Pedro, ya eres libre." (Pedro, you are now free.)

The message of *Romper cadenas* is that White abolitionists are all but powerless before the *negrero* and his factions: only the armed, rational Black man is able to enact a revolution that produces his own freedom and draws the emancipated into a modern political society. The final dialogue of the play makes clear that Pedro's actions may be revolutionary, but they do not threaten Spanish control of Cuba. Quite to the contrary, they strengthen it. Like the Negro Tomás who fights in the barricades of 1854, Pedro works to reform society in the image of European progressives and promises fidelity to "good" White men, assuring everyone, "Que los negros tienen / corazón amante / y quieren al blanco / si mal no les hace" (that the Blacks have / loving heart / and love the White man / if he does them no harm).

For their part, the Spanish Abolitionist Society in Madrid was, like much of European abolitionism, self-congratulatory. On the occasion of parliamentary debates in February 1880 over the *patronato* apprenticeship scheme following the abolition of Cuban slavery, the senator from Santiago de Cuba, Bernardo Portuondo, credited Spanish abolitionists for granting freedom to colonial slaves: "A ella en primer término, a la Sociedad Abolicionista Española, se debe la iniciativa y la propaganda de la abolición de la esclavitud." (Qtd. in Vila Vilar and Vila Vilar, 20; We owe the initiative and the propagation of the abolition of slavery primarily to the Spanish Abolitionist Society.) Such self-congratulation in the metropolis ignored the participation of slaves in their (sometimes armed) struggle for emancipation. But at times, Spanish literature allowed a wider perspective than did political discourse. While the trope of a *negrero*'s redemption was common, many of the works discussed here acknowledged the protagonism of Afro-Cubans as legitimate political players in the fight against the monstrous slave system, albeit only in terms palatable to the metropolitan public: civilized by good Spanish governance, Afro-Cubans were adherent to the values of the liberal regime and malleable in their rebellion. It is clear in this literary version of the facts that slaves' actions were crucial, even as it assimilates, reshapes, and silences the actual motivations of the rebellious Afro-Cubans (slaves and free) into a European liberal story of social change.

§2 The Colony in the Capital
El amigo Manso and *Lo prohibido*

Historical work has offered new insights into nineteenth-century Spain's metropolitan attitudes toward the overseas provinces.[1] But, as Cora Kaplan has argued for the British case, beyond factual knowledge, creative works made empire legible and vivid to readers in Europe. The language and narratives of fiction, poetry, and drama that dealt with the everyday relations between metropole and colony recreated (or undermined) an imperial mind-set at home. Literature does much more than illustrate a case proven through fact-driven analysis; rather, it is the place where political and human relations can be taken to imaginative conclusions. In the case addressed here, such a creation gives form and character to the idea of the nation as empire at the end of the age of slavery (Kaplan, 192).

The Spanish realist novel represents and creates the modern nation in the cultural realm; yet, in Galdós's novels examined in this chapter, the colonies at the margins reveal the (autonomous, modern) nation to be a myth. Paradoxically, the nation that Galdós represents in his novels is a demonstrated fantasy. There were many models of the nation available to Galdós, from Pi y Margall's federalism to a Carlist monarchy, but he remains committed, here, to a particular liberal model and questions the place of the colonies in it when capitalism returns to the metropolis from them and corrupts nation formation. The history of Spain in the nineteenth century is inextricable from colonialism. On an economic level, Angel Bahamonde and José Cayuela in their *Hacer las Américas* have uncovered the striking degree to which major players in the national economy were involved in wealth generation via the slave economies of the Antilles. Additionally, as Chris Schmidt-Nowara has written, "colonial exploitation was not an afterthought but a cornerstone of Spanish liberalism, decisively shaping the political economy, and the political culture, of the metropolis and the colonies" (*Conquest*, 9). Literary works mediate in the rupture between nation building and the realities of the centrality of the colonies to the metropolis. According to Jo Labanyi, the major Spanish realist novels construct modernity as representation, and the critique of representation inherent in the project of the novel comments on the very process of representation that "constructs" the nation. That is, the realist novel is aware of its own processes of representation (Labanyi, 385), and the novel examines modernization as a process whereby reality is converted into representation. Galdós crafts a story of the Spanish nation and the capital city that underscores the very constructedness of Spanishness. He reveals and censures colonial practices in the Peninsula and probes the limits of faithful depiction of national society in a realist novel when the nation is dependent on its corrupt colonial base. Realism exposes that there is no national reality based on an intrinsic or "natural" coherence of the elements of Spain as nation. A representation of the economic truths of the colonial roots of Spanish modernity in an outlawed slave trade (or at the very least the colonial slave economy) undermines the idea of a coherent, emerging Herderian nation-state.

Here I focus on the two novels that were highly contemporary and, as opposed to all of Galdós's other novels, were not reflections on the past, as the action of the plots took place shortly before the publication of the novels. *El amigo Manso* and *Lo prohibido* impart a sense of immediacy and urgency as the bourgeois nation and empire fall apart. Galdós's progressive disappointment with the bourgeoisie to keep the nation afloat in the other contemporary novels is exacerbated by the rapacious mentality of colonialists that is penetrating the tissue of Spanish society, the very heart of the nation. The revolution of 1868 in Spain had represented a moment of hope, but the Bourbon Restoration that squelched the chances for a progressive nation arose from both the failure of the Gloriosa and the success of the Ten Years' colonial war. Spain defeated Cuban insurrectionists but lost in the long run from its win, in these novels. Thus, the crisis of the nation is shaped by the uncertain future of a volatile empire.

Exactly how the Spanish realist novel addressed or avoided the thorny question of Cuban slavery has been the subject of debate. Germán Gullón has argued that the scholarly treatment of the "Generation of '98," the group of writers characterized as addressing Spain's response to the "disaster" of imperial decline, has had decisive implications for Spain's understanding of itself as nation and empire, with Cuba seen as little more than pawn in a battle over control of the Atlantic between two imperial powers (the United States and Spain). Gullón tackles the complex relationship between late nineteenth-century Spanish literature and current widespread cultural ignorance about Spanish policies in Cuba, identifying the sources of misinformation in both literary production and the subsequent criticism of works from the late nineteenth century (91–116). Gullón perceives an overall absence of engagement with Cuba in nineteenth-century Spanish literature and mentions in particular the works of Benito Pérez Galdós (outside the Generation of '98 proper) as part of a refusal by nineteenth-century Spain to recognize Cuba's political or cultural protagonism. The suggestion that turn-of-the-century works are at best devoid of discussions of Cuba (and at worst purposeful misrepresentations of imperial abuses) is a welcome invitation to reconsider the realist novel as a space where the empire was depicted in imaginative terms. Indeed, in his novels Galdós depicts a metropolis fully at ease with empire but explicitly criticizes its policies. The imperial power, violence, and exploitation behind the tinseled grandeur of Galdós's Spain are central to the development of his (and historical) Spain and erupt at crucial moments in his novels to drive the plot and shape narration. In these novels, we catch Galdós thinking about the problem of empire during the Restoration as society is rapidly changing on the heels of the colonial war and the return of the Bourbons.

Galdós published seventy-seven novels during his long and prolific career and nearly all of his *novelas contemporáneas* are realist explorations of life in Madrid. The city he depicts is an often self-absorbed urban sphere. But in certain works, Madrid is dislodged from the center to become just another site of empire, controlled by Cuban fortunes networked across various cities in Spain and in North America. In these works, corrupt colonial administration generates an inescapable rapacity, which threatens to destroy the capital that ostensibly runs the empire. In *El amigo Manso* (1882) and *Lo prohibido* (1884–85) in particular, Galdós underscores the dangerous role played by representatives of the overseas colonial interests (the so-called colonial lobby; see Jacobson) in the economy of Madrid and, metonymically, all of Spain; the attempts at disentangling these interests from "native" peninsular life shape the fantastical plots of these two novels. These two works are by no means the only ones in which Galdós explores the place of the colonial, specifically *negreros*, in a Spain pulled between the real and the ideal. Galdós returned to the *negrero* character in later novels but never changed his position.

Negreros are an eye-catching tessera in the author's realist mosaic. They, and the colonial society they represent, disquiet Galdós's world. Slave traders distinguish the Spanish empire from the British empire; the former relies on their interventions while the latter, the modern nation par excellence, has actively condemned them. The existence and indeed overt embrace of the *negrero* in contemporary Spain is not only illegal but also a moral problem for the too-forgiving bourgeoisie. In Galdós's world, slavery or the slave trade cement moral character, punctuate observations of economic realities, and amplify anxieties about Spain's international image. Francisco Caudet has proposed a link between a certain type of corrupt self-made man from the colonies and the artistic possibilities of the naturalist mode in Galdós's late *episodios nacionales*.[2]

Galdós simultaneously creates and undermines an imperial mind-set at home, and his novels represent the corrupting force of the *negreros* on literature itself. Galdós's sustained preoccupation with the relationship among the printed page, the public sphere, and historical knowledge (or the influence of fact versus fiction on readers) was at the foundation of his *episodios nacionales* project. The same concerns take on farcical dimensions in the playful "La novela en el tranvía" and motivate a metaliterary experiment in *El amigo Manso*, but in the much later *episodio Amadeo I* that returns to the Restoration period, the misuse of the press assumes a menacing tone when the narrator describes plans for a newspaper run by slaving interests that would undermine the entire project of public education through print. In a Spain teetering between attempts at liberalism and the power of the colonial lobby, "ricos hacendados de la Isla [Cuba]" (rich landowners from the Island [Cuba]) intended to

> crear aquí [España] una opinión favorable a sus intereses. . . . Quieren los buenos españoles que si se ha de quitar la esclavitud, nos contentemos ahora con *el vientre libre*, dejando lo demás para mejores tiempos. Si así no se hace, peligrará la riqueza, la propiedad, y los ingenios serán pronto montones de ruinas. . . . Para meter estas ideas en las cabezas alocadas de acá, los hacendados desean tener aquí órganos de la opinión sensata. (Galdós, *Amadeo*, 490)

> (create here an opinion favorable to their interests. . . . If slavery is to be abolished, these good Spaniards want us to be content for now with the Free Womb Law, leaving the rest for better times. If it is not done like this, wealth and property will be jeopardized and the sugar mills will soon become heaps of ruins. In order to introduce these ideas into the crazy heads over here, the landowners wish to have mediums of sensible public opinion in place.)

Juan Manzanedo's *La Reforma* was exactly such an organ intended to sway public opinion, squelch abolitionist sentiments, and defer reform. Opposition newspapers were integral to nineteenth-century politics, but here, Galdós satirizes the ideas of common sense, an informed public, and even the literary-cultural project, when compromised by the colonial lobby. Unlike the aesthetic concerns of a previous generation over a cultural invasion of page and stage by France, Galdós presents a society in which both public opinion and language itself are conquered through the misleading logic of colonial economics. As with Pito's stories of the low-life of a slave trader on the high seas in *Ángel Guerra*, newspapers (and the novels themselves) trade in a literary marketplace, peddling stories palatable to a national (or local) readership sick with nostalgia for its maritime past. The realist novel writes the Spanish nation into being for the readers who confuse its message with reality. In *Amadeo I*, Spain is portrayed as less a nation created by the metropolis through the process of centralized legislation (as the modern bourgeois nation claims itself to be) than a cultural and political sphere controlled by the periphery: the men and money born of slave interests in Cuba. Spain is similarly enchained in *Cánovas*, where, as Francisco Caudet has pointed out, Tito Liviano reflects on the savage capitalists emerging from the colonies who have enchained the nation, thus necessitating a future revolution (99).

> Me reventaban los condes y marqueses, mayormente los de nuevo cuño, sacados por don Amadeo y don Alfonso del montón de indianos negreros, de mercachifles enriquecidos o de agiotistas sin conciencia. . . . Detestaba, en fin, todas las vanidades que se habían mancomunado para contener los progresos de nuestra patria, y encerrarla dentro de unos moldes que no podría romper sin nuevas y más iracundas revoluciones. (Galdós, *Cánovas*, 570)
>
> (The counts and marquis repelled me, especially the newly minted ones, picked by don Amadeo and don Alfonso from the pack of slave-trading *indianos*, of new money peddlers or speculators without a conscious. . . . I hated, in a nutshell, all the vanities that had come together to contain the progress of our country, and confine it in molds she could not break away from without new and more enraged revolutions.)

Galdós returns here to themes he had explored earlier in *El amigo Manso* and *Lo prohibido*. But when he wrote these novels in the 1880s, this process was happening before his eyes, and Galdós did not yet know how it would turn out. Their narrative frame is grounded in an immediate fear of the implications of the colony in the capital. Writing with his habitual hindsight at the turn of the century, the novelist returns to the ideas of these earlier novels in *Cánovas* and *Amadeo I* and reflects that, in fact, their nightmares have come true. The later novels suggest that the imperial turn necessitated revolution.

Mary Coffey has analyzed Galdós's references to Spanish colonialism as part of the author's exploration of "the perceived obstacles to a successful establishment of national identity" (50). In her view, the lack of discussion of the colonies in the first series of the *episodios nacionales* presents a strategic attempt to "forget colonial history" and imagine Spain simply as a nation grounded in Europe, while the contemporary novels address the colonies' metropolitan problems (52, 57). Indeed, Galdós depicts, in literary terms, what the well-known colonial corruption looks like and recasts overseas misgovernment as a domestic affair. But empire not only undercuts nationalist projects, it also constitutes them. Spain as nation was inextricable from its entanglements with Cuba in economics, society, and demographics. Significantly, *El amigo Manso* and *Lo prohibido* do not question Spain's basic right to be an imperial nation-state but do fiercely criticize the effects of a calamitous empire on the metropolitan population. The problems of modern Spain are, in fact, compounded by the imperial process, for flaws in the Spanish "national character" that had been exported to the colonies were exacerbated there and now return to a peninsular nation too weak to keep them out.

Domestic Ruptures in *El amigo Manso*

El amigo Manso (1882) is the story of a *profesor de instituto* (prep-school teacher), Máximo Manso, whose tranquil existence as a bachelor-philosopher in the capital is disrupted shortly after the end of the Ten Years' War (a failed war of Cuban independence, 1868–78), by the arrival in Madrid of his *indiano* brother José María with his Cuban family. The philosopher must narrate the colony into his daily existence. Despite the centrality of José María and his family to the plot, Germán Gullón considers the novel's references to Cuba and the economic logic of empire as merely anecdotal: "el gusto por los colores de la mujer cubana, el frío madrileño comparado con el calor del trópico, etcetera. Poco y muy poco se menciona la riqueza" (109; the Cuban woman's preference for bright colors, the cold of Madrid compared with the heat of the tropics, etc. Very rarely is wealth mentioned). None of these references, according to Gullón, addresses the heart of the problem of Cuban-Spanish relations. However, while the references may not be extensive, the novel as a whole treats the imperial situation with both irony and gravity even as the transatlantic story is scaled down to a domestic dispute between an *indiano* husband and a Cuban wife. The trope of the imperial family remains, but by shifting the gendered relationship between capital and colony from the traditional paradigm of metropolis and "daughter" (from the original Greek definition of a metropolis as the mother city to a colony) to a quarreling married couple, Galdós resets the frame for considering the property, affections, and cultural relations between them.[3] Affiliations thus become affinities—paternity is replaced with matrimony—and property relations appear within the emblematic structure of nineteenth-century bourgeois life and the master narrative of the realist novel.[4]

José María's Cuban family is composed almost exclusively of women and politically and socially emasculated males and thus initially appears to replicate the traditional definition of colony as daughter. Its Cuban members include José María's wife, Lica; her sister, Mercedes; his two small daughters and young son; and Lica's mother, Niña Chucha. They, in turn, are accompanied by a *mulata*, Remedios, and a *negrito*, Rupertico. In addition, José María's family unit is sustained by the participation of three other adult women: the *castiza* Irene, whose role as governess is to civilize his savage children, and two provincial wet nurses who provide basic nourishment to his infant son. All three of these Spanish women function as a sort of "madre postiza y mercenaria" (Galdós, *Manso*, 237; false and mercenary mother), similar to what Spain has become for Cuba, not a mother tied by affection but an authority figure attracted by money and employing the practices and discourse of maternity. Through a dissection of the relations among women in creating nations/homes/families, the novel exposes fissures in the gendered logic of empire. In other words, a deformation of the motherhood-metropolis paradigm remains in the background of the marriage/divorce plot.

However, the Cubans' clashes with Spain in this family stem from marital disagreements over moral behaviors, the performance of "Spanishness," and the governance of resources. Capitalizing on his colonial connections and Lica's money, José María will progressively enter first Madrid society, then politics and the aristocracy, and build his reputation on "el gastado eje de los asuntos públicos, y especialmente de los ultramarinos, que son los más embrollados y sutiles que han fatigado el humano entendimiento" (Galdós, *Manso*, 201; the spent axle of public affairs, and especially the overseas issues, which are the most embroiled and tenuous that have ever fatigued human understanding). Significantly, José María Manso's political aspirations bear fruit and by the writing of *Ángel Guerra* he is fully transformed into a respectable member of society. In spite of his apparent success, Jose María is, as Harriet Turner has written, so useless that one questions which brother is fictional in the literary game of the novel (56). He lives in a dream world and in fact accomplishes nothing material. In the ascent of this self-interested, ineffectual, and unethical character, we clearly see the uneasy balance between metropole and colony—if the *indianos*, created through empire and relying on Antillean money, reputation, and clout, become stronger than the citizens of the capital city, then it is unclear exactly where the source of power lies. John Sinnigen reads the novel as highlighting the national project of incorporating the capital acquired abroad through war and marriages (117), but this incorporation is mediated by "men on the spot" who treat the capital itself as ripe for opportunistic exploitation. As a result, Galdós's nation-building project is on shaky ground in *El amigo Manso*. Will Madrid simply become another body in the orbit of Caribbean *negrero* interests, effectively displaced from center to a periphery organized around Havana? Indeed, is the Spanish nation (and its core identity as an imperial state) a fiction?[5] Galdós represents this type of political reshuffling in an innovative way through the story of a marriage, whose potential dissolution on moral grounds would run counter to the realist marriage plot, just as the disintegration of ties between Cuba and the Peninsula would destabilize the constitution of modern Spain.

At the time Galdós wrote, overseas possessions were not spoken of in terms of empire; as in his novels, this political structure was articulated as a delicate national unity whose constitutive elements were plotted in dysfunctional relations across the globe. The concept of "national integrity" comprising both European and American lands was born out of the resistance to the Napoleonic invasion (Fradera, *Colonias*, 64, 66). This nation was then superimposed onto the lands of the formerly uneven monarchy, sidestepping the terminology of colonialism, making it all, rhetorically, part of a single unit even through a wide variety of practices continued to exist in the different dominions, not least of all slavery and racially informed overseas governance. After 1837, the Philippines, Cuba, and Puerto Rico were referred to officially as "Ultramar," as the overseas elements of a modern liberal nation (Fradera, *Colonias*, 77). The concept of national integrity was reinvigorated in the second half of the nineteenth century as part of the patriotic discourse of empire and the economic policy of protected markets. The overseas possessions were legally "Spain" although in practice they were ruled by a series of Capitán Generals granted absolute power under special laws and were cut off from even the most limited democracy.[6]

In *El amigo Manso*, Lica, her sister, and her mother represent a Cuba that is "fundamentally foreign to the metropolis, but, ironically, more positive" (Coffey, 59), thus upsetting the centrist hierarchy, yet Lica demonstrates split loyalties—unlike either her Cuban mother or Spanish husband. Nevertheless, the island of Cuba is distinctly unique in *El amigo Manso*, and this difference written into the "Spanish" novel gives lie to the contemporary battle cries of "integridad nacional" (national integrity) and "defender España" (defend Spain) that jingoistically punctuated Spain during the Ten Years' War, much as others—including José Martí—had done before. Colonial society in the novel is sensual and grounded in the real in a way that the shady world of Madrid never attains (R. Gullón, 62; Turner, 56). According to Coffey *El amigo Manso* reflects the fact that the metropolis no longer exerts "a civilizing influence on the colonial subject" (59). Galdós had explored this idea earlier: in *Tormento*, the *indiano* Agustín Caballero returns to Madrid in search of correct Spanish, modesty, and female chastity in contrast to the linguistic chaos, vice, and masculinity of the former colonies. Agustín had been deceived and discovers that, in fact, the moral woman at the heart of the metropolis exists only in works of sentimental fiction.

The same *peninsulares* who dictated the terms of the Ten Years' War and ran Cuba as a lawless fiefdom protecting slavers' financial interests move in the shadow of Galdós's city.[7] Although aware of these unpleasant truths, the narrator's world is grounded rather insistently in "home"—domestic space, women, and family—even as he frets over the nature of the true or "apocryphal" nation. The narrator utters this borrowed concept, "home," in ecstacy over Irene's nascent domesticity: "Tenía afanes de decorar bien el recinto donde viviese y de labrarse el agradable y cómodo rincón doméstico que los ingleses llaman *home*." (Galdós, *Manso*, 218; She desired to decorate the place in which they lived well and to carve a pleasant and comfortable domestic retreat that the English call *home*.) In other words, Manso believes that Irene, the governess for his brother's children, holds the promise to create a profoundly rational protected space, sealed off from the exterior. In nineteenth-century Europe, the home exists outside of the public sphere yet is the source of the nation's citizens; presumably Irene's "home" would provide the basis for the variety of modernization that Manso aspires to for Spain, free from external (colonial) forces that are (paradoxically) officially national. Manso hopes that Irene might embody the ideal bourgeois domesticity that is failing in Spain; were it to succeed, then the empire might have been kept at bay.

Manso does not use the common Spanish term "hogar" (hearth) for the private sphere that he projects into Irene's domesticity, opting instead for the British term with its imperial overtones and fantasy of enclosed, homogeneous spaces. As Catherine Hall and Sonya Rose have written in the case of England, the cultivation of home, with its coherence and sense of belonging, goes hand in hand with the creation of nationalism as a similarly imagined space of belonging and enclosure (25–26). The empire, then, exists beyond these firmly established borders. It bears noting that Galdós's oft-noted anglophilia should be read alongside contemporary Spanish admiration and fear of the (perceived) effectiveness of the British empire that had largely replaced it on the Atlantic. In the Spain of *El amigo Manso* such a sense of propriety and divisions, proper to a modern, idealized metropolis, is lacking. Ultimately, the home that Irene creates at the end of *El amigo Manso* conforms to traditional Spanish values and leaves the narrator utterly disillusioned. But it stands in contrast to Lica's distinct and ultimately permeable house that is more a stage than private sphere.

As opposed to what Manso imagines that Irene could have created, Lica's home, in a rented property, is realistic and messy. Catherine Jagoe argues that Lica is a model of poor housekeeping, the antithesis of the ideal domestic angel (96–97). In terms of its Cubanness, however, ideological limits are not so clear-cut and empire becomes part of everyday life. The boundaries of traditional domesticity are blurred by the existence of this Cuban household in the middle of the Spanish capital where the relations of both economic power and cultural assimilation are in constant negotiation. The narrator finds this a troubling space and his desire for a modern yet Spanish home under Irene's direction is his fantastical antidote.

Home and abroad are particularly confused when metropolitan life depends on Cuban money channeled through *indiano* mediators whose rapacious behavior has its roots not in colonial "barbarity" but in the Peninsula. Galdós dramatizes this political and economic reality in *El amigo Manso* with a pact between José María and Cándida (a proud but destitute widow) in order to seduce her niece and his children's governess, Irene. The fate of Spain is transposed onto this overseas claim of control over Castilian women. As Coffey has persuasively argued, José María's attempts to seduce Irene suggest that "the corruption of values is part of the metropolis itself. The seeds of José María's immorality lie in the fact that he is a truly metropolitan subject" (59). Indeed, his plans for Irene are only slightly less chivalrous than those that motivated Manuel Peña in his initial pursuit of the young governess. For her part, Cándida is part of a parasitic Madrid scraping by through the subjugation of the provinces (in this case, a fictitious holding in Zamora) while she plots to defraud Lica and her Cuban family of their money. At the same time, she is just as willing to prostitute her own niece (who claims her aunt wants to sell her) to the *indiano* as she is to prey directly on Lica. Metropolitan fears notwithstanding, Spain was not corrupted by Cuba, but rather by its own policies and a political environment that had gotten out of hand in the Antilles (see Jacobson; Quiroz).

It is significant that Máximo and José María plan their projects for what Spain should become (metaphorically reproduced in their personal projects of domesticity and seduction) by means of Cuban and Castilian women and through marriage plots. Women of both Spain and Cuba, like male Cuban-born Creoles, were all but excluded by the government in Madrid from the political and economic privileges granted to peninsular Spanish men. By the late nineteenth century, the modern state recast the relationship between Madrid and the Antilles (and Philippines) of "national integrity" in a way that implied a particular type of economic and political subordination, characterized by Galdós as akin to marriage. In modern Europe, marriage was the contracted subjugation of woman to man, with the accompanying passage of property to male authority, even while marriage—at least in the nineteenth-century realist novel—represents an intriguing drama of women's freedom of choice (Labanyi, 39). As Labanyi has written, "The realist novel is so interested in married women because it was not clear where they stood, particularly if they were members of the property-owning classes which by definition constituted 'society'" (40). In *El amigo Manso*, marriage structures the utterly domestic story of the modern empire-nation where a discourse of "love" (which will coalesce as *hispanidad* in the twentieth century) replaces one of filial (dis)obedience.

Cuban heiresses dot the literary landscape of Galdós's Madrid as well as the historical nineteenth century. Such transatlantic family alliances were one of the primary means by which Caribbean wealth was injected into metropolitan society. Antillean birth troubled neither the metropolitan identities nor the imperial allegiances of these women. A striking articulation of this imperial nationalism by 240 women born in Cuba and Puerto Rico and resident in Barcelona was written in 1873. These White Creoles petitioned the central government to halt the abolition of slavery in Puerto Rico, presenting themselves as Spanish women authorized to make a political statement based on their firsthand knowledge of "so-called slavery."[8] The islands are the beloved "patria" of these women whose American birth and participation in the slavocracy promised to guarantee national unity.

Lica, the Cuban wife in *El amigo Manso*, initially appears to be from this same mold: she is wealthy, the daughter of a *voluntario* (defender of Spanish imperialism),[9] and married to a Spanish *indiano* who also contributes to a corrupt policy of imperial governance (in the guise of rigged parliamentary elections). Yet her husband is displeased with her limited Europeanization. The Cuban "colonia" in Madrid—significantly, authorized to measure degrees of Spanishness—snubs Lica outright.

> Lica no había logrado hacerse simpática a la mayor parte de las familias cubanas que en Madrid residen, y que en distinción y modales la superaban sin medida. No veían su alma bondadosa, sino su rusticidad, su llaneza campestre y sus equivocaciones funestas en materia de requisitos sociales. A mis oídos llegaron ciertos rumores y chismes poco favorables a la pobre Lica. Por toda la colonia corrían anécdotas punzantes y muy crueles. Lo menos que decían de ella era que la habían cogido con lazo. . . . El origen humildísimo, la educación mala y la permanencia de Lica en un pueblo agreste del interior de la isla no eran circunstancias favorables para hacer de ella una dama europea. (Galdós, *El amigo Manso*, 208)

> (Lica had not managed to ingratiate herself with the majority of Cuban families residing in Madrid that surpassed her beyond measure in distinction and manners. They did not see her kindhearted nature, but her rusticity, her rural simplicity and her fatal oversights in matters of social requirements. I heard certain rumors and gossip that were unfavorable to poor Lica. Caustic and very cruel anecdotes traveled throughout the entire colony. The least unpleasant thing that was said about her was that she had been caught with a lasso. . . . Lica's low-born origin, her poor education and time in a rural village of the interior of the island, were not favorable circumstances for making her a European lady.)

Initially, it seems that Lica's difficult adaptation to Madrid is a version of the story of urban cruelty toward foolish peasants, or suggests that meaningful cultural distinctions between center and periphery prevent her assimilation. However, Lica is not rejected by Spaniards, but rather by the Cuban families who reign over the metropolis from their colony in Madrid and are more European than European Spaniards themselves.

Lica's Cubanness is at odds with the dominant imperial codes. She is not from a sophisticated Western city; rather, as a *guajira* from the interior, Lica personifies a type of Cuban invisible to the metropolis after the victory of the Ten Years' War—one who is unable to submit completely to metropolitan domestication. Lica and her sister (although not their mother) evoke *esclavista*, criollo Cuba in their attempts at integration, but in what is yet another domestic rupture, Lica is excluded from the sphere of power of "lo español" born in her own homes, first in Cuba and now in Madrid. Although it has been transformed by colonial elites, the metropolis still presents itself as the origin of imperial power.

Lica is, moreover, the result of an unusual *mestizaje* of family lines. All we know of her father is that he was a *voluntario* (Galdós, *El amigo Manso*, 285). The detail is brief but significant. As such a militiaman, Lica's father presumably maintained a conservative political position regarding Spain's hold on Cuba, supporting "integridad nacional" (a calculated engagement with popular ideas of "Spanish nationalism" for commercial interests) but operated outside of the limitations of the Spanish state (see Schmidt-Nowara, *La España ultramarina*, 191–214). For, as Domingo Acebrón has written, "aunque todos sus integrantes eran denominados voluntarios, bajo esta denominación se encubrieron los verdaderos intereses políticos, que estaban muy lejos del patriotismo tan aireado por la prensa más reaccionaria. Si bien pudiera ser cierto que algunos de sus integrantes luchaban por la patria, unos pocos defendían intereses mucho más reales y concretos." (119; even though all of its members were designated as *voluntarios*, under this denomination the true political interests were concealed, which were far from the patriotism that was much publicized by the most reactionary press. While it may be true that some of its members fought for the country, a few defended much more real and concrete interests.) Most *voluntarios* were from the Peninsula, although Domingo Acebrón counts Creoles, Blacks, Asians, deserted Spanish soldiers, peasants, and powerful slave traders among their numbers.

The *voluntarios* were much more than volunteers in a civilian militia. To some degree, they were the Spanish counterpart to the rebel Mambises as they, too, were a set of troops and interests that disrupted Madrid's governance of the island, from a position more imperialist than that of the metropolis itself. They embodied uncontrolled violence (often tacitly approved by Spanish authorities) in the name of the Spanish nation (empire) but operated outside the direct command of the central government. For example, they were responsible for driving General Domingo Dulce from the palace of the Capitán General in Havana within five months of his commission by the government in Madrid (because he was open to limited concessions to rebels) and successfully refused to allow the bishop, Jacinto María Martínez, to disembark after his return from Rome out of fear that he would be lenient on revolutionaries (Amores, 81). While the imperial army was unarguably ruthless, the *voluntarios* unleashed sheer terror in the island. In the Peninsula they were viewed as functioning somewhere between the fiercest patriotism and gruesome anarchy. By royal decree, in 1871 a silver medal was granted to 18,340 *voluntarios* in Cuba who were credited with keeping Cuba Spanish. Yet, European Spaniards who opposed these forces, including the federal republican Senator Díaz Quintero and future President Nicolás Salmerón, considered their actions as "assassinations," beyond the rule of law by Spanish Cortes (Cortes Constituyentes, *Diario*, 8914). In sum, during the Ten Years' War, the *voluntarios* fought against the 1868 rebellion that was a rejection of the *negreros* and a government controlled by corrupt *peninsulares*. Lica's father represents this type of fanatical Spanishness beyond the reach of the Spanish state (yet an aspect of the apocryphal nation (Galdós, *El amigo Manso*, 201) evoked in the slogan of "integridad nacional"; thus, he adds another layer of complexity to the Cuban-Spanish family relations in the novel.

Lica's mother, Jesusa, or Niña Chucha, recalls a culturally non-Hispanic Cuba, one that is markedly Taíno and African. She longs for Afro-Cuban dances and music (the *maruga, el guiro, el birimbao*) (Galdós, *El amigo Manso*, 200) and misses Cuban cooking, especially *ajico*, the dish that only decades later Fernando Ortiz would designate as the dish of Cuban identity par excellence for its *mestizaje* of ingredients. Specifically, Niña Chucha misses American and African tubers: "el moniato, la yuca, el ñame, la malanga y demás vegetales que componen la vianda" (Galdós, *El amigo Manso*, 198; yucca, yams, sweet potatoes and malangas and other vegetables of her meals)—they are literally the roots of Jesusa's ties to Cuba, not only what she wishes to eat but also the connections to the earth that she has broken when uprooted to Europe. Niña Chucha's palate is independent of European influence: significantly, she often eats alone in her room. Her body and her domesticity are discordant with metropolitan fare. In her homesickness for non-Spanish Cuba, Niña

Chucha challenges the logic of the *madre patria*, showing that not all imperial subjects find their home in the metropolis. The complexities of domesticity and the gendered notions of authority encompassed by the character of Jesusa ruffle the smooth imperial story. In one of his many nods to Galdós, Pío Baroja reincarnated "Niña Chucha" in the *mulatta* servant to the *baronesa* in his 1904 novel *Mala hierba*. But Baroja externalized cultural difference in terms of conventional race: whereas Galdós's Niña Chucha's non-Spanish Cubanness is cultural, the later Niña Chucha is not only marked sociolinguistically ("etá etudiando") but also is physically black (Baroja, *Mala hierba*, 203).[10]

Lica embodies this complex Antillean past and upon her arrival in Madrid, her Cubanness is recast in contemporary political terms when her husband mistreats her. She is humiliated by José María's infidelities and his use of her money and home to promote his own political career. Over the course of the novel José María weaves himself into the fabric of metropolitan power structures through narcissistic displays of social importance in the family home in the center of Madrid during parties and social hours with a court poet to boot. Initially, as the head of the ironically named "Comision de melazas" (the "molasses commission"), he metaphorically works to express every last bit of advantage out of Cuba that he can. Later, as an elected official representing Cuba, he literally absconds with his constituents' political (democratic) voice. This "neophyte" in politics is completely unprepared to deal with the scope of imperial governance (Galdós, *El amigo Manso*, 230), but his Cuban funds (Lica's money) all but guarantee his entrée.

Lica oscillates between outrage and resignation toward her husband's marital infidelities in what is a clear allegory of the unequal political situation between Cuba and Spain. Where and what is "home"? Where does power reside? From where does it emerge? In this novel, Galdós looks behind the façade of political rhetoric, through the frame of domesticity, to find a gendered Cuban sphere that is silenced, ignored, and humiliated. The Spanish world of *negreros* has no more legitimacy in Cuba than it does in Spain. José María has legal claims over Lica, is scheming to seduce Irene, but has moral authority over neither. The normally docile and complacent Lica reflects angrily on autonomy at key moments in the plot, threatening to return to Cuba, fed up with her husband's wasteful spending and marital infidelities. Speaking as a Cuban, with "palabras exóticas," "claúsulas truncadas," "hipérboles americanas" (Galdós, *El amigo Manso*, 262; exotic words, truncated phrases, American hyperboles) she accuses her husband of affairs and indeed all of Madrid for similarly abusing her domestic generosity and treating her with general disrespect. "Aquí no le hacían caso más que los que venían a comerle los codos, y después de vivir a su costa se burlaba de ella." (Galdós, *El amigo Manso*, 263; Here she was ignored except for those that came to feed off of her, and after living at her expense they made fun of her.) Legitimate autonomy awaits Lica in Cuba where she is mistress of her people (263) and where nary a "madre postiza y mercenaria" (Galdós, *El amigo Manso*, 237) would interfere in her home and her affairs. Calling upon matrilineal authority, she proclaims, "Yo soy madre, y yo me voy a mi tierra, yo me ahogo en esta tierra, yo no quiero que la gente se ría de mí, y que con mi dinero echen fantasía las bribonas. . . . ¡Mamá! Mamá!" (Galdós, *El amigo Manso*, 314; I am a mother and I'm going to my country, I'm suffocating in this land, I do not want people laughing at me or gold-digging women living out their fantasies at my expense. . . . Mama! Mama!) If José María "no se enmendaba, ella se plantaba de un salto en su tierra, llevándose a sus hijos" (Galdós, *El amigo Manso*, 264; did not mend his ways, she would immediately go to her country, taking their children.) For Lica—as for Spanish realist fiction more broadly—belonging to Spain is generated from role-playing ("fingir y ponerse en tormento para hacer todo a la moda de acá" [264; pretend and torment oneself in order to do everything as it is done here]). For his part, Manso considers Lica and her sister as "emblemáticamente la flora de aquellos risueños países, el encanto de sus bosques poblados de lindísimos pajarracos y de insectos vestidos con todos los colores del iris" (Galdós, *El amigo Manso*, 195; symbolically the flora of those cheerful countries, the charm of its forests populated with very pretty birds and insects dressed with all the colors of the rainbow).

In Manso's mind, Lica, a fertile and generous image of innocent bounty, seems to give selflessly to all who ask without demanding accountability or even moral behavior in return. According to this perspective, Lica is, as a result of this excessive generosity, partly responsible for her poor state of affairs. She allows herself to be taken advantage of by the self-serving Spanish "savages" (the wet nurse's family) and Cándida, who simply wish to seize her riches. In terms of political allegory, her children require mother-substitutes because Lica doubts her ability to nurture her own children and calls upon the narrator to staff her home. Spanish women (the governess Irene and the nursemaids) intervene in Lica's family affairs, for Lica appears unable to claim control over her children while in the capital. Manso's description of the desperate mother after the departure of her baby son's wet nurse infuses the portrait of the loving mother with the sadness of the *pietà*: "Encontré a Manuela [Lica] desesperada. Con mi ahijado sobre las rodillas, rodeada de su madre y hermana, era la figura más lastimosa y patética de aquel cuadro de desolación. Maximín chillaba como un becerro . . . las tres aturdidas mujeres invocaban a todos los santos de la Corte celestial." (Galdós, *El amigo Manso*, 322; I found Manuela [Lica] in despair. With my godson on her knees, surrounded by her mother and sister, she was the most piteous and pathetic figure in that desolate scene. Maximín squealed like a calf . . . the three bewildered women invoked all the Saints of the heavenly court.)

The narrator Máximo Manso claims he is not a political actor but a philosopher, above the fray of empty rhetoric and party politics. Nevertheless, Lica's situation so moves him that he suspends his usual disinterest. He realizes that if Lica knew the true extent of her husband's abuses, she would demand a "separación de bienes" (division of property) and return to Cuba, much as her mother predicts (Galdós, *El amigo Manso*, 349). Divorce was illegal in nineteenth-century Spain, but the power accorded to Lica in a legal separation, a concept rooted in Roman law, was still significant, for the process formally recognized a husband as incompetent and forbade a later marriage by either party. The state, following ecclesiastic law, accorded women this avenue of self-protection in an era in which domestic abuse was not prosecuted.[11] "La mujer puede pedir la separacion, si el marido la trata con crueldad o sevicia" (a woman can request a separation, if her husband treats with cruelty or brutality), which is certainly the case for Lica and indeed for Cuba, too (Escriche, 565). Specifically, if a woman envisioned her husband facing bankruptcy, she could recover the properties she had brought to the marriage. In terms of the novel's political analogy, this type of "separación de bienes" (and necessarily the "separación de habitación") is both distinct from and stronger for Cuba than armed rebellion, for in this situation Cuba would necessarily be prevented from committing itself to the United States or any other maritime power. In this way Galdós questions whether Cuba (Lica) should be subjected to a corrupt capital. As much as Galdós favors empire, he would rather have an ethical nation, even if the price of such a nation is the loss of its colonies. Galdós makes his case with a very sympathetic Lica who maintains her moral authority throughout the novel. (Significantly, only the Havana colony and her husband reject her.) Galdós, of course, is concerned about the colonies only insofar as they impact Spain, but through Lica Galdós makes visible the difficult situation of a White

Creole population. At these moments in the novel, Galdós comes shockingly close to advocating for American independence. But he also uses the story of marital separation as a way to imagine what imperial rupture might look like and to allow readers to make sense of what many in Spain considered to be an inevitable loss (the recent Spanish victory notwithstanding). If the bourgeois novel consolidates nation, property, and narrative through stories of marriage and shared experiences, in *El amigo Manso*, Galdós unravels these very same threads to envision the dissolution of the empire-nation's ties to Cuba.

By positing a rupture in the terms of a "separación" between Lica and José María, Galdós makes clear that the dominant models for understanding successful colonial independence movements and imperial failures were inadequate. Spain as the empire-nation is not just a relationship of power negotiated between Europeans and White Creole males, under a false rubric of "brotherhood": the ruling classes—and men—are not the only members of society that decide the political future. The determination of the characters of Lica and Chucha in this novel suggest that it may be another Cuba that is ready to walk away from the *madre patria*, and that rebellion in Cuba is not only a diplomatic issue but also a moral and "feminine" one. Through Lica, Chucha, and their female family, Galdós collapses the imperial and the domestic into a single space, confusing the lines between center and colony in a struggle for control over the *home* (and its limits). Galdós recreates a very real anxiety over the loss of Cuba as one where the island could use juridical tools to sever ties with Spain, as the novelist transposes imperial practices onto the novel's familiar terrain of family customs and law. The *madre patria* and its "mercenary" wet nurses would be challenged if, as in the case of the female characters in *El amigo Manso*, the Cubans were to choose to sever family ties with Spain using the juridical tools available within the discursive space of domesticity. On the heels of the peace treaty of Zanjón and preoccupation over the health of the empire with the cessation of the slave trade and the promise of abolition, Galdós suggests a paradigm in which the rupture of nation from home throws the centrality of Madrid into question and begs a reinterpretation of the domestic space created by the women in the novel. If Madrid is not home for the nation's subjects, then the familial structure around the *madre patria* is false. Moreover, for a Spain reinventing itself as a modern nation, in the face of the Restoration, the inability to impose boundaries to prevent the periphery from colonizing its center leads to the chaos of overlapping "authentic" and "aprocyphal" nations.

In this novel, Galdós takes the rhetoric of imperial domesticity to its logical conclusion: an injured wife who departs with her wealth and her children effectively destroys the imperial family by choosing to find *home* in the colonies. Theirs is not violent revolution, or a claim for juridical selfhood (for men) or national self-determination, but a female-coded censure of immorality. If the immorality of the capital were unmasked, Spain would lose its grip on the colonies because the logic of "home" could, paradoxically, triumph overseas. Through the story of the ever-faithful Lica, Galdós inscribes gender into the discourses of independence—not as a concept supported by metropolitan women who proclaim a sense of solidarity with imperial subjects abroad in terms of a shared oppression, but instead a questioning of the source of colonial discontent and an expression of the need to revisit the terms of the empire and its constituent parts.[12] This potentially subversive power of the moral code of domesticity implies an existential crisis over the place of the center in national identity. Such Cuban disgraces are a constitutive element of the contemporary Spanish realist novel, but the discourse of realism and the plot structure of marriage (and its inversion as separation) allow for other ways to conceive of political independence.

Gender, of course, complicates the discourses of both nationalism and empire. Labanyi argues that the realist novel was so interested in women, especially propertied women, because of their problematic relationship to the nation as public sphere. Women were members of the nation but existed outside of civil society or the realm of civil rights (Labanyi, 10). Husbands, in theory, represented their wives legally and politically. In this sense, Lica, the Cuban wife, is a synecdoche of the entire island in that both are crucial elements of the nation, but without rights of representation or civic participation. The fraught divisions among gender, domesticity, and political authority shadow the plot. For example, the announcement of José María's election to congress interrupts Máximo Manso and his student Manuel Peña as they are sharing anxieties over girls' education in Spain as well as the role of the mother in the home and society. Peña envisions the imminent destruction of the family and individualist society and the passage of power over the nation into the hands of women: "la patria potestad en la mujer" (Galdós, *El amigo Manso*, 244). Peña's fears over separate spheres aside, José María Manso astutely—and correctly—proclaims that he will serve the nation from the home. His first words as an elected official are surprising for a public man: "Yo no quiero salir de mis cuatro paredes." (Galdós, *El amigo Manso*, 245; I don't want to leave my four walls.) While José María certainly spends his days in the streets, the real power remains at the family residence that Niña Chucha describes as a "trapiche" (sugarcane mill) on evenings when José María stages his career as a series of tableaux of power and influence before a handpicked audience in Lica's ostentatious house (Galdós, *El amigo Manso*, 247). The narrator describes this same scene as "un rinconcito del Salón de Conferencias" (246; a corner of the conference rooms of the parliament). The two complementary images solidify the relationship between these two spheres of power and confirm, as Peter Bly has argued, José María as the "personification of the Restoration parliamentary system, despoiler of colonial Cuba" (26). Home and periphery collapse as Lica's home in Madrid itself symbolically becomes a sugar factory in its generation of parliamentary power.

Lica's "Noah's ark" (Galdós, *El amigo Manso*, 196) of a home is a metonym for the empire as a whole: metropolitan power is generated in a Cuban Creole sphere whose inhabitants are seen by the capital as little more than the raw materials of empire. The center (Madrid) wields power through the framework of the nation, while constantly negotiating with differences from the various peripheries, defined in terms of language and race. In Lica's home, one sees a little bit of nearly everything as the family, in turn, is wholly dependent on Black and mixed-race slaves and dehumanized domestic servants from the Peninsula, none of whom is (literally) versant in Castilian Spanish, the language of empire. But as we learn through the characters' interactions, the ability to speak normative Castilian is not a marker of national allegiances but rather of the right to wield metropolitan power (much as it had been the official language of administration for centuries). Indeed, Lica's home is packed with Spanish nationals who speak everything from Rupertico's nonstandard Cuban Spanish to the first wet nurse's "ladrido entre vascuence y castellano" (Galdós, *El amigo Manso*, 227; bark, somewhere between Basque and Castilian), to the unintelligible cawing by Robustiana (Galdós, *El amigo Manso*, 326; "graznó"), who all give lie to the national model of unity through linguistic homogeneity.

Language and the need to homogenize are part of the national project. In contrast, race and the attending need to draw sharp distinctions—in other words, the racial component of liberalism—were written into Spain at its reconceptualization as "nation" during the Cortes of Cádiz. Race was, of course, the logic by which Spain justified the slave trade both to maintain sugar production, but also to manipulate populations and colonial control over its Caribbean colonies. Abolition and reform of empire were inseparable, but the place of the enslaved themselves in the metropolitan imagination was marginal. Máximo Manso speaks of his abolitionist inclinations, but slaves are all but invisible in the novel. Rupertico and Remedios blend into the background of José María's family, simultaneously seen and not seen.

Manso created himself and his novelistic world self-consciously through the act of narration, through his own will. But, as Linda Willem has written, whereas Máximo Manso embraces his fictionality and thus attains autonomy, José María Bueno de Guzmán, the narrator of *Lo prohibido*, achieves it "through the segmented memoir format of the text which seems to endow him with a life outside the narration as well as within it" (192). *El amigo Manso* disintegrates when Máximo, disillusioned and frustrated, departs society: he relinquishes control over his narrative and wills himself into inexistence, and the novel dissolves. In contrast, José María Bueno de Guzmán will cease to be able to narrate the world around him when he realizes the discursive limits of the bourgeois fictional mode.

Imperial Glamor: *Lo prohibido*

The tension between pride and unease over colonial practices in Cuba and late nineteenth-century Spanish life is perhaps most subtly depicted in Galdós's *Lo prohibido* (1884–85). The novel's representation of attitudes toward Cuba on the part of monied interests is not a reflection of actual public opinion, but rather a creative contemplation of metropolitan Madrid's hopes and nightmares about its own fiscal and imperial morals. In *Lo prohibido*, Galdós traces the shifting imaginative terms of the connection between Spain and Cuba in the early 1880s. In *Lo prohibido* Galdós draws from the biographies of both prominent and lesser-known *negreros*, but he doesn't simply give these famous men cameos. Rather, their presence and influence are fully embedded in the quotidian as part of the novel's imaginary moral landscape.

Lo prohibido presents the memoirs of José María Bueno de Guzmán who has come to Madrid in retirement at age thirty-six to live off his investments. José María recounts his high life in the capital from his arrival in 1880 to his death in 1884. The son of a virtuous Englishwoman and an Andalusian *señorito*, José María derives his wealth principally from viticulture in Jerez—an enterprise quite literally rooted in Spanish tradition and English exploitation. A "shameless" character (Gilman, 143), he amuses himself by seducing married women (the forbidden fruit of the novel's title)—specifically, his three cousins: María Juana, Eloísa, and Camila. Amid the adulterous trysts, the novel is also a tale of finance. Labanyi has characterized it as a "novel about unfaithful wives going into circulation, seduced by a representative of capitalist modernity," alongside the stock and currency crises of 1881–82 (Labanyi, 129)—spawned, significantly, by the death of the singularly influential colonial financier Antonio López. At the same time, *Lo prohibido* explores not only infidelity complicated by forbidden fruit (married relatives), but also the crimes that motivate subsequent sins. By drawing together exchange values and invisible labor, the language of finance presses on the representational possibilities of narrative. This combination of language and exchange is presented in the novel through the voice of the not entirely reliable narrator whose fortunes in love and money rise and fall. Although a veritable debauchee, José María is initially a geographic and ideological outsider to the novel's circle of metropolitan vice. Ricardo Gullón measures his *pecadillos* as relatively minor within the novel's scale of vice. He argues that in spite of the protagonist's appearance as a small-time libertine, José María has surprising and profound psychological depth and complexity (159–60). Indeed, José María is never as depraved as other male characters in the novel, such as Fúcar or Botín, nor (in the published version) does he share financial interests with them.

José María dabbles in colonial finance, yet he remains outside of it. However, the narrator does move in concentric circles and interacts with the pro-slavery, antireform lobby of peninsular interests in the Antilles. José María's banker in Paris is Mitjans (Galdós, *Lo prohibido*, 160)—(historically, the *indiano* financier par excellence for Spaniards residing in France as well as both partner and in-law of the leader of the colonial-*negrero* lobby, the Duke of Santoña). Galdós refers to both Antonio López and Mitjans to set the novel's banking scene firmly within the parameters of colonial finance, although José María himself does not have Cuban revenues. The detail is significant, for James Whiston uncovered that in the draft version of the novel, José María's position wasn't that clearly defined: Carrillo (Eloísa's husband) chastises José María for his involvement in "negocios sucios" (dirty deals) with the Marqués de Fúcar (28). In the published version, the lines of colonial interests are more heavily drawn and the narrator retains only social relations with the colonial lobby, becoming, consequently, a more ambiguous character but also a more reliable narrator.

The first half of the novel is an accounting of José María and Eloísa's consumption of a significant percentage of the narrator's savings on luxury items. The second recounts his campaign to seduce Camila and his speculation on the stock market—both ultimately disastrous. Obsessed with destroying Camila's husband as well as with seducing her, he fails to attend to his investments and suffers great losses. After Camila dramatically rejects his attempts at rapprochement, José María suffers a stroke and is left speechless. His moral degeneration is thus accompanied by physical deterioration and sexual exhaustion, according to some scholars, a result of his "excess consumerism" (Labanyi, 132–33). Utterly weakened, he consequently hands over authorship of his memoirs to the ubiquitous Ido del Sagrario, who is charged with writing the life that José María can no longer articulate, beginning with his illness and including his final encounter with Eloísa.[13]

Conspicuous and uncontrolled consumption is at the heart of the novel and is realized through the relationship between women addicted to fashion, the men who support them, their sources of wealth, and the illicit desires that underwrite the whole enterprise. The moral temptation of Cuba to the male bourgeois and aristocratic characters is nearly as strong as fashion is to the novel's female characters. The overseas economy comprised a widespread network throughout the world, in many ways anchored in Barcelona, but Galdós reduces the question of colonial finance to a dichotomy of Cuban *indianos* and Madrid. The scant finances found in Madrid are constructed, to a great extent, upon the ethically questionable opportunities available in Cuba and a fetishistic belief in the power of the stock market. The narrator's cousin Raimundo articulates society's anxieties over the scarcity of money in Madrid. He maintains that "no existen, contantes y sonantes, más que veinte mil reales. Cuando uno los tiene los demás están a cero. Pasan de mano en mano haciendo felices sucesivamente a este al otro, al de más allá." (Galdós, *Lo prohibido*, 220; there does not exist, in cold hard cash, more than twenty thousand reales. When one person has them, everyone else has nothing. They circulate from hand to hand, successfully making each person happy.) The rest is chimerical, a vast financial network built around a miserable base, either through stock-market gambling or necromancy in Cuba. The city suffers from its "locura crematística" (Montesino's felicitous term for uncontrollable, cannibalistic spending), which is inseparable from the shadow economy that buffers it from total collapse (see Montesinos, vol. 2). Labanyi reads the references to finance in Galdós's work as characteristic of "a realist writer in the . . . sense that he is responding to the increasing abstraction and self-reflexivity of the modern capitalist monetary system, which detaches value from 'things'" (Labanyi, 395). The historical and aesthetic intersect in the denouement of the novel, which is a response to the ethical and representational problems that arise when value and "thing" are reconnected through the link of labor.

References to colonial finance are direct in the novel, yet their importance to the plot are not immediately evident, particularly to a twenty-first-century readership. Edward Said's analysis of Jane Austen's *Mansfield Park* has become the model of contrapuntal reading in which the marginal and invisible binding colony and metropole (often through slavocracy) in a novel is rendered central and visible. His is one model of framing center and periphery, discovering the colony's constitutive presence at "home" and, consequently, dissolving the distinctions between the two realms. Such an analysis makes explicit, for example, the significance of the mention of a colonial sugar plantation in sustaining a life of refined elegance in England (Said, 78). Ever since Said queried the silence around the slave trade in *Mansfield Park*, contrapuntal readings have encouraged a deeper exploration of the fissures and complicities between domestic policies and European literature.[14] Like Austen's novel, *Lo prohibido* simultaneously reveals and occludes imperial desires, but Galdós does much more, dramatizing the discursive difficulty in articulating economic realities in ethical and aesthetic terms. Indeed, the contradictions in his society's ethics of empire culminate not in uncomfortable silences, but rather in a silent scream that paralyzes the narrator upon his realization of the colonial source of the Cuban riches that save him—and Madrid—from fiscal collapse.

Like other European novels that have been read contrapuntally, *Lo prohibido* appears fully grounded in metropolitan life. Save for brief excursions to seaside resorts or Paris, where *madrileños* consort among themselves, the action takes place in the capital city. The vanities of the self-absorbed leisure class ensconced in its metropolitan cityscape nearly eclipse the novel's references to an external world. Galdós makes frequent mention of Cuba and the morally suspect sources of the comforts of home, but the corruption associated with the island does remain something of an iceberg just below the surface supporting the novelistic world. There is more slave policy in Madrid than meets the eye, although the colonial subplot of *Lo prohibido* was more explicit in the first draft. For example, Galdós had originally included an *indiano* cousin for the narrator, whose wealth was dissipated in a "ruinous family spending spree" (Whiston, "Change and

Creativity," 33). Its traces remain in the published version, most patently in Sánchez Botín's "extreme miserliness" (Whiston, "Change and Creativity," 34), but also in the destruction of the great Cuban fortune of the Casa-Bojío clan (Galdós, *Lo prohibido*, 207) that prefaces the potential collapse of the monstrous imperial economic system.

Galdós depicts a wretched—albeit elegant and fabulously well-dressed—spendthrift society that (as Said has written about Austen's characters [94]), would have been impossible without *negrero* money, the slave trade, and sugar. But as opposed to the respectable Bertram household and the moral authority it represented to contemporary readers, Galdós makes clear that the disgraceful society he depicts should come to an end. Said famously found Austen complicit with the growing empire and read *Mansfield Park* as "part of a structure of an expanding imperialist venture, . . . the novel steadily, if unobtrusively, opens up a broad expanse of domestic imperialist culture without which Britain's subsequent acquisition of territory would not have been possible" (95). *Mansfield Park*, of course, was written at the beginning of the nineteenth century; in contrast, *Lo prohibido* renders visible the functioning of empire within a nation aware of its dissolution, although denying its demise. In 1880, an apprenticeship scheme (*patronato*) was legislated and complete abolition was a foregone conclusion. At the end of the Spanish empire's American lifeline, Galdós narrates a morality story that imagines a way to disengage from Cuba—not necessarily politically, but psychically—and address the aftermath of Spain's coloniality.

Marriage and property are the bedrock of the nineteenth-century novel. Yet in Galdós's Madrid, marriage is a sham (save the hopeful Miquis couple) and property is treated as a sort of parlor game. Bourgeois values are less the foundation of modern society than a poorly executed backdrop to the tragedy of modernity. In other words, in no way does *Lo prohibido* affirm the moral authority of the modern nation-empire. Rather, *Lo prohibido* depicts an infirm metropolis in counterpoint to its terminally ill imperialism. Clearly, Spaniards have not succeeded in imposing a rigid moral order at home any more than they have been able to do so in the colonies, which they first established through corruption and the slave trade and subsequently ruled through the twinned vices of greed and cruelty. Yet again the question of the corrupting influence of colonialism on the capital is raised. Galdós's bourgeois characters reincarnate the Black Legend, with a polished veneer over a world of aristocratic (now bourgeois financier) fatuity. Race, an equally fundamental nineteenth-century concept, further complicates the exploration of global and local finance and the liberal societies they support.

Fully entrenched in Galdós' "segunda manera," *Lo prohibido* nevertheless has a clear moral message. In his letter to Clarín of May 5, 1885, Galdós expressed doubts about having made these points too bluntly, writing of the novel, "Lo que sí resulta es de una moralidad gruesa que salta a la vista hasta de los más ciegos. Por eso quizá le he tomado tirria a este libro, no me gusta que la moral de una obra sea de las que están al alcance de todas las retinas." (Qtd. in López Baralt, 17; It clearly is of a blunt morality that is obvious even to the blindest of readers. Perhaps that is why I have taken a dislike to this book, I do not like that the moral of a work is within the reach of all retinas.)[15] Galdós is disillusioned by the bourgeoisie that abandoned its promises at the 1868 revolution, made a pact with the Bourbons, and ushered in the reign of the colonial lobby. To a great extent, Alfonso XII owed his throne to Cuban interests (on this point, see Jacobson, and also Espada Burgos) and Galdós depicts a Restoration Madrid that has come to live by these same *negrero* values. In *Lo prohibido* and *El amigo Manso*, Galdós's *negreros* are not simply slave traders, but are generalized to comprise a particular type of *indiano*, whose corruption and perversion of liberal ideas have infused conservative Restoration politics with the worst impulses of colonial exploitation. They are among the few self-made men to emerge from a nineteenth-century world that oppressed, rather than supported, individualism. The *negreros*, ironically, only serve to exacerbate this oppressive system by consolidating existing power in their personal networks.

José María's memoirs are usually characterized as accounts of his attempts to seduce his three married cousins. However, the novel also follows one of these cousins, Eloísa, through her relationships with her husband and three lovers. In a descent reminiscent of that of Isidora Rufete (*La desheredada*), each affair with men involved with various aspects of the economy moves Eloísa progressively closer to the truth at Madrid's financial core: Where exactly do Raimundo's "veinte mil reales" come from? Marriage to the impoverished aristocrat Pepe Carrillo de Albornoz and his ancestral honor (he refuses a lucrative "buen destino en Cuba" [Galdós, *Lo prohibido*, 101–2; a good position in Cuba]) shares space with an extramarital affair (with José María) based on affection and conspicuous consumption. Her relationship with José María ends when Carrillo dies; she quickly replaces her lover with the Marqués de Fúcar. Her socially recognized financial-physical arrangement with the colonial financier is later followed by straightforward prostitution with Sánchez Botín, suggesting that the relationship with Fúcar was also a form of prostitution to the corrupt ideology of the slave trade.

There are no secrets about the slave trader, the Marqués de Fúcar, in Galdós's Madrid. As Montesinos noted, "para nadie era un misterio, por ejemplo, el orígen de la fortuna del Marqués de Fúcar" (32; it was a mystery to no one, for example, the origins of the Marques de Fúcar's fortune). In spite of his shady dealings and unattractive physique, however, Fúcar is generally well-liked by members of polite society and enjoys wide personal and business connections.[16] This is because, similar to the historical Fuggers, who granted loans to Charles V ("quisiera ser un Fúcar," wishes Don Quijote), Galdós's *marqués* is crucial to the solvency of Spanish society, which has come to depend on massive corruption schemes and disregard of human rights in the pursuit of profit (Cervantes, 827).

We first learn of Fúcar's repellent appeal in *Lo prohibido* during a conversation between José María and his cousin María Juana, who voices her disgust at her sister's choice of the *marqués* as José María's replacement. Specifically, she is shocked that Eloísa has managed to overlook the source of his perversely attractive riches and the foolishness of his exterior mask: "no comprendía que hubiera mujer capaz de echarse a pechos [textual] al carcamal asqueroso del marqués de Fúcar, sólo por estar forrado de oro; un adefesio que había sido negrero en Cuba y contrabandista por alto en España, y que, por añadidura, ¡se teñía la barba!" (Galdós, *Lo prohibido*, 304; she couldn't believe that there was a woman alive capable of throwing herself at a disgusting, decrepit old man like the Marqués de Fúcar, simply because he was loaded; a miscreant who had been a slave trader in Cuba and a smuggler in Spain, and who, to top it off, dyed his beard!) In his cosmetics, he is much like Spain itself, embellishing the surface of its economic relations, making what is old, decrepit, and from a former age appear young, vigorous, and contemporary. In the morally inverted Restoration Madrid represented by María Juana (who commits adultery with José María in order to save him), slave trading is less of a crime than using hair color.

With José María, Eloísa learned to act on her desires and to spend conspicuously, but Fúcar instructs Eloísa in the fundamentals of modern speculation. With her second lover, Eloísa discovers the mysteries of bank notes, through which value becomes detached from a moral code, labor, or even objects themselves. Even before she begins her sexual relations with the *negrero*, Eloísa often spoke with him about finance, fascinated by the fabulous fortunes that certain men manage to create overnight. As Fúcar remarks to José María, Eloísa learns the basics of capitalism quickly. "Me ha preguntado lo que es *comprar a plazo*, en *voluntad* y en *firme*. He tenido que darle una lección de cosas de Bolsa sin olvidar las triquiñuelas del oficio. . . . Mucho ojo, que la señora piensa demasiado en el dinero." (Galdós, *Lo prohibido*, 180; She has asked me to explain how the private sale of shares is done, what it is to buy stocks in installments, at a fixed predetermined price, or at a price determined by the buyer. I have had to give her a lesson on the Stock Exchange without omitting the tricks of the trade. . . . Be very careful, this lady thinks too much about money.) Ultimately, Eloísa does not invest, but she does learn how great wealth is made and is willing to accept whatever means are necessary to maintain it. Galdós parodies the avaricious *negrero's* economic theories of Restoration Madrid as Eloísa repeats her financial lessons from Fúcar, speaking of extortion, fraud, damage, and civil war, all detached from a moral framework. The gendered caricature of a (relatively) uneducated woman learning the bases of Restoration economics is an effective narrative tactic by which Galdós spells out imperial and national corruption in the most simple and direct of terms. She explains to José María:

> Durante la guerra, Fúcar y otros como él triplicaron su fortuna en un par de años. . . . ¿Por qué no te haces amigo, muy amigo de los ministros, para ver si cae un empréstito de Cuba, ya que en la Península no se hacen ahora? Con que el ministro de Ultramar te encargara de hacer la suscripción, dándote el 1 por 100 de comisión, o siquiera el medio, ganarías una millonada. De este modo ha ganado Sánchez Botín muchos cuartos . . . lo sé . . . me lo contó Fúcar. Di que eres un perezoso, que no quieres molestarte. Eres diputado y no sabes sacar partido de tu posición. . . . ¡Lástima que no hubiera guerra civil! Pues si la hubiera, o te hacías contratista de víveres o perdíamos las amistades. (Galdós, *Lo prohibido*, 216)
>
> (During the war Fúcar and others like him tripled their fortune within two years. . . . Why don't you become friendly, very friendly, with the ministers, and see if a Cuban loan comes your way, given that in the Peninsula they aren't doing them now. If the Overseas Minister charges you with drawing up the subscriptions, giving you a 1 percent commission or even half a percent, you would make a million. This is how Sánchez Botín made his big bucks . . . I know . . . Fúcar told me. Admit you are lazy, that you don't want to be bothered. You are a member of parliament and you don't know how to take advantage of your position. . . . It is a shame there isn't a civil war now! If there were, either you'd get the canteen contract or we would end our friendship.)

Fully instructed in the complex relationships among political authority, social unrest, war, finance, imperialism, and corruption, Eloísa dreams of a future for the Peninsula feeding off the El Dorado of Cuba. "Esa isla de Cuba es todavía, aun de capa caída como está, una verdadera mina que no se explota bien. ¡Ah! se me ocurre ahora que lo que debe hacer España es venderla. Y mira, nadie mejor que tú [José María] se podría encargar de las negociaciones en los Estados Unidos, en Alemania o en el Infierno. Con que te dieran el medio por ciento de corretaje . . . " (Galdós, *Lo prohibido*, 217; That island of Cuba is still, even as run down as it is, a goldmine that we have yet to fully exploit. Ah! I just realized that what Spain ought to do is sell it. And, of course, no one would be better than you to lead negotiations with the United States, Germany, or Hell itself. As long as they gave you a kickback of half a percent . . .)

Eloísa has lost her innocence yet remains fantastically naïve. Her anachronistic views are not only comical but also tragically realistic for a society unable to imagine a postimperial world without recourse to Cuban riches, regular civil wars, and government kickbacks. Yet, for his part, José María fails to act as a national representative in his inability to look beyond the borders of the Peninsula.

Fúcar manages his resources well and thus breaks with Eloísa before she consumes much of his fortune.[17] His successor, Alejandro Sánchez Botín, also became wealthy from Cuba, and he lives off of the "booty" of the defrauded on both sides of the Atlantic.[18] Both men prey upon Spain as they preyed upon the colony. But unlike the affable Fúcar, Botín is barely tolerated by other characters in the novel; part of his unattractiveness is because most of his connections lead back, unmasked, to Cuba. By blood and marriage Botín is linked to other *indiano* families in Galdós's universe: his sister is the Marquesa de Tellería whose son-in-law, Leon Roch, maintains a long-term amorous relationship with Fúcar's daughter Pepa. Botín's nephew is married to Susana of the Cuban Casa-Bojío fortune. Sánchez Botín himself appears in numerous novels, always aligned with colonial schemes. In *O'Donnell* (1904) he is a promising young man with a well-connected uncle in Cuba. In *Miau* (1888) his influence over administrative workings in Alfonsine Spain constitutes one of the occult colonialist powers that dictate political and personal life in the metropolis. In *La desheredada* he is Isidora Rufete's jealous second lover and personifies the disgraceful speculation that took place during the Ten Years' War when he made an immense fortune trading in soldiers' *abonarés* (promissory notes) and shady government loans, embezzling directly from the state.[19]

Miquis enlightens Isidora (and the reader) on the intentions behind the *indiano*'s clamorous nationalism: "No hay dos Botines en el mundo. Si los hubiera, ¿dónde estaría ya nuestra querida patria? Desde Pirene a Calpe habría sido devorada, y todos los españoles nos agitaríamos en una cárcel de tela, ¡ay!, en los bolsillos de ese afanador de naciones . . . " (Galdós, *La desheredada*, 339; There are not two Botíns in the world. If there were, where would our beloved patria be? From the border to border it would have been devoured and all of us Spaniards would be suffering in a prison of cloth. Ay! That is in the pockets of this corruptor of nations . . .) Botín is also presented with great irony in the dramatis personae of part II of *La desheredada* as a "padre de la patria" (founding father). This is, ironically, the real man behind the mask of Botín, whose fierce support of the *patria* behind Spain's "national integrity" destroys both metropolitan and Antillean societies.

In *Lo prohibido*, Botín's patriotic schemes give shape to a monstrous administrative reality. A caricature of historic *esclavista* interests, Botín's jingoistic patriotism thinly disguises the vested interests at the heart of *españolismo* (see Schmidt-Nowara, *La España ultramarina*, 191–214). "Tres veces había desempeñado en Cuba pingües destinos, y cada vez que volvía con media isla entre las uñas, repetía la sagrada fórmula 'España derramará hasta la última gota de su sangre en defensa *etcétera*' . . . " (Galdós, *Lo prohibido*, 189; Three times he had been given miserable positions in the Cuban administration and each time he came back with half of the island in his hands and he repeated the sacred formula "Spain will give the last drop of its blood in defense, etc." . . .) Throughout the nineteenth century, fears ran through the Peninsula that European Spain would become the victim of its colonial agents: a monstrous nation-state. For example, much earlier in the century when General Espartero assumed the regency during Isabel II's reign, his American past was reevaluated and he was considered an "Ayacucho"—judged to be governing the Peninsula with the same barbarity that he had exhibited in colonial wars of South America, ruling through fear, executing rebellious generals, and bombing Barcelona and Seville. These anxieties were not totally unfounded for, in terms of administrative corruption, as Alfonso Quiroz has amply documented, bureaucratic malfeasance went both ways: by engaging in these practices in Cuba, these bureaucrats fostered corruption in Spain itself (474). Following the independence wars, the Cuban dissident Juan Gualberto Gómez published numerous treatises arguing that the colonial system and its political, administrative, and moral codes were responsible for corruption and immorality in Cuba that were, in turn, inseparable from colonial oppression and *indiano* power in not only the Antilles but also the Peninsula.[20] Galdós draws upon these very fears in the figure of Botín.

Galdós reintroduces Sánchez Botín, "uno de nuestros primeros reptiles, y sin género de duda el primero de nuestros antipáticos" (431; one of our leading reptiles, and undoubtedly our most disagreeable) in *Lo prohibido* as the last resort for Eloísa and her monstrous society. Botín is less a full-fledged character than a grotesque compendium of human vice. Galdós's detailed descriptions of Botín's nauseating habits dehumanize the character, even while, as John Kronik has written, such extreme "grotesque portraiture" in fact "arrives at reality through distortion in order to project a vision of its falseness" (44). Because no façade of good manners can veil his vice, Botín is both clownishly monstrous and terrifyingly real. Throughout the novel he lurks amidst Eloísa's circle as a potential menace. Indeed, he begins to lay siege to Eloísa long before their final transaction. "Sánchez Botín le hacía la rueda con la pegajosa tenacidad que siempre ponía en todas sus empresas; pero que mi prima declaraba a todo el que la quisiera oír, que jamás descendería hasta un ser que consideraba muy por bajo de todos los envilecimientos y de todas las prostituciones posibles." (Galdós, *Lo prohibido*, 415; Sánchez Botín circled her with the sticky tenacity he always employed in his transactions, but my cousin proclaimed to anyone who would listen that she would never descend to the level of a being whom she considered beneath all defilements and all possible prostitutions.) At this point in the novel, even before Eloísa has accepted his "groseras ofertas de dádivas," Botín represents ominous, unspeakable crimes that José María cannot quite articulate (see Kronik): "Era un hombre que me repugnaba lo indecible; odiábale sin saber por qué, pues jamás me hizo daño alguno." (Galdós, *Lo prohibido*, 431–32; He disgusted me in unspeakable ways; I hated him without knowing why as he never harmed me personally.) José María's incomprehension prevents him from describing his revulsion; after Eloísa's unexpected sale of herself to Botín, however, the narrator's speechlessness stems from knowledge.

The patina of bourgeois honor and the glamor of frivolous Spanish life in the capital that fill the pages of the novel like reports in a society column are captivating, but *Lo prohibido* dares the reader to scratch the gilded surface. At a moment of great tension and falling action in the plot, the narrator has lost his own fortune and faces economic ruin. When his friends and relations are unable to cover his debts, Eloísa sells herself to Sánchez Botín and José María is ultimately saved from disgrace through her intervention.[21] At this point—a Cervantine slip from the ideal to the real—José María undergoes an anagnorisis during one of his many reversals of fortunes, recognizing the true state of affairs in his society, discarding his previous ignorance.

José María has lost money, honor, and health, yet he is reluctant to accept Eloísa's money. Alda Blanco reads his reaction as a result of the fact that "lo considera dinero sucio y teñido de la inmoralidad de su antigua amante" (16; he considers it dirty money, stained by the immorality of his former lover). Indeed, initially, it is the recognition of his own role in the commerce in bodies and luxury that makes the money repulsive to José María: "Parecíame que los tres, Eloísa, Botín y yo éramos igualmente despreciables, odiosos y viles, y que formábamos una sociedad de envilecimiento comanditario para socorrernos por turno." (459; It seemed to me that the three of us, Eloísa, Botín, and I, were equally disgusting, odious, and vile, and that we formed a company of bedfellow defilement where we came to each other's aid in turn.) But his discomfort goes beyond Eloisa's sale of her own body to comprise previous transactions by Fúcar and Botín before they knew her, as well as to a deeper perception of the traffic of human bodies and the relationship between bodily transactions and the circulation of money.

Eloísa traffics her own body in order to access Botín's fortune. As Arthur Terry observed, the economic metaphor linking sexual vitality and economic prosperity prevalent in nineteenth-century thinking is implicit in this novel—sexual energy becomes a matter of spending or conserving; promiscuity may be compared to rash investments (75). But in this instance the body is literally for sale. European prostitution and colonial slavery were often compared in nineteenth-century Spain, culminating in reform movements that called for the abolition of both institutions for similar reasons (see P. Fernández, ch. 6). Within *Lo prohibido* José María's awareness of one type of trafficking allows him to perceive the other. Eloísa's body is contaminated by the financial enterprises of the various men with whom she enters into an economic relationship and becomes a contagion by which the men infect each other with their various forms of corruption. By accepting Eloísa's money, José María would be complicit with the financial schemes of all the men who had trafficked her—including with the slave trade itself.

José María is, in fact, slowly struck dumb with his knowledge. His anagnorisis of the unsayable is accompanied by a loss of voice (initiated after his fall down the stairs following a final rejection by Camila).[22] When he first hears of Eloísa's "prostitución elegante," he bites his tongue, begins to spit blood—"Empecé a echar sangre por la boca, porque me mordí la lengua" (Galdós, *Lo prohibido*, 459; I began to spit blood, because I bit my tongue)—and reflects on his role in his lover's finances. The next paragraph begins with a parallel description of silence and violence. His friend, "no se mordió la lengua para darme detalles" (459; didn't bite his tongue and gave me all the details). José María bites his tongue (literally and figuratively) as a consequence of inner conflict and is unable to articulate what is actually at stake in accepting Botín's money; Severiano, who does not remain silent, shares the sordid details of Eloísa's transactions without recognizing the deeper moral implications of her actions. He does not bite his tongue for he is oblivious to the ramifications of the story he repeats as anything more than gossip. At this point in their conversation José María can still speak, but when he realizes the impossibility of returning Eloisa's gift and forfeiting his fiscal solvency, José María moves closer to muteness: "La lengua me hacía cosquillas y se declaraba en huelga completa, negándome hasta los monosílabos." (461; My tongue became ticklish and declared itself on strike, refusing me even monosyllables.)

When José María sees Eloísa for the first time after she has saved him from social and financial infamy and his fortunes are yet again reversed, he refuses to speak: "Calleme ante la prójima." (461; I stayed silent in front of the floozy.) Refusing language, he comes to understand by sensorial, rather than intellectual means the true state of Spain's affairs. The artifice of "civilization" is unmasked as he senses that the only source of wealth in Madrid vast enough to rescue the narrator has left symbolic traces on Eloísa's body. He takes her hand: "¡Ay! me olió a estafermo sucio y perfumado con ingredientes innobles; olióme a baratería, a barbas mal pintadas, a dinero amasado con sangre de negros esclavos, a infamia y grosería, a sordidez y a ojos de carnero agonizante." (461; Oh! It smelled like a filthy dummy, perfumed with vulgar ingredients; it smelled like cheap stuff, like an ill-dyed beard, like money amassed with the blood of Black slaves, like infamy and coarseness, like sordidness and the eyes of an agonizing ram.) In this moment of clarity, José María connects Eloísa, glamor, Fúcar, speculation, Sánchez Botín, and himself to slave trading, infamy, and a sordid underworld that goes well beyond Eloísa's immediate transactions. With this whiff of shock, the truth about metropolitan glamor—indeed, even decency—is acquired through olfactory knowledge, beyond the verbal or the visual. His knowledge is closer to animalistic intuition than those of intellectual observation or discourse that have permitted the inhumane into human civilization. Finally, José María claims he has been struck dumb (although he does not lose the ability to speak definitively) (462). He admits he is ashamed of the effeminate sound of his voice after his stroke, but in fact, he no longer trusts what he says and is worried about what he might say.

Elena Delgado has emphasized the importance of the social meaning of language in nineteenth-century Spain. Those without the power of not just speech as a physical action but language as a social and rational system were considered primitive and savage (304), distinguished from those bearing reason and civilization: that is, they were "monstrous." Monsters in late nineteenth- and early twentieth-century literature threaten to disrupt the hegemonic order (Delgado cites Stevenson's Mr. Hyde and Kafka's Samsa) but lacking language, they ultimately fail to contest the reigning systems on their own terms. Delgado builds upon this premise to develop a provocative analysis of the characterization of Galdós's *indianos* in *Tormento* and *La loca de la casa*, poised between civilization and barbarity, Europe and the colonies, embodying some of this modern monstrosity of linguistic incompetence (305).

José María's knowledge of the barbarity of civilization accompanies his rejection of spoken language and confirms his departure from cultured society. Unlike the *indianos* that Delgado analyzes, José María is fully versant in Spanish language and society. Rather, it is upon acquiring perspective on the monstrosity of the *negrero* basis of Restoration finance that he loses facility in the language of civilization (Spanish)—the linguistic code that normalizes the truth about money that he cannot articulate. A physical deficiency fuses with a fissure in imperial logic: his loss of speech is accompanied by a paralysis that culminates in his death.

José María becomes unable to articulate a critique of the fundamental moral imperial code of Madrid in its own language either at his first interaction with Botín or after his money buys the narrator's honor. "Monsters by trade" takes on a new guise as José María Bueno de Guzmán becomes a monster by recognizing his complicity in the *negrero* world. He is left a drooling invalid and the novel implodes, leaving behind the bourgeois tale and transforming into sheer melodrama under Ido del Sagrario. With the transfer between narrators, Galdós writes the impossibility of narrating bourgeois society once one no longer believes in marriage, property, the logic of race, or the value of trading in monstrosity.

Previous scholarship has dedicated much attention to the reliability of José María as narrator and the veracity of his moral turn during crucial chapters of *Lo prohibido*, in particular given his previous behavior, narrative style, and the fantastical nature of his amanuensis, Ido del Sagrario (Terry; Whiston, *Ironía*, 1990; Willem). Ido is a known scribbler in the *novelas contemporáneas* and his folletinesque and melodramatic tendencies heighten tension and often transform the quotidian into the melodramatic. Ido's considerable role in the production of the third segment calls into question the depth of José María's moral conversion (Willem, 194). José María's anagnorisis very well may be such an embellishment of the narrator's more account book-entry recollections, all the more convincing for its sharpened emotion. The anagnorisis is plausible, to be sure, especially given José María's carefully crafted moral position on the edge of imperial Spain, which he has maintained throughout the novel. Nevertheless, what is at stake is not the ethical bounds of José María's confessions but the narrative possibilities of such an event in the realist novel. *Lo prohibido* stages a breakdown of novelistic discourse by suggesting that only the melodramatic mode can effectively communicate such an unthinkable story. The plot resolves its moral tensions precisely through the collapse of mimesis, a discursive rupture executed by Ido del Sagrario. When Eloísa pays José María's debts with money from Botín's corrupt ventures, bourgeois respectability has been temporarily saved, but the possibility of this class (and its literary discourse) to make sense of this world, without recourse to fantastic melodrama, has not. As Timothy McGovern pointed out in regard to other novels, Galdós habitually turns to melodrama "in order to highlight events which are impossible to explain as rational throughout his production" (15). In *Lo prohibido*, however, there are no magical, peripheral worlds, only the savagely realist world of finance. As Wadda Ríos-Font has argued, "Galdós comprehends reality as an essentially dynamic *economic* phenomenon in which patterns of exchange and credit govern not only individuals' financial and social positions, but even deep structures of desire and language, and thus ultimately thought and being" (167). Thus Galdós's elaboration of an economic realism does demonstrate the contours of reality, but at the price of dismantling the political myth of the modern nation built on liberal values that is woven into its logic.

The sections of the novel narrated by José María depict the interactions of characters who desire—and acquire—what is prohibited by either law or morality. Galdós's Sánchez Botín, José María, Fúcar, and Eloísa characterize various aspects of what immorality means—and what it looks like—and present to readers a way to conceive of a city that has become immoral on a global scale. The slave trade and colonial fraud are neither the source nor the result of the immorality of Madrid society that Galdós depicts in this novel, but rather wholly inseparable from it. In *Lo prohibido*, Galdós shows the monstrous effects of an entrenched complacency toward practices in Cuba that supported these morally and physically indolent *madrileños*.

José María's inability to narrate (and the transposition of orality to written narration is not automatic) goes beyond the verbal. He can no longer write the modern novel, even in its guise as autobiography. For a contemporary bourgeois novel to function, certain secrets cannot be stated, lest the novel reveal society's basic monstrosity. Race is one of these secrets. In *Lo prohibido*, traces of race (even where it is invisible and unspeakable) allow us to appreciate the extent to which race holds the novel together and informs its foundational logic.

Vilashini Coopan has written that race "operates as the fantasy element through which the social meaning of various historical structures and ideologies understood to make the novel are regularly routed. . . . The nationalism, capitalism, and individualism supposedly generative of the novel [are] themselves ghosted by the structures of colonial capitalism (empire), racial capitalism (slavery), and finally, by the spectral category of race itself" (82). Indeed, José María's lesson is also a racial one. Galdós emphasizes not only corruption, but also a particular type of colonial capitalism that provided the logic for a book like *Lo prohibido*, where the truth about how race and capitalism function can only be written in melodramatic form, as the narration of the acknowledgment of the ideologies of the bourgeois life of the nineteenth-century novel. Conceptualizing race as an avenue of understanding corruption and capitalism within the Peninsula is also a way of reconceptualizing Spain's place in the Atlantic world through the *esclavista* system. *Lo prohibido* is one of a handful of books in a global literary history where, as Coopan has written, "the logic of capital, the imaginary of race, and the technology of genre all converge" (81).

Galdós's narratives are fictional representations of a political concept ("Spain as modern European nation") that coexisted uneasily with the (by then) shameful and (to Galdós) problematic practices of late nineteenth-century empire. Spain acts like an empire but justifies its practices through the language of nationalism, thus revealing the danger of patriotic discourse and, indeed, the misuse of the concept of the nation, and more specifically, a particular conceptualization of the nation as innocent, pure, and a force for good in the Iberian Peninsula. Galdós constructs the nation even as he illustrates its perilous ruptures personified by Spanish *negreros* who are at the root of modern Spain and whose influence is woven into its political and economic structure. In *El amigo Manso* Galdós writes his disillusionment at the recognition of the ultimately fictive nature of his idealized strong "home" nation that, somehow morally edified, could counter the centrifugal influences of *esclavismo* on the state. This home (and the educated, civilized woman who could create it) are merely fantasies: Irene turns out to be "como todas."

These fictional depictions of colonial corruption by no means approach the condemnations by exiled Cubans such as Juan Gualberto Gómez or Antonio Saco. Nevertheless, the supposed silence identified by other critics around imperialism, injustice, and *indiano* control of the metropolitan government in the work of the great Spanish realist is less a result of lack of interest in the colonies than part of Galdós's pro-Spanish literary project exploring the limits of the nation. In *El amigo Manso*, he staged the uneasy positions of the empire at home, the invisibility of Black Cubans to peninsular progressives, and the relationship between law and fiction to create, deny, or abolish personhood, leaving political rhetoric firmly in the hands of the *indiano* José María Manso and the self-interested Mañolito Peña. The polite society of *Lo prohibido* survives on corruption at home and abroad, as apt to foment civil wars as to traffic human labor, or swindle the state. Spain—whatever it may be apart from its imperial lifelines—seems unlikely to survive its nineteenth-century empire in better shape than the Antilles.

§3 Baroja's Atlantic, Beyond Slavery

Whereas Blanco White, Ayguals de Izco, and Galdós were generally concerned with "Spain," largely defined, Pío Baroja (1872–1956) wrote a more intimate story of the role of Basque seamen in nineteenth-century Spanish colonialism. The *negreros* in this author's works are not the slick capitalists depicted by Galdós; rather, they are hardworking sailors. Twenty-five years after the abolition of slavery in colonial Cuba and less than a generation after the spectacular naval defeats at Manila and Santiago de Cuba during the War of 1898 ended Spain's political hold on the Antilles, the Philippines, and Guam, Baroja launched a series of four novels titled *El Mar*.[1] Three of these—*Las inquietudes de Shanti Andía* (1911), *Los pilotos de altura* (1929), and *La estrella del capitán Chimista* (1930)—revisit one of the murkier chapters of Spanish imperial history, narrating the lives of fictional Basque mariners who transported Africans across the Middle Passage to Cuba after the transatlantic slave trade had been outlawed.[2] Firsthand memories of the slave trade had all but disappeared by the first decades of the twentieth century, and Baroja's novels present a highly self-conscious attempt to use fiction to reverse a growing social amnesia and retain knowledge of a crucial aspect of nineteenth-century Basque culture. In the process, he suggests a reconsideration of the Atlantic as a sphere of the Spanish empire.[3] The double-decker of *Los pilotos de altura* and *La estrella del capitán Chimista*, in particular, is an explicit attempt to commit the past to paper, so that a Spain that is beyond slavery, beyond empire, and beyond the concerns of the nineteenth century might not completely condemn its past to oblivion.

Baroja's ambitious maritime series is of greater importance than the slight critical attention it has received might suggest. Its significance stems from the author's geographic focus, generic choice, and assessment of Spain's recent imperial missteps. Baroja departs from the general practice of his contemporaries by shifting his focus from the center of Iberia to the northern coast and beyond, moving from landscape to seascape and by adopting an outmoded subgenre whose popularity had peaked a century before.[4] *Las inquietudes de Shanti Andía*, *Los pilotos de altura*, and *La estrella del capitán Chimista* stand out in their rejection of the narrative possibilities offered by the landscape of Old Castile and in their cultivation of the style, mode, and discourse of the English maritime novel to write about the sea as the means by which Spain arrived at its overseas colonies.

Baroja's choice of form not only provides a sense of authenticity for his historical novels set in the nineteenth century but also subverts English maritime supremacy by appropriating its celebratory fictional discourse and creating a counternarrative. Although Baroja's narrators never pose the central question of many early twentieth-century intellectuals based in Madrid—"Why did Spain lose its colonies?"—the *Mar* novels offer an answer to the parallel question, albeit never posed by these same writers: "How did Spain retain any of its former empire after the 1820s?"[5] While Baroja was certainly not an apologist for Cuban nationalism, nor did he offer favorable depictions of Africans, Asians, or Creoles, he did examine in great detail the inhumane mechanics of empire that kept Spain in the Antilles: corruption, violence, dishonesty, slavery, and crime. He reveals his answers in the open secret of what actually happened at sea and who carried it out. His truths are less than agreeable to a vanquished nation, and the scant attention that these novels have received is a consequence of their subversive character. Baroja finds responsibility for a nineteenth-century empire not in the power of the Spanish navy or the political savvy of its government (both recently defeated in the battles of 1898) but rather in the merchant marines who functioned as free traders on the open market of the high seas but were never commemorated as national heroes.[6]

The narrators of these three novels are Shanti Andía and Ignacio Embil; both are ship captains from the fictional coastal towns of Luzaro and Elguea (respectively), in the western end of the province of Gipuzkoa, but each presents a singular perspective on maritime life. Andía belongs to the officer class of sailors and is urbane, educated, and correct in his morals, language, and actions. As the narrator of the *Las inquietudes de Shanti Andía*, he both recounts his own, rather conventional, travels and simultaneously unravels the mysterious life of his uncle who sailed the world at the margins of legitimate trade. In contrast to Shanti Andía, Ignacio Embil is a rough self-made man of the seas with no moral compass. Embil is the narrator of *Pilotos de altura* and *La estrella del capitán Chimista*; these works follow his and his childhood friend Chimista's pursuit of wealth through the transatlantic slave trade, travels to the Pacific, and maritime trade routes throughout the globe. Like Andía, Embil remains at the margins of the adventures he relates, but only because his attempts end in failure.

Baroja and the Basques

The Spanish nineteenth-century empire implied a control of land (those colonies lost in 1898), but was guaranteed by the oceanic presence of both the navy and merchant marines. In Baroja's version, their Atlantic turns out to be anything but "Spanish." The empire may have claimed maritime supremacy, but the actual sailors working within it eluded a straightforward affiliation. At sea, slave ships could bear any number of flags or names and the same was true for the sailors. From temporary impersonations to the outright buying and selling of men for labor to identity theft, the boundaries of personhood are impossible to demarcate. The idea that it was possible to ascertain the nation or state to which one belonged was challenged when individual identity was pure invention. In spite of international treaties regarding the oceans, what actually happened was beyond the reach of the signature nations.[7] It is here where Baroja finds a homeland of sorts for his cohesive group of Basque sailors and suggests an appreciation of the nineteenth-century Atlantic as a Basque one.

Nevertheless, Baroja's narrators, Ignacio Embil and Shanti Andía, are not Basque separatists and have multiple allegiances. For example, Shanti Andía and a *capitán* from Guéthary acknowledge this as they exchange toasts "Por el país vasco. –Por España. –Por Francia" (*Shanti*, 187; To the Basque Country.—To Spain.—To France). Baroja famously undermined Basque claims for national status on land, particularly in his satirical work on Basque nationalism, *Momentum catastrophicum*. But in the *Mar* novels, his approach to the idea of a unified Basque identity, as well as the significance of its integration into Spain are much more nuanced. The maritime world would seem to promise an autonomous sphere for Basque individualism. However, as Ignacio Aldecoa has written, in spite of the "romanticism" of adventure, life at sea is not entirely enviable, and a narrative "denigración del mar" (denigration of the sea) leads to "el canto a la tierra natal" (hymn to the land of birth) in these works (159). In sum, the sailors long for a Basque homeland that exists only in childhood memories, but Baroja keeps Basque culture offshore, at sea, and presents an alternate view of nation-building that has little to do with landscape or national boundaries. Rather, language is the foundation of this variant of Basque diasporic culture.

Like all of his classmates, the young Shanti Andía growing up on the Basque coast found his schoolmaster ridiculous. Don Hilario, a *castellano viejo* who taught the curriculum through the prism of the propriety of the Spanish language and a loathing for everything Basque, "odiaba el vascuence como a un enemigo personal" (hated the Basque language like a personal enemy). To his pupils, in contrast, "nos parecía una pretensión ridícula el que don Hilario quisiera dar importancia a las cosas de tierra adentro . . . le temíamos y le despreciábamos al mismo tiempo" (67; it seemed ridiculously pretentious to us that don Hilario wanted to give importance to inland things . . . we feared him and despised him at the same time). Rather than learn of "las viñas de Haro, de los trigos de Medina del Campo" (the vineyards of Haro, the wheat fields of Medina del Campo), they want to be at sea where they speak *vascuence* and live in freedom from everything their teacher represents. In their innocent view, the sea is a means to escape the impositions of Spanish society and language; ironically, these Basque boys will grow up and indirectly serve the same empire upon the oceans.

For the adult Shanti, knowledge continues to be categorized linguistically. He has difficulties creating commercial, amorous, and social ties outside of the Basque Country because he is unsteady in Castilian. Comparing himself with other young men and women in Cádiz at the beginning of his career, he notes:

> Un nuevo idioma es una nueva alma, y hay algo de verdad en esto; yo comprendía, al oír a aquellos muchachos, que no sólo no sabía el castellano, sino que mi alma era distinta a la suya. Yo me sentía otra cosa, pero no tenía el valor ni la fuerza para creer que mi espíritu, más concentrado y más sobrio, valía tanto como el de ellos, toda expansión, palabras y muecas. Mi humildad me inducía a creerme un salvaje entre civilizados. (*Shanti*, 117)

> (A new language is a new soul, and there is some truth in this; I understood listening to those boys, that not only did I not know Castilian, but that my soul was different from theirs. I felt different, but I did not have the courage or the strength to believe that my spirit, more concentrated and more sober, was worth as much as theirs, all expansion, words and grimaces. My humility induced me to believe I was a savage among civilized individuals.)

In contrast to this alienation produced by his linguistic constitution, offshore, as the Gascon sailor avows, "ser vasco . . . constituía gran ventaja. El capitán lo era; lo mismo que su camarilla o guardia negra, con quien se entendía en vascuence." (192; being Basque . . . was a great advantage. The captain was; so too was his inner circle or black guard, with whom he spoke in Basque.) This is particularly true on slave ships and in his commentary on Embil's *Diario*, Shanti's friend, the historian Cincúnegui, delves further into power of the close-knit Basque community that existed within the international crews.

> Entre los españoles, los peores marinos para los viajes negreros eran los catalanes y los vascos. . . . Los vascos se mostraban indisciplinados, desesperados, marineros rebeldes, marineros tigres. Creían, sin duda, que fuera de su país y de su pueblo y en un barco dedicado a la trata, no quedaba en pie ni leyes ni respetos humanos. Probablemente, de ser marinero, yo hubiera creído lo mismo. Esta condición se sabía entre los negreros, y una tripulación completa de vascos no la hubiese aceptado ningún capitán, de miedo a la rebelión. (*Pilotos*, 143)

> (Among the Spanish, the worst mariners for the *negrero* voyages were the Catalans and the Basques. . . . The Basques showed themselves to be undisciplined, desperate, rebellious sailors, tiger sailors. They believed, undoubtedly, that outside their country and their village and in a boat dedicated to trafficking slaves, there were no longer laws or human respect. Probably, if I had been a sailor, I would have believed the same thing. This condition was known among the *negreros*, and no captain would have accepted an entire crew of Basques, for fear of rebellion.)

Back on land, but investigating maritime stories, bilingualism becomes indispensable to Shanti Andía as he recovers the double lives of his uncle Juan de Aguirre/Tristán de Uribe. What is generally known (but not necessarily true) about his uncle's mysterious life is available in Castilian while many of the secrets that emerge are in Euskara: for example, the French Gascon shopkeeper's report on Aguirre's participation in the Asian coolie and African slave trades or Juan's treasure map written in a code based on *vascuence*.

For his part, the narrator of *Pilotos* and *Estrella*, Ignacio Embil, emphasizes that his friend, the idealized José Chimista (also known as Bizargorri), "dominaba el vascuence y no lo quería olvidar; era una manera secreta de entenderse con los paisanos, cosa que a él le interesaba" (*Pilotos*, 85; dominated Basque and did not want to forget it; it was a secret way to communicate with his countrymen, which interested him). Among themselves, the sailors choose to speak their native language because of its utility in preserving knowledge—a fundamental theme of these novels—but in their case, it is in order to exclude others rather than educate them. Whether for pirates or legitimate merchant marines, the elite, secret language of Baroja's Atlantic was Euskara, impervious to interpretation by speakers of the usual maritime patois.[8]

Baroja's Basque sailors are merchant marines. While their objectives were not explicitly to promote the empire, their participation in the lucrative slave trade was indirectly patriotic.[9] Agents of a wider Western, racially justified imperial and slavocratic ideology, Embil rationalizes their participation in these very terms. Neither Basque nor European, but specific to the framework of their particular empire, "los españoles, entonces, tenían grandes colonias y necesitaban brazos" (*Pilotos*, 133; the Spanish, at that time, had large colonies and needed manpower). The modern Spanish empire as a whole existed in doublespeak as pertained to the slave trade. As late as the 1860s, there was tacit approval of it on the part of Spanish colonial authorities. Not only did the slave trade provide loyalist planters with fresh labor, but also corruption around the trade stymied a healthy society and economy that could have accelerated Cuban independence. Colonial governance integrated both of these practices, as Alfonso Quiroz has argued.

> Offenders often justified this type of corruption originating at the top as a patriotic effort to keep Cuba under a re-centralized colonial rule buttressed by divisive racial policies. For example, the lieutenant governor of Guanabacoa, separated from his post in 1853, for collaborating with slave traders and gamblers, argued that he was being punished for his patriotic gestures and services. (Quiroz, 491)

Baroja situates his merchant marines within this larger frame of vice and depicts an empire afloat through corruption by officials as well as by freelance sailors. *Pilotos de Altura* and *La estrella del Capitán Chimista* explore the degree to which indirect patriotism—criminal acts against international treaties and the (then unrecognized) human rights of Africans—by José Chimista and his kind served the imperial project. Such was the glory of the "Hispanic Atlantic." Nevertheless, the novels are ambiguous about the "poco patriotismo de los vascos" (*Estrella*, 264; minimal patriotism of the Basques) until the end of the series when an aged Chimista delivers a riveting speech confirming Basque contributions to Spain's maritime greatness (266).

The *Mar* Novels at Sea

Margaret Cohen dates the launch of maritime fiction to 1823 with the publication of James Fenimore Cooper's *The Pilot* and charts the "boom" in European and North American sea fiction to the 1830s and 1840s, although it remained popular throughout the nineteenth century (483–84). The Anglo-American sea novel ascended concurrently with the United States' and England's custodianship of the seas. As a genre, it belongs to dominant, not vanquished empires, serving to provide images of life at sea to readers on land. By the publication of *Las inquietudes de Shanti Andía* in 1911, Spain no longer ruled the Atlantic nor had to transverse it to reach its remaining colonies; maritime novels could no longer facilitate armchair participation in the exploits of overseas adventure. Thus when Baroja adopts it in the twentieth century, he uses an anachronistic mode to relate an antiquated story. On an aesthetic plane, the choice is appropriate: as his narrators live in the nineteenth century, the tone of the maritime novel cultivates a salty air of temporal authenticity. Moreover, Baroja's choice resonated with a publishing trend: during these same years, Vicente Blasco Ibáñez published a translation of Mayne Reid's 1858 novel *Ran Away to Sea* as *El barco negrero* in the "Novela Ilustrada" series in 1910, the same novel was republished in 1930 (by Ameller in Barcelona), and the Galician-Cuban writer Lino Novás Calvo published his masterpiece, the fictionalized biography of Pedro Blanco, *El negrero*, in Madrid with Espasa-Calpe in 1933, "at the suggestion of the publishers who were interested in a book of adventures" (Luis, 177). But politically, Baroja's choice of the maritime mode produces a disjuncture between the genre and reality for early twentieth-century Spain that results in lessons about life at sea (Spain's past "glories") for postempire readers through a discursive mode created by a culture that defeated it.[10]

Spain, of course, had written its imperial history of the seas in other genres. But when Great Britain gained hegemony over the seas it also assumed the right to write. In addition to the emergence of the maritime novel, English models of cartography eclipsed Spanish ones. Spain's attempt to map itself as an Atlantic empire was a relatively recent endeavor, but the Hapsburgs carefully guarded its cartographic treasure (Padrón, 12–13). As Ricardo Padrón has argued, during the early modern period, linear and itinerary thinking shaped cartographic practices. The ideologies aligned with a scientific perspective on global representation and mapping superseded the arbitrariness that characterized itinerary-based conceptualizations of space. Indeed, as Ursula Lamb explains, Spanish cosmographers and hydrographers had long been respected throughout Europe and their authority was not seriously contested before the early nineteenth century (Lamb, passim). Until the middle of the nineteenth century (when longitude finally became a consistent measurement), the sea was navigated primarily by either "derrota" (dead reckoning) or "altura" (latitude fixed by star gazing), with the assistance of the astrolabe and quadrant (Padrón, 65), and *pilotos de altura*, possessing a highly specialized skill for exploring and expanding the empire, were held in high esteem for their knowledge and intelligence. During the first decades of the nineteenth century, the scientific charts promoted by the English hydrographic office were gaining ground, and by the late 1820s, Spanish nautical cartographic methods, its navy, and influence of its merchant marines ceded superiority to England (Lamb, XVI–327).[11] Shanti Andía reflected upon the intellectual and physical challenges of the sea before English cartography conquered it scientifically. "Entonces, en la mayoría de los buques, se deducía la situación más por conjeturas que por cálculos" (*Shanti*, 40; At that time, on the majority of ships, location was deduced more by conjectures than calculations) and his musings inform us that the sea, "una esfinge incomprensible" (38; incomprehensible sphinx), is not knowable the way that land is. By definition, those who understood it best had to invert their gaze to dominate it: *pilotos de altura* looked to the stars in order to read and navigate the sea. But the Spanish *pilotos de altura* were written off the oceans by English scientific progress until Pío Baroja appropriated the British literary form to reinscribe them. Shanti Andía's poetic idealization of the sea is part of a dialectic of nostalgia and repulsion for the Spanish empire (and its high-seas adventures) that ebbs and flows throughout the novel.

In various texts, Baroja insisted upon the need to integrate the stories of Basque seamen into high literature. In his essay "El mar y el marino" Baroja points out that "en ningún [momento], el hombre del mar, el marino, se ha destacado, ni ha sido puesto a plena luz por la literatura. Un personaje tan importante ha quedado siempre en la semioscuridad." (785; at no [time], has the man of the sea, the mariner, been highlighted, nor has he been placed in broad daylight by literature. Such an important character has always remained semiobscured.) Both the *marino* and the sea itself had been overlooked as an obstacle to the "real" story of a hero in Spanish literature. "El mar, el marino y el marinero, en su época de misterio . . . se han escapado a la observación del escritor. Los hombres iban y venían por el océano, sufrían sus embates y sus cóleras y no le concedían importancia." (787; The sea, the mariner, and the sailor, in their time of mystery . . . have escaped the writer's observation. Men went and came by the ocean, they suffered its pounding and its rage and did not grant it importance.) Throughout the *Mar* series, Baroja demonstrates that both the sea and its sailors are full of dramatic appeal and that Basque mariners are just as interesting as French and English fictional sailors. Citing the works of Eugène Sue, Fenimore Cooper, Captain Marryat, and Walter Scott as models, Baroja then reclaims the Atlantic for Spanish fiction. "El mar ya no es una exclusiva de los autores ingleses." (787; The sea no longer belongs exclusively to English authors.) Politically, the sea may belong to Anglo-American navies, but the right to narrate it is now contested.

Chasing History

The three *Mar* novels exhibit a strong sense of responsibility both to retell nineteenth-century history and to teach readers the correct way to interpret it. Moreover, an anxiety about access to knowledge goes beyond that of the slave trade to a generalized dismay at public ignorance about the past. Shockingly, even official history may not be learned—an exasperated Cincúnegui notes that Blas de Aristondo, a Basque sailor from Elguea, had never heard of the Invincible Armada (*Estrella*, 283)—and crucial personal histories are more elusive yet.

Historiography is not only the task of professional writers but also the responsibility of the Basques themselves, who learn the skills during childhood. For example, the young José Chimista convinces veterans of the War of Independence (1808–14) to tell him their experiences, "de los cuales no podía tener idea por otro conducto" (*Pilotos*, 72; of which he could not have any idea by any other means). Shanti Andía, too, hears fantastic tales from the old *negrero* Yurrumendi (76) and folklore shared by his nanny Iñure before he learns to read. The young boy subsequently enters the world of literature through chronicles of his family at sea and his Aunt Ursula's library of foreign maritime adventure novels.

The upstanding and honorable Shanti Andía's "inquietudes" stem, in part, from his unease about the past and the difficulty in knowing what happened between his uncle's social death (during Shanti's childhood) and his actual, physical death many years later. Juan de Aguirre was a fearless sailor, captain of a slave ship that transported Asian coolies and Africans, a convicted pirate, and an escapee from an English prison. His life is a compendium of Basque participation in the global transportation of forced laborers in the nineteenth century. Although Shanti knew and conversed with the old sailor (initially identified as Tristán) while he was alive, it is only after the man dies that Shanti discovers Aguirre's true identity. The novel's historiographical tension is a result of this missed opportunity to access a living primary source and his familial connection to the dark side of the imperial seas. Shanti's story is one of discovering and rediscovering the truth, interpreting the past, and integrating it into his understanding of himself, his town, his culture, and his nation. Moving beyond slavery in this novel is about understanding personal, family, and cultural history and acknowledging responsibilities for past actions and crimes as well as reconciling them with the present and with official versions of history.

Formally, history is a composite of multiple voices, each with a unique perspective and ideology. For example, the conversation with a *vasco-francés* sailor and shopkeeper provides Shanti with an eyewitness account of his uncle's adventures with a coterie of Basque sailors; later access to Juan's deathbed letter to his illegitimate son corroborates the testimony. Shanti comes to understand history as a "colaboración espontánea [que] adorna los grandes hechos y los grandes caracteres. El uno insinúa: 'Podría ser'; el otro añade: 'Se dice'; un tercero agrega: 'Ocurrió así,' y el ultimo asegura: 'Lo he visto . . . ' De este modo se va formando la historia, que es el folletín de las personas serias." (*Shanti*, 37; spontaneous collaboration [that] adorns the great events and the great characters. One insinuates: "It could be"; the other adds: "It is said"; a third adds: "It happened like this," and the latter one asserts: "I've seen . . . " In this way history is formed, which is the serial novel of serious people.) History has literature's meandering narrative and is molded as much by commentary and dialogue as by plot. Shanti Andía's reflections on history are replicated in the structure of his memoirs. The novel harmonizes discordant voices and hops across historical time zones, alternating between drawing readers close to the truth about Juan de Aguirre and disorienting them. According to Biruté Ciplijauskaité, distancing is a recurrent stylistic motif in Baroja's oeuvre, including the distortion of time, a dimension that she identifies as a protagonist in *Las inquietudes de Shanti Andía.* "Los excursos en el pasado—ya no sólo de Shanti, sino también del tío—amplían el horizonte temporal. El sostenido tono nostálgico contribuye a mantener vivo el pasado como tal." (360; The digressions into the past—not only Shanti's, but also the uncle's—amplify the temporal horizon.

The sustained nostalgic tone contributes to keep the past alive as such.) That is, the jumping around in time underscores the mechanics of history as well as its place in the present.

In contrast to *Shanti Andía*'s emphasis on oral history, *Pilotos* and *Estrella* are structured around a found document. The framing device is a favored technique for an author who wishes to avoid accountability or establish authenticity. But a found manuscript is often, as in Baroja's case, one that has been lost. Its fortuitous recovery draws attention to the precariousness of knowledge and the author's importance in creating new written history to sustain memory. The two novels have three frames, each entailing a recovery of the document and the inclusion of a new narrative and interpretive voice. In the "Introducción" to *Pilotos*, set around the time of World War I, the first narrator, a "manufacturer of novels" (or "fabricante de novelas"), a genealogist, and a book collector visit the Basque coast. In the small town of Elguea, the three men stumble upon the abandoned library of the deceased Domingo Cincúnegui, a local historian and friend of Shanti Andía in *Inquietudes*. Cincúnegui's sister urges the narrator to take a document he finds there: "Sí, sí, puede usted llevárselo, si quiere. ¿Para qué sirve?" (*Pilotos*, 42; Yes, yes, you can take it, if you want. What is it good for?)

The narrator of this first frame illustrates how society devours and destroys knowledge, ingesting it without digesting or even retaining a flavor of its message. Assessing Cincúnegui's decaying library, the *fabricante de novelas* conjectures:

> Muchas de las páginas faltas y otras de papeles del archivo fueron, probablemente, a parar a la tienda del piso bajo, a la carnicería y a la confitería de enfrente para envolver clavos, chuletas, bolos y dulces en una época menos preocupada de la higiene que la actual. Quizá algunas de las hojas las emplearon las vecinas en hacer papillotes. La hermana de Cincúnegui aseguró que muchos papeles habían ido a la buhardilla y se los comían las ratas. (40)

> (Many of the missing pages and other file papers, probably, ended up at the store on the ground floor, at the butcher shop and the confectionary in front to wrap nails, chops, ninepins, and candy in a time less concerned with hygiene than the present. Maybe the neighbors used some of the sheets to cook in *papillote*. Cincúnegui's sister asserted that many of the papers were in the attic and were eaten by rats.)

The townspeople of Lúzaro packaged their lives with this history without absorbing its meaning. The three scholars pessimistically predict a similar fate for their own work: "Lo mismo nos pasará a nosotros. . . . Nuestras bibliotecas se dispersarán; nuestros papeles se los comerán los ratones." (42; The same will happen to us. . . . Our libraries will be scattered; our papers will be eaten by mice.) Their labor and, in particular, the preparation of the novel in hand is futile. "Realmente, en España . . . el público no necesita escritores." (*Pilotos*, 42; Really, in Spain . . . the public does not need writers.) Nevertheless, the *fabricante de novelas* will write a set of spell-binding, action-packed novels (*Pilotos de altura* and *La estrella del capitán Chimista*), based on a rigorous historical study of the document found in the disarray of Cincúnegui's archives.

Moving back in time, the "Prólogo" presents a second frame in which Domingo Cincúnegui and a descendent of the Basque sailor Ignacio Embil meet at the turn of the century to talk about Bizargorri, a legendary red-bearded pirate whose fame has been kept alive through storytelling. Embil's descendent explains to Cincúnegui:

> —Yo soy el único que tiene datos de ese famoso capitán Chimista, llamado también Bizargorri—dijo el doctor Embil—. Este capitán tuvo alguna fama en el pueblo, hace muchos años, y se contaban de él muchas anécdotas.
>
> —¿Y siguen acordándose de él?
>
> —No; su fama se eclipsó. Yo tengo buena memoria, y le oía hablar de este hombre a mi padre, que tenía también una memoria excelente. (61)

> ("I am the only one that has information about that famous captain Chimista, also called Bizargorri," said doctor Embil. "This captain had some fame in the village, many years ago, and many stories were told of him."
>
> "And they still remember him?"
>
> "No, his fame was eclipsed. I have a good memory and I heard my father, who also had an excellent memory, speak of him.")

Doctor Embil then gives the historian his great-uncle's *diario de navegación* where his ancestor had known and written of the pirate.[12] His objective was to save Bizargorri's story from perdition, but he and Cincúnegui tread dangerous waters by reading Embil's navigation journal only to access information about Chimista. Everything else in the *diario*, including the author's own story, is dismissed as packaging (much as the townspeople use the pages from Cincúnegui's library to wrap their own lives). However, the survival of Embil's *diario* is astounding, not because of its references to Bizargorri, but because the events Embil narrates, the illicit trade, were officially undocumented. There were no examination papers required for sailors, no certificates, no set positions; in their place a certain "bohemia" reigned (119). Slave ships' crews existed beyond paper, with no written trace of their lives. Cincúnegui's oversight of this archival gem reflects his ideological bias for retelling local history only as a series of glories.

Ignacio Embil started his *diario* when he first embarked as a *piloto de altura* at age eighteen and kept it through his retirement. The first half of the diary, which forms the basis of *Pilotos de altura*, recounts his career as a pilot and captain on no less than eight slaving trips across the Middle Passage—all of them after Spain had agreed to English pressure to outlaw the trade and after no data or statements by traffickers were officially written or formally acknowledged. While these two novels constitute a confession, as autobiographies often do, our narrator is wholly unrepentant. A very old Embil, keenly aware of the significance of his story, inserts this commentary into his *diario*: "Como ya no puede quedar vivo nadie que haya presenciado con sus propios ojos cómo se creaba y cómo funcionaba una empresa de trata de negros, lo explicaré yo con detalles." (120; As no one can still be alive who witnessed with their own eyes how a slave trade company was created or how it functioned, I will explain it in detail.) Embil's consciousness of being the last tie to this past prompts him to give details and exact statistics, without hiding unpleasantries.[13] For example, he reports that a ship of three hundred tons could carry "entre el sollado y la cubierta, de quinientos a seiscientos negros. Claro que iban estibados como si fueran vacas o caballos." (121; between the primary and lower decks, from five to six hundred Blacks. Of course they were stowed like cows and horses.) Cincúnegui complains that such commentaries clutter the story, pushing the more exciting Chimista to the side, without acknowledging the rarity of the primary source in his possession.[14] Embil's manuscript is unique in explaining the conditions of these sailors who officially did not sail and Africans who officially were not sold.

Pilotos and *Estrella* are, then, the *fabricante*'s rewrite of Cincúnegui's edition of Embil's *diario*, written in first person, although the "I" of the novels refers usually, but not always, to Embil. Each of these authors offers a different perspective and contradictory prejudices. Rivera identifies the source of the excitement in these novels around the "magical world of adventure" as a profound nostalgia for the former age of "action" on the part of Baroja (159). But if we refrain from reading the characters as stand-ins for Pío Baroja the author (Rivera, 160, explicitly collapses any distinction), the nostalgia becomes more complex and reflects an understandable fantasy that once upon a time one could celebrate the thrill of empire without considering its consequences.

As readers, we quickly find Embil a despicable character, impossible to like or feel compassion for in any way. His *diario* (especially part III of *Pilotos*) gives a frightful description of the trade and its actors and actions in a system rotten to the core. These episodes are wholly devoid of adventure (the supposedly lighthearted material for evasion). It is tedious to read through Embil's workaday prose and unglamorized violence, but the promise of voyeuristic pleasure at Chimista's antics rewards readers who can digest Embil's brutal realism. Here, history chases readers of adventure novels.

Embil is also unappealing because of his extremely close-minded view of the non-Basque world. In the *Mar* series, Baroja weaves the Basque story into that of the Western imperial oceanic enterprise with numerous references to not only European and Brazilian powers but also the British in India. Characters like Embil work in all arenas, from transporting forced laborers to shipping goods for supranational commercial interests in areas officially independent from European administration. Embil, Chimista, and to a lesser degree, Aguirre move in an oceanic sphere that comprises the entire geography of the Spanish empire. In spite of this comprehensive view of Spanish colonial and postcolonial involvement across the global oceans, Baroja's representation of the former colonies is superficial. His depiction of Africa is, as Corrales Egea aptly put it, "archiconvencional, tópica, de reyezuelos de bazar . . . el África barojiana, aislada del complejo mundial e histórico del que forma parte y por el que está determinada en lo mejor y en lo peor, resulta una irrealidad en la que sólo existe una dimensión; la de lo curioso, lo raro, lo extravagante" (189; very conventional, clichéd, one of bazaar barons . . . Baroja's Africa, isolated from the global and historical complex of which it is part and which shapes it, for better and for worse, results in an unreality in which only one dimension exists; that of the intriguing, the strange, the extravagant). The same is true for Embil's descriptions of Asia in *La estrella* (Corrales Egea, 190). That is, Baroja does not cultivate an interest in knowing these areas for his readers, or incite them to consider interregional relationships, but rather limits himself to a European story of exploitation. Whether Embil's perspective mirrors Baroja's personal prejudices is debatable, but aesthetically, it does reflect contemporary Spanish attitudes regarding the colonies as little more than an easy route to riches. When placed in the mouth of the discredited Embil, this attitude that defined Spanish nineteenth-century empire is clearly miserable.

"Un capitán negrero mucho desgraciado"[15] Versus Bizargorri

In her study of a range of novels by Baroja and others, Denise DuPont analyzes their structure as one of tensions between realism and romantic idealism, or between a supposedly accurate representation of life as opposed to an image of how we would like life to be (see her introduction to *Realism as Resistance*). In a general sense these two modes form the organizing principle of the *Mar* novels, with a sharp divide between "protagonists" and "heroes" (Rivera, 153) and their corresponding interpretations of life at sea. Shanti Andía begins his autobiography noting the blandness of life: "La generalidad de los hombres nadamos en el océano de la vulgaridad." (*Shanti*, 35; The majority of us men swim in the ocean of vulgarity.) Juan de Aguirre, in contrast, is adventure personified. Embil and Chimista are similarly opposed with Bizargorri embodying an idealized fantasy that readers wish were representative of Spanish empire while Embil considers his life as mundane. Embil echoes Shanti when he reflects, "No he podido salir del charco de la vulgaridad de la vida cotidiana." (*Pilotos*, 58; I have not been able to get out of the puddle of the vulgarity of everyday life.) Indeed Embil breaks completely with established imperial narratives, for not only does he live a miserable existence and divulge unsavory facts, but also he refuses to complete even the most basic *indiano* story line: upon his return to Spain he does not pay off his family's mortgages, invest in their town, or marry within the clan of friends and relatives (*Estrella*, 274).

The conservation of Embil's navigation log by Cincúnegui and Embil's family members has everything to do with access to his friend. These readers hoped to find, discover, and recover the image of effortless imperialism and only accept Embil as the necessary vehicle by which they can reach Chimista. However, Embil presents a complex and compromised view of Chimista. Obviously in awe of his friend, the narrator nevertheless introduces him thus: "Yo, a veces, pensé si sería el diablo. Tales cosas hacía." (*Pilotos*, 59; I, sometimes, wondered if he was the devil. Such were the things he did.) But Chimista is not an omnipotent supernatural being. His success is the product of good relations with "canalla" (149; scoundrels), and Embil's comments throughout the novel suggest that Chimista is a scoundrel, too, but one who manages to refashion himself. Apart from insinuations of vice, Embil explains that the sometime pirate also worked as a slave trafficker and a witch doctor, among other questionable professions.

The persona that José Chimista creates around himself conforms exactly to what we would expect in a pirate hero: young, handsome, successful, intelligent, carefree, brilliantly skilled at avoiding capture, likeable, and rich. He is aware of his appeal and cultivates his own myth by authoring and perpetuating tales, poems, and newspaper notices about himself (164); indeed, the double-decker concludes with a description of an oil painting of Bizargorri. It might have been thoroughly enjoyable to read a lighthearted version of Chimista's life and legend, but Embil makes that impossible.

Much as Embil conscientiously reports even mundane details about his navigations (such as shuttling bat pelts and salt water (*Estrella*, 227) in order to produce a very faithful reflection of his life, Chimista, too, is aware of the power of words to make sense of life at sea. During one of their voyages together, Chimista and Embil disagree over the importance of poetry to sailors. An Andalusian quartermaster charmed the crew by singing (in heavily accented Spanish):

> Yo tengo una cabaña
> a la oriyita der ma,
> y una bancale de caña
> y un corasón para amá.
>
> Mi niña es una princesa
> rubia como el mismo so,
> con unos labios de fresa
> y colores de arrebó.
>
> (I have a cottage
> at the shore of the sea
> and bit of sugar cane
> and a heart to love.
>
> My girl is a princess
> blonde like the sun
> with strawberry lips
> and colored aglow.)

Embil finds no value in this unrealistic poetry, "A mí hasta asco me producían estas melosidades.—No somos angelitos, sino negreros—decía yo—, piratas que habría que ahorcar." (*Pilotos*, 153; These sweet [verses] even disgusted me. "We are no little angels, but slavers," I said, "pirates that ought to be hanged.") In contrast, Chimista reflects wisely on the verses' function as a salve, "Déjalos—contestaba Chimista, riendo—. Están ahí pensando en su cabañita y en su princesa, pero si viene el caso son capaces de abrirle a cualquiera las tripas, lo mismo que nosotros." (153–54; "Leave them," Chimista answered, laughing. "They are there thinking about their little cottage and their princess, but if the case arises they are capable of slicing open anyone's guts, just like us.") Imperialism itself survives by masking its reality in lyricism and heroic fiction, and Chimista recognizes that sailors need their fantasy as much as readers on land did. But peel away the romantic patina of adventure and the blond princesses offered by a certain kind of literature, and we find that the heroes of nineteenth-century empire are brutality itself.

Chimista's story is similar to that of any hero of maritime fiction or glamorized violence. He is lucky in love and war, and he demands respect yet rejects authority; moreover, he commands a secret band of pirates. Chimista may be handsome and charming, but his "gatadas" (93; sly tricks] remind readers of the nefarious impact that beguiling Spaniards like him had on daily life in Cuba. Embil does not divulge the specifics of Chimista's crimes; however, it was an open secret that Spain kept its hold on Cuba through reliance on clandestine slave traders and criminals of all types (Quiroz, 489).[16] By association, we comprehend the degree of Chimista's vice: for example, his fellow pirate the Vizconde openly states that he rapes both *negros* and *negras* (*Pilotos*, 177). Embil's textual protection of Chimista is characteristic of the cultivated ignorance toward life at sea and beyond that Shanti Andía reports in his memories.

> A la gran barbarie del mar correspondía la barbarie de su servidor el marino; a la brutalidad del elemento salobre, la brutalidad humana. . . . Un marino, entonces, era algo extrasocial, casi extrahumano; un marino era un ser para quien la moral ofrecía otros aspectos que para los demás mortales.
>
> —Te preguntarán cuánto has hecho—decían los padres a sus hijos, que se lanzaban a la aventura—, no cómo lo has hecho.
>
> Y los hijos se hundían en los abismos de la vida intensa, sin preocupaciones ni escrúpulos. . . . el Destino, en su misterioso molde, vaciaba esta humanidad y sacaba intrépidos mareantes o feroces negreros, exploradores audaces, o vendedores de chinos. (*Shanti*, 41)

> (The great barbarism of the sea corresponded with the barbarism of yours truly the mariner; to the brutality of the brackish element, human cruelty. . . . A mariner at that time, was something extrasocial, almost extrahuman; a mariner was a being for whom morality offered different aspects than it did for other mortals.

> "You will be asked what you have done"—fathers said to their sons that took to adventure, "not how you did it."
>
> And the sons sank into the abysses of their intense life, without worries or scruples. . . . Fate, in its mysterious form, emptied this humanity and drew out of it intrepid seafarers or ferocious *negreros*, bold explorers, or sellers of Chinese coolies.)

Our admiration for Chimista, the legendary character, is misplaced once we know of the historical personage (within the novel). Nevertheless, his appeal is real. Chimista represents what Spain in the early twentieth century (and, perhaps even today) wants to believe about its past: that this admirable, free-spirited individualism drove the empire. As Christopher Britt Arredondo has written about Baroja's contemporaries, the practitioners of what he calls "Quixotism" chose to deny the reality of their nation's imperial decline "rather than promote a critical understanding of the historical events that had led to Spain's demise as a world power" (13). Indeed, it is this type of negation of the historical facts of Spain's decline that Cincúnegui and other readers are hoping to find in Embil's diary. But this quixotic illusion will forever eclipse Embil's realism and keep Spain ignorant of the reasons why there was a nineteenth-century Atlantic empire in the first place.

At the end of the second novel, *La estrella del capitán Chimista*, after an exciting series of warfare between pirate crews, voyages to distant lands, and fabulous wealth, Chimista disappears. His father, an English count who had spent a short time in Elguea after he had been shipwrecked off the Basque coast upon his return home from British India, recognizes Chimista as his son in his will. Chimista inherits the name, title, land, and culture of the count, and he becomes completely absorbed by England. With him, "la *estrella* del Capitán Chimista" or the good fortune of empire vacates Spain and becomes entrenched in a landlocked estate in England. Chimista, the self-made literary adventurer of the Atlantic no longer works for Spain: there is no place for him there as England adopts the mantle of maritime glory.

In counterpoint to the glamorized crime protagonized by Bizargorri, in Embil's story of maritime adventure, there is no swashbuckling; in its place are large sections of extremely detailed descriptions of life at sea, the tools and conditions of the slave ship, the means by which slaves were procured in Africa, the death rates in the Middle Passage, the salaries earned by the ships' crews, and the type of men who chose to work on them. Whereas Chimista holds the story together through plot, Embil contextualizes and describes. Embil's routine, his small-minded bourgeois desire for personal wealth and accumulation, and his willingness to engage in a monstrous trade are the real spirit of nineteenth-century Spanish empire. This is what kept Cuba Spanish, not an "Espronceda-like" free spirit of piracy in which one's only homeland is at sea. In the face of the general opinion in nineteenth-century Spain and Cuba that abolition would bring about Cuban independence, it was the work of slave traders who prevented this from happening earlier than it ultimately did.

Los pilotos de altura narrates eight transatlantic voyages that the Basque sailor Ignacio Embil undertook as captain or pilot of slave ships. However, Embil is a failure when he tries to import slaves without Chimista's help; he is intercepted and arrested by the English six times. Historically improbable, English success here is a parody of their failure to stop the most famous trader of the mid- to late nineteenth century: Julián Zulueta. The Basque businessman didn't pilot the ships himself but bankrolled them with impunity. He also pioneered the importation of coolies as forced Chinese labor in Cuba and owned the largest and most modern plantations on the island. He became one of the wealthiest Spaniards alive in his day, governed as *alcalde* of Havana, was granted the title of Marquis of Álava as compensation for his services to the crown (repressing independence in Cuba, general conservative politics), and became a senator in 1876.

Where Chimista is spontaneous, Embil is ruled by routine; where Chimista is gallant and dashing, Embil is insipid and uncreative; where Chimista searches out adventure, Embil is motivated by money. Where Embil gets arrested by the English, Chimista deftly escapes through brilliant maneuvering. The title of the third novel defines the reason for his success: Capitán Chimista's "star" is not the astronomical guide of a *piloto de altura* but rather luck. Embil's mediocrity glorifies Chimista's heroism and action, but only to a point. Chimista's story can offer no real answers but instead contributes to Spain's outdated and inflated sense of global importance. As Carl Schurz, the US ambassador to Spain, reported as late as the 1860s, the official line of the Spanish government was that theirs was the most important country in Europe.[17] Chimista's story fails to invite the reader to interpret and offers no challenge to what she believes she already knows. For the nineteenth-century empire to function, Spain needed both Embil and Chimista: the myth of adventure and a belief in Spanish imperial infallibility as well as an amoral mind-set to carry out the slave trade in the face of global protest.

Baroja and His Critics

In his provocative article reconsidering the Generation of '98 and Galdós, Germán Gullón has argued that the discourse around the "Disaster" of 1898 as an imperial battle with the United States elides the role of Cuba and the realities of the nineteenth-century imperial hold on the island. He emphasizes that in spite of what the public may believe, the primary reason to retain Cuba was economic, and horrible human rights violations were carried out in order to do so (94). But, according to Gullón, the mea culpa of the famous Generation of '98 led to a literary smoke-and-mirrors cover-up of the cultural reality and gave a more palatable version of the war and its causes (95). Gullón criticizes these writers severely and chastises the Spanish public for not knowing more about its colonial past (96). In particular, this critic denounces "unos señores muy serios, dos vascos [Unamuno and Baroja]" (two very serious gentlemen, two Basques) who he deems responsible for "la mal denominada generación del 98, que a modo de un gran tapiz intelectual se utiliza para cerrar el paso a toda indagación seria sobre qué pasó en nuestras colonias. Es como si estos señores hubieran pensado por el resto de la ciudadanía del país y con eso las gentes hispanas quedamos exentas de mayores preocupaciones." (98; ill-termed Generation of '98, that like a great intellectual tapestry is used to shut out all serious inquiry into what happened in our colonies. It's as if these gentlemen had thought for the entire citizenry of the country and with that, we the Hispanic people were left free from major concerns.)

José Chimista's story seduces Domingo Cincúnegui and other readers within the novel while corresponding to what Gullón identifies as the version of empire that Spaniards want to remember. Nevertheless, the *Mar* series is neither nationalist nor widely read. It has remained beyond critics' interest, perhaps because the novels evade an easy categorization into the standard definition of literature by the Generation of '98. I certainly don't mean to imply that some of Baroja's works did not participate in regenerationist ideology. But his views toward Spain's "glorious" past across his corpus are more nuanced. Aguirre is humanized by Shanti Andía, and Chimista is anchored by Embil. Unlike what Gullón has identified for Baroja's contemporaries, whose literature "silencia, en fin, los abusos imperiales españoles" (96; silences, succinctly, the Spanish imperial abuses), these novels shock readers with the naked truth.

Early in *La estrella del capitán Chimista* Baroja spells out yet again the calculated economic interest that held the empire together behind official declarations of love and familial harmony. Embil is living in Cuba, unhappily married to a Creole. Society is deeply divided by rampant corruption by all parties. Both *Los pilotos de altura* and *La estrella del capitán Chimista* are flush with descriptions of contraband and details of Creole commerce that were the landlubber's equivalent to the maritime crimes that kept Cuba a Spanish colony (*Pilotos*, 130–31; *Estrella*, 168–69). Chimista describes the hierarchical system of vice as "*Aundiac naidutena chiquiac aldesateguena* (Los grandes, lo que quieren; los pequeños, lo que pueden)" (*Estrella*, 51; the great, what they want; the small, what they can). Embil and his father-in-law sustain an extended debate over who holds greater blame, Creoles or Spaniards, and the fragile relationship of frigid tolerance between Embil and his wife, Panchita, represents the contentious marriage between Spain and Cuba. Only economic interests and mutual disdain unite this couple that does not even understand one another. To illustrate this equality in animosity, Embil's wife Panchita teaches him an adage popular among Cuban ladies: "Los españoles para maridos; y los criollos, para amantes" (*Estrella*, 44; Spaniards for husbands; and Creoles, for lovers). Even Chimista, who claims he is exclusively interested in adventure, recognizes his role in protecting metropolitan investments and helps Embil by proposing a fraudulent scheme to release him from his financial ties to Panchita. The unhappy husband does so immediately and willingly (66). Clearly, if Spain could recover its investments, it would similarly walk away from its marriage with Cuba. There is no love holding the empire together.[18]

Criticism has favored Baroja's nationalist works and, as a consequence, overlooked the imperial aspects of his novels. In the aforementioned article, Germán Gullón rightly identified "falangista" scholars of the mid-century as responsible for interpreting literature of this generation "de una manera demasiado estrecha, nacionalista" (too narrowly, nationalist) and carving out a path for criticism that must be adjusted today (98). While the *Mar* trilogy and *Shanti Andía* in particular received a moderate amount of critical attention in the first half of the twentieth century,[19] the preferred way to deal with these other novels is either to ignore them or to regard them as idle entertainment or as pure evasion from the precise topics that they so openly address: the slave trade and its place in Spanish history. Nor has Rivera's alternate interpretation, that Baroja uses the *negrero* as the means to reject the hypocrisy and mediocrity of liberalism, been followed (126).

In his introduction to the recent Anaya edition for younger readers (published by Nueva Biblioteca Didáctica) of *Pilotos*, Juan María Marín offers some surprising remarks:

> Raramente aparecen en la literatura española novelas cuyo principal atractivo sean las aventuras, y más si ocurren en el mar; ese tipo de relato de aventuras es, en cambio, frecuente en la literatura inglesa, con la que se emparenta *Los pilotos de altura*. Pío Baroja nos ofrece en este caso a unos personajes (los tratantes de esclavos) a los que sucede en sus viajes toda suerte de peripecias: tempestades, persecuciones, enfermedades. . . . Su relato carece de un plan general que lo articule para llevarlo a un desenlace determinado que, por ejemplo, pudiera confirmar la validez de unas ideas o de un planteamiento filosófico. Ni *Los pilotos de altura* ni su continuación, *La estrella del capitán Chimista*, persiguen convencer al lector de ninguna tesis, sino que son novelas puramente entretenidas que buscan poner en sus manos historias que le permitan evadirse u olvidarse de la vulgaridad del mundo en que viven, viajar con su imaginación por los océanos, por el Atlántico y por el Pacífico, sin moverse de su cuarto y hacerle vivir azarosas peripecias y los más peligrosos lances, cuya sucesión va constituyendo la novela. (28)

> (Rarely do novels whose main attractions are adventures appear in Spanish literature, and even less if they take place at sea; that kind of adventure story is, however, common in English literature, which correlates to *Los pilotos de Altura*. Pío Baroja offers us in this case characters (slave traders) who experience in their trips all sorts of unforeseen vicissitudes: storms, persecutions, diseases. . . . His story lacks a general plan that would articulate it in order to take it to a determined outcome that, for example, could confirm the validity of some ideas or a philosophical approach. Neither *Los pilotos de altura* nor *La estrella del capitán Chimista* seek to convince the reader of any thesis, but rather are purely entertaining novels looking to put in his/her hands stories that allow him/her to escape or forget the vulgarity of the world in which he/she lives, travel the oceans with his/her imagination, the Atlantic and the Pacific, without moving from his/her room and making him/her live random vicissitudes and the most dangerous incidents, whose sequence constitutes the novel as it goes along.)

Does Baroja consciously censure imperial myth? Marín seems to echo earlier scholarship that insisted, with little disagreement, that Baroja wrote to provide escapism from contemporary reality, without demanding contemplation or critical intervention on the part of his readers. For example, Rivera summarizes Baroja's perspective as an "actitud de constante afán de evasion de la realidad, a fin de mantenerse íntegramente dentro de sí mismo e incontaminado con respecto al medio social" (99; an attitude of constant eagerness to evade reality, in order to keep himself entirely within and remain uncontaminated by his social environment).[20] However, it seems these critics either protest too much or have not read the *Mar* novels carefully, for the novels make it difficult to retain a glorified version of empire, even for readers who adopt the same attitude and turn to literature to evade reality.

Marín's resurrection of this traditional reading of Baroja confirms Gullón's opinion that a fascist interpretation, à la Laín Entralgo, has forged the approach toward these authors so that we now find it difficult to find anything else. Nevertheless, Marín's introduction is astonishingly naïve. English sea narratives and adventure tales have all manner of ideological stances. But most importantly, Marín fails to explain exactly how one can read about the slave trade in graphic detail and simply be entertained. In what interpretive circumstances is it possible to read about how Africans were bought, sold, and abused and still be seduced by the adventure in Embil's nauseating detail, without finding a philosophical message? Discussing *Shanti Andía*, Bretz has identified stylistic characteristics that impede pure escapism for its readers (370). But Marín's unstated position is more moral than intellectual, and the fact that this introduction (pitched to approximately a high-school-level audience) declares that the novel is about evasion and forgetting, suggests that its readers may do just that. *Pilotos* and all of the *Mar* series offer rare opportunities to remember and philosophically engage in the question of the slave trade, the mechanics of empire, and the literature that has enshrined it. Aversion, not diversion, is the theme of the novels. In Gullón's words, culture is not taken seriously when it is only "entretenimiento para ociosos, que quieren saber lo que pasó en resumen, en líneas generales, porque los detalles aburren. Esta pasividad del lector debería estar de moda en la sociedad del presente." (96; entertainment for the idle, that want to know what happened in a nutshell, in general terms, because details bore them. This passivity from the reader must be in vogue in the present society.) Yet this received view is now transmitted to another generation of readers who, at most, are asked to write their own "diario de navegación como si fueras tú el capitán del barco [negrero]" (Marín, 297; navigation log as if you were the captain of the slave ship) as part of their classroom activities.

The terms by which critics have defined and dismissed these novels are intriguing. Marín's ultimate estimation of *Pilotos* is that it is an "entretenida novela de aventuras" (30; entertaining novel of adventures). However, the concept of "adventure" should not shut down conversation about the work, but rather provide a means of exploring how the quest is conducted and what its aims are (see Nerlich). Indeed, an adventure novel is not a flat form. The adventure mode (especially for juvenile literature) in the English model educated its readers to appreciate the values, fantasies, or "ethos" of imperialism (J. Richards, 9), and it is precisely this pro-imperialist fantasy that Baroja undercuts by telling Chimista's story through Embil. Chimista insists to Embil that he has no goals in life, that he is simply amused by "aventura y peligro" (73; adventure and danger). But his use of the term can only be taken as a parody, for, as Embil explains at some length, Chimista's band of pirates and *negreros* were bereft of honor.

> Todavía el marino de este tiempo, hijo predilecto de la aventura, era un hombre atrevido, violento e inconsciente. Impulsado por una esperanza de riqueza y de placeres, pensaba encontrar países fabulosos como El Dorado, y tenía para el final de su vida el sueño de volver a su tierra, a su aldea, tranquila y plácida. Aquellos hombres, niños grandes la mayoría, sin rencor, consideraban alcanzado el fin de su vida por haber pasado algunos días en la taberna de un puerto, al lado de una mujer, bebiendo y derrochando el dinero. (*Pilotos*, 119)

> (The mariner of this time, favored son of adventure, was still a bold man, violent and unaware. Driven by a hope of wealth and pleasures, he expected to find fabulous countries like El Dorado, and had for the end of his life the dream of returning home, to his village, calm and placid. Those men, mostly big boys, without rancor, considered the purpose of their life to have been reached if they spent some days in the tavern of a harbor, next to a woman, drinking and squandering their money.)

In observations such as these, Embil demystifies the sailors' brand of adventure and shows it to have been liquidated of any trace of honorable action. The ideals of these men, motivated by a grotesque mix of lethargy, violence, and fantasy, inspire neither virtue nor admiration. In contrast, Chimista actively cultivates a legend around himself that inserts him into a romantic literary tradition of the free-spirited pirate who flaunts society's rules.

Embil expands his reflections on portside hedonism with descriptions of a grim life at sea.

> La vida en el mar no es más que una serie de emboscadas. Todos los hombres en el mundo viven en estado de guerra. El que más puede, más consigue; yo no he visto en la vida del mar más que una lucha terrible, en la cual los contrincantes emplean todas las armas: la fuerza, el valor, la inteligencia, la intriga y la mentira. El hombre es mal bicho, digan lo que quieran. (*Pilotos*, 59)

> (Life at sea is nothing but a series of ambushes. All men in the world live in a state of war. He who is more able, attains more; I have not seen in maritime life anything but a terrible fight, in which opponents use all weapons: strength, courage, intelligence, intrigue and deceit. Man is an evil creature, whatever they might say.)

The maritime novel that we read only has a hero if we look for him in spite of the reliable narrator's facts and descriptions. With his characteristic frankness, Embil reflects upon his identity as a slave trader during the era of piracy: "Yo no soy un aventurero—dice en una nota preliminar de su diario—; yo he sido solo un buen piloto y un hombre trabajador. Allí donde me puso la fortuna trabajé con todas mis fuerzas." (*Pilotos*, 75; "I am not an adventurer," he says in a preliminary note of his diary. "I have only been a good pilot and a hardworking man. There where fortune placed me I worked with all my strength.")

Cincunegui punctuates Embil's statement, "Esta declaración de Embil nos lleva a pensar en lo subjetivo de la idea de la aventura. Un marino como Embil, que recorrió el mundo de negrero, de bohemio del mar, metido con frecuencia en empresas difíciles y arriesgadas, no se consideraba aventurero; era un hombre con un oficio, un técnico, casi un burócrata." (76; This declaration by Embil leads us to ponder the subjective nature of the idea of adventure. A mariner like Embil, who roamed the world as a *negrero*, as a bohemian of the seas, frequently in difficult and risky ventures, did not consider himself an adventurer; he was a man with a trade, a technician, almost a bureaucrat.) Cincúnegui provides the key for unlocking the code of adventure in these novels. Living as an adventurer is all about a sense of spirit, not action. If adventure is a prism for understanding life on the seas in this novel, readers, too, must choose whether to continue to privilege adventure over Embil's story of a man who is consciously a monster by his trade. "Lo que en uno tomó el carácter de vulgar y cotidiano, en el otro apareció como extraordinario y anormal." (76; What in one became a vulgar and routine attribute, in the other appeared as extraordinary and abnormal.) Should the empire be remembered as extraordinary, vulgar, or both?

Conclusion

An early twentieth-century reader may have found herself uninspired by Shanti Andía's restlessness or tempted to abandon Embil's technical and mundane prose, but what kept her reading was the promise of pirate tales and adventures on the high seas. The dual historical perspectives at play in the *Mar* series allow the reader to choose her own version of the Spain's modern empire, but encourage her to filter the romantic through the prosaic realism. If she reads history with Chimista and an idealized Aguirre, favoring legend and adventure, she'll become a Quixote, enraptured with romance, but wholly unaware of reality—a situation both dangerous and delusional, no matter how attractive it may be. All histories must be recovered, preserved, and read critically and in concert, for only in this way can we know the past and understand the present.

Metropolitan governments made policies, but actors in the nineteenth-century Atlantic made and unmade national and imperial identities. That is, Basques became agents of Spain through the confluence of economic incentive and the appeal of freedom on the high seas, cultivating a fantasy of Basque independence at sea even as they supported the fantasy that was the grand Spanish empire. Unofficial complicity among sailors dreaming of instant wealth, Spanish policy, Capitán Generals' corruption, and plantation owners' avidity for retaining Cuba for Spain kept the empire alive well beyond its expected lifetime. The *Mar* novels recreate these aspects of the former empire for a generation of readers who never knew it and were likely to allow the role of Basque sailors and the brutality of the illegal slave trade to fall into oblivion.

But perhaps the novels tackle a universal problem, for does any empire have a metropolitan population fully aware of the human oppression that keeps it afloat? In the modern era, the education of the populace has been understood to be instrumental in bringing about social and political change. Such were the tactics of nineteenth-century English abolitionists, Ayguals de Izco, or any number of dissidents of modern nation-states, including the United States, today. Imperialism requires lyrical representation, and it is through literature that the *Mar* series inverts this phenomenon and attempts to release fact from fiction's fast grip, to promote a revisionary historiography of a past just beyond living memory.

§4 Postimperial Detours and Retours

The Ruta del Indiano

Debates about the place of slavery and empire in nineteenth-century Spain, and, by extension, the second empire project and the state's geopolitical position, were tightly woven into contemporary literature. Awareness of the Spanish role in the illegal transatlantic slave trade, however, gradually disappeared along with the last generation of traders. Thus, in spite of a deep engagement with the *negrero* in literature, these aspects of the past are at present largely absent from public discourse about Spanish history. In this chapter I explore representations of the nineteenth-century empire in northern Spain today in order to demonstrate that we must reevaluate the nuanced and complex literary representations of slave traders in the nineteenth century, when the relationship between imaginative literature and contemporary events was cast in terms unlike those of the current political or economic sphere. Such representations encompassed both fear and fantasy.

Why and how is the past erased? Oblivion is much more complex than a whitewashing or obliteration of memory. As Michel-Rolph Trouillot reminds us, celebrations, too, are "part and parcel of the process of historical productions. Celebrations straddle the two sides of historicity. They impose a silence upon the events that they ignore, and they fill that silence with narratives of power about the event they celebrate" (118). Celebrations of the triumphant *indiano* have shaped newly established tourist itineraries organized around *casonas indianas* in Asturias and Cantabria along the Bay of Biscay, which are, in turn, reorienting public consciousness of the country's post-1808 imperial past. These new *rutas* are among the most accessible means for people today to learn about Spain's overseas legacy; however, in keeping with the current veneration of the self-made man, the *rutas* often treat the past in ways that simplify the complexities explored in nineteenth-century literature. For example, an exquisitely photographed guidebook published in December 2010 suggests nine routes to discover the "nueva y esplendorosa conquista de América" (Braña, 5; new and splendid conquest of the Americas) by Asturians in the tobacco, sugar, and textile industries.[1] The routes are local sites connected by a narrative that is made both physical and geographical. The story that connects the routes in this book from 2010 depicts wealthy *indianos* as reincarnations of the early modern conquistadors who endured great hardships in the Americas before dominating industry and returning to Europe to improve their hometowns. But the appeal of this new metanarrative threatens to shut down any real inquiry into exactly what "conquest" comprised. This contemporary version consumed by tourists today subverts Galdós's careful dissection of Restoration politics for nineteenth-century readers. In such ways, tourism is influential in refashioning the narrative of the second empire, a move that has exacerbated its expurgation from public discourse today. The redefinition and resignification of an *indiano* legacy is both factual and visceral. As Christopher Matthews has written regarding public archaeology, "The pasts that come to light become the result of an effort to define a politics for the present" (162). This chapter first reviews the changing perceptions of *indianos*, whose wealth was generated during the empire, and that of their homes. It then analyzes the phenomenon of route tourism, reading specific points on these newly established *rutas* as texts and understanding the *indianos*' palaces as the sites where their founders created their personal stories and today are intimate substitutes for the people who built them.

The American Dream led millions of Europeans to cross the Atlantic over several centuries. The Asturians and Cantabros who attempted to "hacer las américas" (make the Americas) in the nineteenth century did so out of a sense that there was little opportunity in Spain.[2] Some fled economic hardship, others lengthy military service (emigration was markedly tied to the wars in Africa) or individual oppressive situations. Many thousands of Spaniards crossed the Atlantic in the nineteenth century in search of a better life, and the majority of those who returned were neither sugar barons nor insatiable imperialists, but rather members of lower- to middle-class families whose gains in the New World were significant but not necessarily tremendous. Many worked hard; few met great wealth. Nevertheless, the *negrero* arc shaped the archetypal *indiano* story. In part this is because his was the most spectacular tale of rags to riches (often culminating in an aristocratic title), but also because he embodied the contemporary dialectical thinking on empire. Spain's hold on the Antilles was simultaneously problematic (if not outright horrific) and productive as the source of wealth for individuals, towns, industries, and the national treasury.

In the nineteenth century, the conquest of new lands was no longer part of the emigrant discourse, although the presence of *peninsulares* in the colonies was always a factor in imperial governance. Before 1765, residents of most parts of Spain were simply prohibited from relocating to the Americas, in what constituted a means of channeling colonial finances through Castile (see Martínez Shaw, 169–70).[3] Emigration to the Americas was tightly controlled until after the 1830s, when the government began to adjust its tactics in order to keep its remaining colonies loyal (Sonesson, 14). (Notably, after the independence of most of Latin America, emigration to the new republics was officially banned for several decades.)

During the late eighteenth century, the reigning economic logic cautioned against the departure of Iberian youth as part of the guarded attitude toward the heavy price of empire. Gaspar Melchor de Jovellanos, for example, defined emigration as a bane to the modernization of Asturias and warned of the danger of those few rich *indianos* who returned and made a "funesto ejemplo de su fortuna" (290; disastrous example of their fortune), thus inspiring further departures of potential laborers. Jovellanos's concern with stimulating Spain's economic development in manufacturing and agriculture, grounded in a satisfied and stable working class, set the tone for intellectuals' disregard of *indianos*' substantial contributions to local economies for nearly a century.[4] In reality, great economic change was created through *indiano* money, both on a grand scale and via small remittances; nevertheless, they and their *casonas* symbolized the impoverishment of Asturias through emigration and the stagnation of idle wealth.

Midcentury fears of an "Africanization" of Cuba as well as concerns over the island's annexation to the United States prompted a temporary departure from established policies regarding emigration. A concerted effort by the government to promote the introduction of poor Spaniards to Cuba to both offset the Afro-Cuban population and change the island's racial balance ignited an emigration boom. During the 1840s and 1850s, the government underwrote the expenses of Spanish peasants who moved to Cuba.[5] This racial population policy (*blanqueamiento*) also reaffirmed cultural, "Hispanic" ties between Cuba and Spain that were neither African nor Anglo-Saxon. Much earlier, in 1817, the Junta de Población Blanca had developed a colonizing scheme to balance the influx of African slaves with European Spaniards (Cervantes-Rodríguez, 71) that would simultaneously serve to tighten the ties between the island and the metropolis. Whitening policies reappeared in the Junta de Fomento in the 1830s. Thus from the beginning of Cuba's sugar boom, emigration from Spain was a carefully monitored racial project that had political, linguistic, and ethnic implications (Cervantes-Rodríguez, 72). The mid-nineteenth century witnessed their implementation. Opinions on the utility of Spanish immigration to the Antilles soon changed, however, and within twenty years there was once again little approval of the growing and seemingly unstoppable exodus of youth from the north of Spain.

The storied *indiano* of the nineteenth century was a young, poor man from a small village, usually in Asturias, Cantabria, País Vasco, or Catalonia (or, later, Galicia) who departed across the Atlantic (to the "Indies") to make his fortune. Years later, he returned fabulously wealthy to a hometown that greeted him as a hero, conqueror, or *triunfador*, and he proved his generosity by mending the finances of his extended family. At the same time, divorced from a local framework, the *indiano* became a stock character in novels and theater from the latter half of the century, often representing the most brutish type of nouveau riche and symbolizing the emigration of tens of thousands of young men (and women) during this same period.[6]

Among the works treating *indianos* generally, the slave trader held a prominent position, as countless literary works from both sides of the Atlantic parodied the meteoric rise of slave traders into the sphere of the aristocracy. As Stephen Silverstein has argued, a characterization of the slave trader as a rhetorical Jew often functioned to alleviate culpability among a White (non-Jewish) Caribbean readership (9). In the Cuban novel *Cecilia Valdés* by Cirilio Villaverde, Cándido Gamboa is one such character, shaped almost entirely by his greed as a slave trader and his yearning for the title of Marqués de Casa Gamboa, which he naturally acquires even as his family life dissolves. Juan Valera attacks the phenomenon from the other side of the Atlantic (and with a very different political agenda) in *Pepita Jiménez* (1874), whose *negrero* appears at the end of the novel as a moral foil to the eponymous heroine. In the novel's epilogue we read a series of letters from Don Pedro de Vargas (Pepita's father-in-law) to his brother during the four years following the main body of the story. De Vargas reports that Pepita's brother, an exceedingly rich former slave trader, is "casi o sin casi" (almost or actually) bringing honor to the family with his imminent purchase of an aristocratic title. Pepita is thoroughly scandalized, but her father-in-law, whose indulgent attitude epitomizes the moral relativism and complicity regarding the slave trade that reigned in Spain among most sectors of the population, including the midlevel elite of Andalucía, reassures Pepita that if her brother is going to be a "pillete" (scoundrel) it is better that he have society's approval.[7] Joan Ramon Resina cites the novel's depiction of *indianos* as an example of what he identifies as a structural relationship between vice and the external world, as opposed to the idealized home community. The issue for Resina is not that of the colonies per se, but rather the political implications of Valera's *costumbrismo* in which, additionally, unscrupulous colonial businessmen "contribute to the moral bankruptcy" of the aristocracy (181–82). In terms of the plot and characterization of the novel, this late appearance by the *indiano* is important: the contrast between Pepita's pure, chaste love—although of dubious morality in the eyes of some—and her brother's crimes against humanity underscore with great irony the young woman's virtue.

The standard narrative of the successful *indiano* culminates in the construction of the *casona* built in the emigrant's hometown. Indeed, thousands of such houses dot the small towns of northern Spain even today. The buildings were literally eccentric in that they drew their aesthetic inspiration from the periphery of the empire. Many of the most ostentatious examples were showpieces intended for summer entertainment rather than family homes. Sometimes unheated and quickly built, many of the grandest sacrificed function for glamor. While no two houses are identical, certain features identify the *indiano* house to the nonspecialist tourist.

Paul Connerton has theorized the symbolic and material qualities of a house as cultural text, emphasizing that it is always "more than a shelter and spatial disposition of activities, a material order constructed out of walls and boundaries. Over and beyond this it is a medium of representation, and, as such, can be read effectively as a mnemonic system" (19). The nineteenth-century *casonas* imitated traditional aristocratic houses in size and grandeur; however, even those built in an autochthonous style actually invert the values embedded in the noble *solar*. The great European house, in Claude Lévi-Strauss's theorization of the home, is less a domestic space than an architectural statement of family lines, history, and integration with the land (that is, the family's feudal roots) (6–8). In contrast, the *indiano* house is an architectural monument to a personal itinerary and reflects the founder's fundamental uprootedness. It relates the *indiano*'s departure from the modest family home, his "conquest" of the Americas, and his later return and "conquest" of his native village. In a radical departure from traditional aristocratic styles, there is neither formal nor material harmony between the typical *casona* and the landscape in which it is situated, but rather an emphasis on the transplanted quality of the house and its occupants. Aesthetically, it replaces the representation of descent and alliance in the traditional European aristocratic house with a declaration of the spoils of colonialism, exoticism, and individualism by the self-made man. In other words, the *indianos*, shut out of the means of social ascent in the traditional Spanish system, display their (new) American origins in their homes. But where the *solar* rememorates the social and economic ties of its foundation, the *casona* reveals its geographical sources.

Botanical idioms intersect with *indiano* architecture to evoke the domesticated colonies. Lavish gardens with American plants often circle the *casona*, but by far the most important marker of the *indiano* home, whatever its architectural style, is the palm tree. A symbol of victory in ancient Rome and early Christiandom, in the nineteenth century, the palm became a floral symbol of the *indiano*'s transatlantic transplantation and subsequent regermination in Spain. The palm and accompanying plants on private plots were miniature versions of the imperial botanical gardens of earlier centuries and sensual artifacts from the tropics.[8] The symbolic charge of the tree was such that Spaniards who never left the Peninsula but wished to engage with the image of social and financial ascent associated with *indianos* planted them outside of their homes, too. But the vitality of the palm tree in the temperate zones of northern Spain did not always match the *indiano*'s sometimes uneasy regrafting onto his village. Transatlantic families could be riven by tensions between the *indianos*' wish to reintegrate and his family's wish for continued remittances from abroad, as Clarín depicts in his moral tale "Boroña."

Like the *indiano* himself, the *casona* was originally little appreciated. Clarín (who had little interest in anything coming from America)[9] ridiculed the oneiric modernist structures in *La Regenta*, describing their neighborhood, la *Colonia*, as

> tirada a cordel, deslumbrante de colores vivos con reflejos acerados; parecía un pájaro de los bosques de América, o una india brava adornada con plumas y cintas de tonos discordantes. Igualdad geométrica, desigualdad, anarquía cromáticas. En los tejados todos los colores del iris como en los muros de Ecbátana; galerías de cristales robando a los edificios por todas partes la esbeltez que podía suponérseles; alardes de piedra inoportunos, solidez

> afectada, lujo vocinglero. La ciudad del sueño de un indiano que va mezclada con la ciudad de un usurero o de un mercader de paños o de harinas que se quedan y edifican despiertos. . . . Además los indianos no quieren nada que no sea de buen tono, que huela a plebeyo, ni siquiera pueda recordar los orígenes humildes de la estirpe. (*La Regenta*, 114)

> (dazzling with vivid colors and steely reflections, like some bird from a South American jungle, or a savage Amerindian woman adorned with feathers and ribbons of clashing colors. Geometrical regularity; chromatic irregularity, indeed anarchy. On the roof-tops all the colors of the rainbow, as on the walls of Persian Ecbatana; glassed balconies protruding on every side, depriving the houses of whatever graces they might otherwise have possessed; inopportune displays of stone; sham solidity, vociferous luxury. The city of an emigrant's dreams, combined with the city of a money-lender or draper or flour merchant who stays at home and builds while wide awake. . . . What is more, they refuse to tolerate anything which is not in good taste or smacks of the plebian, or indeed any reminder whatsoever of the humble origins of their stock.) (English trans., *La Regenta*, 33–34)

Clarín's survey of vibrant colors, innovative shapes, and numerous windows is accurate, if disapproving. His aesthetic censure of the *casonas* was inseparable from the prevailing view of the *indianos* since the eighteenth century as detrimental to Asturian agriculture and their *casonas* as irresistible sirens perpetuating emigration. For intellectuals eager to emulate European liberalism, industrialization, and modernity, the reliance on the Americas as a goose laying golden eggs was retrograde, and the *casonas* were a symbol of all that was antiquated in the Spanish economy.[10] But the colonial matrix of power was recognized in Spain when it began to rival local rule. The *negreros* and their influence in Spain upset the distinction between Ultramar as the place where coloniality is wielded and the metropolis as the source of ordering. This complex relationship was built into the *casona*.

It was only after the loss of Cuba that opinions toward *indianos* changed—an attitude that serves as a primary logic in Antonio Machado's "La Tierra de Alvargonzález" (Ott, 112; Conlon, 190). After 1898, *indianos* came to be seen as crucial to the industrial and commercial growth of the "auge de fin de siglo" and understood to change from a passive reintegration (living in their big homes) to active roles in stimulating the economy. However, there was no real "before and after" in the impact of the *indiano* on Asturias; their sustained contribution to the Spanish economy was perceptible throughout the century (Ojeda and San Miguel, 77–78, 97).

But the current unqualified glorification of nineteenth-century *indianos* as heroes necessarily does not question how to "hacer las Américas."[11] Baroja's observation in *Las inquietudes de Shanti Andía* for the early nineteenth century remains valid today: "Te preguntarán cúanto has hecho . . . no cómo lo has hecho" (41).

Today the *indiano* is no longer cast as the social climber or mercantilist rare bird of the nineteenth century, but an Odyssean hero who has come home and been fully integrated into the narrative of his nation's glorious past. The *indiano* story also intersects with current regionalist constructions of identity; for the idea of Asturian emigrants maintaining a "local" identity while abroad is a powerful evocation of Asturian collectivity. Narratively, the return of the *indiano* hinges on a heartfelt pining for his "tierrina" while in America, with "home" as the pivotal player in drawing money and successful men and women back across the Atlantic. Indeed, the daily *El Diario Montañes* stated, in its recent profile piece on nineteenth-century *indianos*, that *every* successful Cantabrian emigrant returned, so drawn were they to the land of their birth (with the implication that the Americas were populated by the losers who, nevertheless, imbued modern America with its Hispanic essence): "Cántabros y asturianos, más que ningunos otros, regresaron a su tierra con el dinero acumulado."[12] Indeed, the same Cantabrian newspaper article proudly reports that northern Spanish businessmen learned their trade in Mexico and brought back refined business skills to Spain, noting the imperial origins of modern Spanish finance—in contrast to the nineteenth-century view of *indianos* as idle mercantilists. While such a story is extremely useful in Spain's present political climate, it simplifies the *indianos*' role as "glocal" agents, working and residing in two economic and cultural spheres. Their actions abroad had decisive ramifications for Spain's internal economic development and twentieth-century neocolonial investments in Latin America (Tortella, 158–81). As Martín Rodrigo y Alharilla has argued for the case of Catalan *indianos*, the dialectic of emigration/return is limited ("Con un pie," 397), and it is more useful to consider the cultural and economic influences as not simply unidirectional but a crisscrossing of transatlantic economic ventures.[13]

Spanish economic emigrants certainly faced great adversity; nevertheless, the profile of the "self-made man" in Cuba begs historical contextualization. First, *peninsulares* in the Antilles had advantages that White Creoles did not. As Joan Casanovas has written, "nineteenth-century colonial society and the slave system sharply divided Cuba's inhabitants by race and by origin (primarily, a division between Spaniards and Creoles). In Cuba these two sources of division were so intense that, until the last decades of the century, they outweighed class or gender" (1). In other words, not only was the transatlantic influence multidirectional, but White peninsular emigrants who met success did so in an environment slanted in their favor. Second, those who went to Cuba entered a booming economy. Franklin Knight has traced the evolution of the Cuban economy in terms of sugar production in relation to its new populations. After centuries of relatively little financial importance, the arrival of immigrants (and their technical expertise) from Saint-Domingue after the Haitian Revolution stimulated the cultivation of sugar. Production then surged significantly after 1830, with the manpower provided by contraband African slaves. These two "catalytic" influxes of French Creoles and African laborers transformed Cuba, especially the western end, into the most profitable place on the globe (Knight, 243).[14] Cuba's emergence as the world's leading sugar producer offered poor Spanish migrants opportunities to create wealth on a scale that would have been entirely impossible in Spain, whatever their sector (252). This is because, in addition to agriculture itself, the robust sugar economy necessitated the construction of railroads, docks, textiles, and food warehouses along with myriad other services and infrastructures. Nineteenth-century *indiano* heroes in the Antilles should be read in terms of these enhanced opportunities, for those who met with success thrived in the candyland of the slave economy. It is all but impossible to untangle a single occupation—for example, that of shopkeeper—from the larger economic framework.

While the *negreros,* strictly defined on the scale of Pau Samà or Julián Zulueta, were numerically small, the relationship between the slave economy that the transatlantic trade created and the economic opportunities for nineteenth-century *indianos* necessitates a wider view of both figures. As the Abbé Gregoire, a fierce critic of the French colonial system, wrote in 1822, "I call *négrier* not only the captain of the ship who steals, buys, enchains, barrels, and sells black and mixed-raced men, who even throws them into the sea to destroy evidence, but also every individual who, by direct or indirect cooperation, is an accomplice in these crimes."[15] His definition, which includes shareholders, insurance companies, and sailors, is similar to what José María comes to believe (but silences) in *Lo prohibido;* this definition is effaced in today's *indiano* story, which melds imperialism, liberalism, and questionable business practices, such that any distinction among them is masked by admiration of the American Dream.

Route Tourism

Route tourism is a contemporary cultural leisure practice, appealing to upwardly mobile tourists who desire to be active and educated even while on vacation (a neo-Enlightenment marriage of pleasure and learning). Pursued around the globe, "themed routes" and "trails" are a market-driven approach to tourism destination development (Lourens, 475–76). Tourism routes have blossomed all over the world in the past two decades, from the Kubaka Heritage Trail in Uganda to the American Whiskey Trail. Major Europe-sponsored tourist routes include the Northern Lights Route, the Baroque Route, the Mozart Route, and the Gypsy Route (Meyer, 5). In Europe, the Cultural Routes Program has developed twenty routes during a period of seventeen years with serious financial backing: government funding to establish routes ranges from 850,000 to 5 million euros (Lourens, 477). Jordi Tresserras, a former member of the Scientific Committee of the UNESCO Slave Route, and Javier Medina have traced this trend in Spain, where immaterial tourist objectives like wine or dance have reframed the goals of travel in recent years. Numerous local routes have sprung up across the country and subsequently linked disparate provinces in a supraregional network in ways distinct from the Spanish state's centralizing impulses. One of the most popular since 2001 is the "Ruta del Vino de España," a nationwide association of local wine routes that was pioneered by the "Rutas del Vino y del Cava de l'Alt Penedès" in 1997 (Medina and Tresserras, 497). Whereas wine tourism satisfies a particular gastronomic niche, neoimperialist fans of the traditional version of the story of the rise of Christian Spain are attended to on the "Ruta de los Castillos, Testigos de la Reconquista," which benefited from three million euros of start-up funds from the Junta of Andalucía and from the local town halls of eleven *pueblos* in the hills between Seville and Cádiz. Finally, routes are not only productive, but are also pliable business structures, open to rearticulation according to political needs. For example, the city of Santoña (outside Santander) proudly announced its recent integration into the Camino de Santiago as a means for garnering enhanced visibility for the town (Santoña, 16).

Indeed, Spain's Camino de Santiago is the leading model of route tourism in Europe. This "linear tourist product" grew out of the Council of Europe's intentions to emphasize Europe's shared cultural heritage (Lourens, 477). Driven by postwar concerns, the Council of Europe imagined supranational tourism as a way to help young people identify politically and culturally as European while at the same time stimulating local economies. All well-designed route tourism complements leisure with cultural or historical education and often engages with the cultural or political identities of its travelers. The Camino de Santiago is ostensibly a pilgrimage: a journey to the sacred. However, in its modern incarnation, the spiritual can be combined with physical fitness, cultural literacy, and culinary adventure. Brian Graham and Michael Murray describe this most refined route as a "pluralist pilgrimage for a postmodern epoch, marrying renditions of the past, physical exertion, and the search for meaning and inner peace in a secular world increasingly bereft of guiding principles" (406). As Dorothea Meyer has written, "the route can function as a regional definition, a theme that transcends geographical diversity and distance to provide a spatially exclusive but integrated, marketable theme" (8). This kind of segmented travel promotes a personal relationship to space and to the geographically specific ways that history and culture are embedded on a local and regional scale.

Today, the fervor for route-based tourism and a recovery of the imperial past combine to create a novel perspective on *indianos*' homes and the colonial regime. These houses can be visited individually, as museums or often as hotels (inhabitable dreams of the late *conquistadores*)—a method that allows the tourist to inhabit the domesticated spaces of a nation *at home with empire*—and, increasingly, on local tourist routes, as part of a "*ruta del indiano.*" Neocolonial tourism is something of a niche product these days. As Claire Williams has discussed, contemporary Portuguese tourists at hotels in former plantation houses of São Tomé are explicitly invited to perform the role of colonists and "inhabit" and "sleep" in the homes of slave owners, a position that allows them to recapture their nation's glory days. The discourse of triumph in many *indiano* hotels is similar, although along Spain's northern coast the locus of conquest can be found without leaving the Peninsula.

In general, these hotels evoke the opulence and luxury of an age just beyond the recent past with an emphasis on an exotic, international feel. Lodgers fill the shoes (or dining rooms or beds) of the *indianos* and actualize the memory of great colonial wealth, utter leisure, and the magic of class ascent, in a country that in the twenty-first century remains stratified and with little class mobility. The opportunity to peek at these pleasures allows the tourist to reenact the *indiano*'s own forgetting of his humble origins and labor in the Americas. Imperial nostalgia is closely tied to a longing for the prospects of social mobility inherent in the idea of "hacer las Americas." Each of the houses is a potential site for an exploration of community values, history, and heritage with meanings that go beyond mere facts. Of course, to foreigners unversed in the stakes of the *indiano* story, the effect offered by these sites is that of a gilded former age.

The *indiano* houses are the primary material artifacts of the colonial period for contemporary Spaniards. They provide a stunning representation of a late and lucrative imperialism even as the stories told about them often efface the truly problematic relationships between the metropolis and the colonies. The *rutas de los indianos* show that an understanding of the complex relationship—and sometimes fear of the arrival and triumph of coloniality in Spain that was evident in the original disdain of the *casonas*—largely has been set aside for a more simplistic understanding of empire as conquest. Visitors are seldom prompted overtly to ask productive questions such as why emigrants left (beyond a general sense of adventure or search for a better life), where they went, how they made their money, and the conditions of their reintegration into Spain. These issues emerge from interaction with the *casonas* at the ground level for those who want to find them, as oblivion is neither uniform nor even one-way. Building an *indiano* heritage is a process of invention. As Matthews argues, the desire for a heritage is a desire to reinvent a community (179), and the stories that the community tells about itself reveal the aspect they wish to change. In the case of many of the *rutas* what is left out of the narratives is as important as the facts that are included. Indeed, in general the discourse tends toward either technical architectural descriptions of the *casonas* or a tone of hollow celebration that only narrowly misses a complete reproduction of old stereotypes of Spaniards' supposed "spirit of adventure," instead of paying real attention to the economic, agricultural, and imperial structures at the national and local levels that prompted emigration, or to the economic, imperial, and racial structures that facilitated the generation of wealth in the Americas. Many modern tourist products reproduce an attitude toward *indianos* that economic historians Germán Ojeda and José Luis San Miguel find generalized in studies of modern emigration: "Gran parte de los análisis que hasta ahora se han hecho sobre la emigración asturiana han oscilado entre la idealización de los que se van y la magnificación de las obras realizadas de los que se vuelven, sin que tales discursos aporten nada a nuestro conocimiento del tema." (14; Most of the analyses that have been made hitherto of Asturian emigration have oscillated between the idealization of those that left and the aggrandizement of the charitable works undertaken by those who returned. Neither tendency furthers our understanding of the issue.) The various *rutas del indiano* connect modernist homes and civic buildings built with American money between 1860 and 1920 and are monuments to Spain's ability to domesticate colonial fortunes. The *indiano* routes draw upon regional, national, and imperial histories yet narrate local stories and events independently. The established *rutas* in Llanes, Malleza, Colombres, Luarca, or Somao are not national or even regional (although they may enjoy regional sponsorship); rather, they are organized by small proprietors or villages at the municipal level. Route tourism actualizes a new memory of past events, constructed around the same *casonas*, and the erasure that they instigate is similarly influenced by local concerns. At the ground level, the meaning of the past is woven into daily life and packaged for its tourist potential differently, at times with some ambiguity.

Successful route tourism builds upon a unified narrative, but—despite an overall metanarrative of self-made triumphs—such coherence is uneven among the *indiano* offerings in Asturias and Cantabria, owing in part to differing perspectives on the causes of emigration and current attitudes toward the role of government in private lives. Consequently, the oblivion in which they participate is equally uneven. The forgetting and reframing of Spain's colonial past of the nineteenth century is not the result of a homogeneous obliteration, but rather an unraveling and reweaving of the materials of emigration, wealth, and social ascent to new ends. The various versions of the imperial story highlight different aspects of an unevenly remembered and documented past. Just as there is no uniform *indiano* story across northern Spain—in spite of an overall metanarrative of self-made triumphs—oblivion, too, is influenced by local particulars. At the ground level, the meaning of the region's past relationship with the Americas (especially Cuba, but also Mexico and Argentina) is woven into daily life and screened for tourist potential differently in each city. At the same time, tourists (many from Madrid) crave a particular story of evasion, wealth, and social mobility. That is, while the Asturian towns may address local concerns, the consumer arrives with a set of larger social questions. Significantly, as Alda Blanco has written, there is a "dearth of commemorative sites to imperial memory in present-day Madrid's urban topography [that] can be read as emblematic of Spain's ambivalence towards its imperial past" (2). The locus for imperial nostalgia is lodged solidly in the north of the country.

This tourism promotes the triumphal story, ridiculed by Clarín, that the original *indianos* had proclaimed in their houses. For example, one very popular book, *Indianos: La gran aventura*, repeats stories from Ramón Argüelles's great-granddaughters, who report that they grew up "como princesas" and fondly recall their grandmother's friendship with Antonio Maura and Antonio XIII, and her ability to order private trains for the family in France (Mencos and Bojstad, 146). Beneath the reverence for wealth, the emphasis on the nineteenth-century empire's "self-made men" in books such as these also celebrates the *indianos*' escape from the oppression of a still-strong ancien régime culture to rise from poverty to a degree of wealth that could humble royalty. In such a tale, the conditions in which this money was made are irrelevant.

As demonstrated in the case of the Camino de Santiago, a route is a consumer good with a story or leisure product to sell. By their very nature, the various *indiano* routes encourage travelers to appreciate the Spanish empire through a series of personal stories framed by the concept of Spain as "home." Theirs is not a history of the massive conquest of foreign lands, but rather a series of very "American" stories of individuals who, through intelligence, perspicacity, and luck changed the status of their families and their hometowns. As a result, a century after the loss of the last vestiges of the American empire and the sense of national "disaster" in 1898, the *indiano* routes offer a different way of considering the nineteenth-century as a great age of empire. The *casona* story upends a profound historical narrative: a century bracketed by two imperial failures is reconstructed as a period of great success. This reframing applies not only to Cuba but also to the colonies that achieved independence early in the century. Argentina and Mexico, in this narrative, continued to produce financial returns for Spain, almost as though the political revolutions had never taken place.

The concept of the *indiano* route evokes the conditions of the *indianos* themselves, albeit on a smaller and more luxurious scale: displacement, return, and the conscious distribution of money made elsewhere to the small towns. But unlike the UNESCO Slave Route Project or even the reconstituted sections of the Historic Route 66 in the United States, which evoke the mass westward migrations of the twentieth century, the Spanish routes do not press travelers to conceive of their actions in relation to the physical displacement of the *indianos* themselves. Left undefined, the relationship between host and tourist opens up several interpretive possibilities of the themes of belonging, ownership, and wealth. Are travelers to identify with the *indianos*, luxuriating in their American mansions? Or are they to be contemporary versions of the Spaniards who remained in Europe, curious about the exotic wealth and keen to partake of it, without asking too many questions? Whereas the *casonas* constitute the staging of a story that happened offshore, at a great geographical distance, the tourist's body experiences gourmet meals, sumptuous decor, and architectural exoticism, but is often detached from an overt engagement with the ideology that it may be performing in them. As a result the *casona* is the theater of a countertheater, staging the formation, reformation, and deformation of empire.

In stark contrast to the *indiano* routes, the "Slave History Trail" of Liverpool and "The Slave Trade Trail around Central Bristol"—both dating from the 1990s—attempt to prompt new understandings of European cities where slavery is present in "the city's streets, architecture, and public memorials" (Kowaleski-Wallace, 30). More than simply revealing the source of the money that made the men that built the cities architectural gems, the Bristol Slave Trade Trail transforms tourists into researchers grounded in historical process. As Elizabeth Kowaleski-Wallace has argued, the routes are designed to create "informed and active interpreters who can learn to see themselves as capable of critical inquiry" (46). Remembering slavery is acceptable (if not always easy) in England today in ways that are impossible in Spain for several reasons. First and foremost, England has had a sizeable Black British population for more than two hundred years, and members of this community in the late twentieth century led new initiatives for a revision of imperial history. Of course, the nation congratulates itself for having been among the first to abolish the slave trade; in contrast, Spain only watched it die out after the end of the US Civil War and under English pressure. Moreover, imperial nostalgia holds a different valence in England, a country that has remained rich long after its Antillean sugar money ran out, and remembering the past is not complicated by a longing to return to an era of wealth. The Spanish "miracle" notwithstanding, Spain is not on the same financial or geopolitical footing as its ancient rival, and the popular narrative around all four centuries of the imperial age is clouded by nostalgia for financial success and global influence. That said, Spain is hardly unique as a beneficiary nation of slavery with a one-sided tourist story. As Sandra Richards has written about emerging diasporic tourism to African Castle-Dungeons, "slavery is not integral to how most Ghanaians define themselves. To attract tourists, Ghanaians must remember a history they learned to forget" (626). African Americans from the United States and other historically slave-based societies in the Americas (as well as some Europeans) form the majority of tourists who undertake this cultural route in search of roots. In contrast, the Spanish *ruta* is by and primarily for Spaniards who no longer overtly identify slave traders as glamorous adventurers, yet do celebrate the story of social mobility of emigrants and those who they believe were able to succeed without state intervention.

Indiano routes have captured the attention of the national and international press of all ideologies. The Spanish author of an article on family travel, published simultaneously in *The New York Times* and *The Globe and Mail*, gushes that such "ostentatious mansions" led her nine-year-old son to "feel rich" (Ojito). A progressive Spanish daily suggests an *indiano* route precisely for those who wish to "Dormir como un indiano" (who presumably slept easy) (Valiña). The travel section of *El País* ("El viajero") recently proposed a *ruta* in Asturias that constructs the story of colonial success and "prosperity" as a product appropriate for a weekend getaway from the pressures of contemporary reality (Arenas). *La Razón* suggests La Casona Azul de Corvera for its readers who wish to partake of the "richness" enjoyed by a nineteenth-century *indiano* who "hizo las Américas" (Aguado).

Casonas indianas appear in the various routes in the guise of memory, recovering the stories of individual immigrants: Mallezas is built upon personal objects; the Archivo de Indianos (even in nomenclature, a counterpart to the massive state archive in Seville, the Archivo de Indias) is a monument to the attempt to document the influence of Spanish emigration on the world in the modern period, in an overtly "Hispanist" discourse that finds each emigrant part of a story of "Spain Beyond Spain," to use Brad Epps's and Luis Fernández Cifuentes's felicitous term. The narratives constructed about these houses go hand in hand with a changing understanding of Spain's place in the Atlantic world. Since the quincentennial celebrations in 1992 revived interest in the empire, these buildings serve as an elegant iconography bridging nineteenth-century grandeur and current economic influence in the former colonies. They provide an image of Spain's continuing relevance and influence in the Atlantic world that both elides the strife of the problematic mid-twentieth century and discourages critical inquiry into what actually happened overseas. Yet, at the same time, historiographical and economic regionalism disarticulates locally specific stories from a larger global story that must be reimpressed onto the cultural spaces of the *casonas*.

I have identified several representative points on the *indiano* routes in terms of the tendencies in contemporary tourism through an analysis of their discussion in the media, localized marketing, their presence at municipal tourist offices, and the presentation of the *casonas* themselves. The first is a route comprising a number of small, site-specific architectural itineraries. The second is a series of three palaces built by well-known slave traders; the third is the small Asturian town of Malleza. The celebratory *indiano* phenomenon comprises all émigrés from before the Spanish Civil War (1936–39); the *casonas* discussed in the following pages were built primarily by men who made their fortunes before 1880, in Cuba, and were complicit with slavocracy, if not direct participants. My reading of the *ruta del indiano* phenomenon is based on my own travels along the Bay of Biscay in October and November 2010 as an informed tourist interested in *indianos* but without any personal ties to their story. I focused on areas where emigrants went to Cuba, but also considered regions with Mexican and Argentine money.

"Hacer las Rutas"

There is a range of *indiano* stops in the various towns dotting Asturias and Cantabria populated with memorable *casonas*. Some are proposed by tourist sites (for example, "desdeasturias.com"), others by individual *indiano* hotels (for example, Hotel Villa la Argentina in Luarca), and several municipalities also promote itineraries. The language is celebratory, but these small routes emphasize the *indianos*' return by claiming status as architectural treasures. That is, the technical language of these routes prompts an artistic appreciation of the house as a synecdoche of the bounty brought back to Spain from the Americas.

In the Asturian villages of Somao and Luarca, the striking *indiano* presence is framed in this architectural vein. The tiny hamlet of Somao is flush with mansions built in the early twentieth century by locals returning from Cuba. The placards on its tourist route highlight the architectural wonders of the homes and public buildings they created. Luarca is similarly the site of a significant number of large and ostentatious *indiano* houses, some of which are open to the public as hotels, while others lie in ruins (see Figures 1 and 2). In lieu of an official municipal route, the Hotel Villa la Argentina provides guests with a map of the *indiano* route within the city limits; the framed story is borrowed from Menco Valdés's "gran aventura," emphasizing "heroismo" and the role of Asturians in the Americas (in this case Argentina) as heirs to the *conquistadores* and "modernos pobladores" who continued to shape society and extract fortunes as if the empire had not come to an end (Casariego).[16]

Figure 1. Villa Excelsior, Luarca. Original photograph by Lisa Surwillo.

Figure 2. Hotel Villa la Argentina, Luarca. Original photograph by Lisa Surwillo.

One hundred miles to the east of Luarca, the Ribadedeva Town Hall created a *ruta* in 2006 called La Huella Indiana in direct response to visitor demand after twelve thousand people visited their tourist office in 2005, many of whom requested information on *indiano* buildings. The Museo Abierto de la Arquitectura Indiana in Ribadedeva offers a series of informative panels throughout the area (including the parish of Colombres) to provide historical, architectural, and anecdotal information about fifteen buildings built with American money in the late nineteenth and early twentieth centuries. Significantly, their stories may be local, but half of the cost of the route's infrastructure was paid by the Culture Ministry of the Principality of Asturias—which saw an opportunity to link this project with others in the province ("El Ayuntamiento estrena").

At the heart of the Ribadedeva circuit, the Archivo de Indianos in the parish of Colombres provides a centralized institution for the *indiano* story based on an unbroken relationship between Spain and the Americas, with the latter depicted as a land of fortune, but also a land enriched by the generosity of Asturians (see Figures 3 and 4). The Archivo de Indianos tells the long tale of emigration from about 1850 to 1950. One small, meaningful room is dedicated to those forced to emigrate during the Spanish Civil War, including the military of the defense of Madrid. However, the lion's share of the museum is dedicated to two neocolonial stories: the "second conquistador" of Mexico and friend of Porfirio Díaz, the millionaire Íñigo Noriega; and the modern colonization of the Americas. Installations communicate the pain of departure from Spain, but the overarching message is of the good that the emigrants did in their new lands, societies that veritably blossomed with the presence and deeds of the Spaniards who kept these lands Hispanic.

The Archivo is a high temple of *hispanismo*. As Angel Loureiro has written, since the nineteenth century, considerations of the relationship between Spain and America have tended to posit that

> Spain performed a civilizing task in America, leaving a lasting legacy perceptible above all in the language, culture and religion of the former colonies. Such a legacy should guarantee Spain's cultural rights over the now independent countries. Thus, the civilizing enterprise, cultural legacy, spiritual debt incurred by the colonized, and the need to fight against the loss or corruption of the Spanish legacy are some of the more salient aspects of the Spanish discourses on Latin America deserving further analysis. (69)

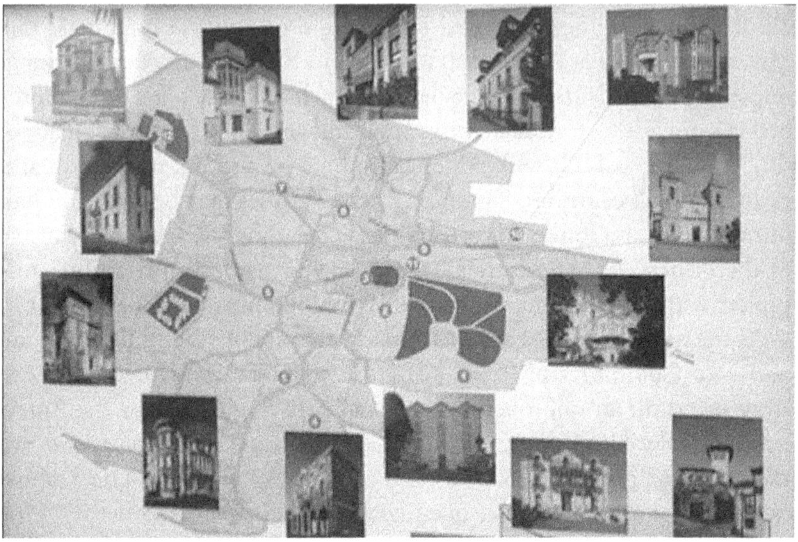

Figure 3. Ribadedeva Route. Original photograph by Lisa Surwillo.

Figure 4. Archivo de Indianos. Original photograph by Lisa Surwillo.

Indeed, the cultural colonization did not cease in the early nineteenth century, although it did change direction, with American money and vision modernizing Spain. But as the Archivo presents it, a Eurocentric imperial Hispanism was reinvigorated several decades after the majority of the Americas gained independence.

While the *rutas* in Somao, Luarca, and Ribadedeva are shaped by their municipalities rather than by a single protagonist, the *indiano* stories of Juan Manuel Manzanedo, Antonio López, and Ramón Argüelles (two Cantabrians and one Asturian) form a natural grouping (Sazatornil, 544). Their life stories forged the ur-narrative of the model *indiano*: birth in humble circumstances, exodus to Cuba at an early age, rapid creation of great wealth through direct or indirect dealings with the illegal slave trade, and a triumphal return to either Madrid and Barcelona, where their sumptuous lives and powerful networks of influence in politics and finance gave them great visibility. All of the men in this group were not simply involved in the slave trade while in the Antilles; after their direct activity had concluded, they continued to intervene in colonial economics and metropolitan government, fiercely adhering to a *negrero* politics.[17] They founded an economic and political world on both shores of the empire that facilitated the ongoing successes of their fellow *indianos*. Finally, all three monsters by trade returned to the towns of their birth with an aristocratic title to found architectural monuments to themselves in the 1870s and 1880s (Sazatornil, 545, 552).

Comillas

Antonio López de Piélago y López de Lamadrid (1817–83) was the epitome of the nineteenth-century self-made man. Born in Cantabria, López moved to Cuba where his commercial rise began with his marriage to the Creole Luisa Brú Lassús. With her dowry, López paid off debts and founded a shipping line for smuggling slaves. He invested his initial profits in sugar and coffee plantations, diversifying and multiplying his holdings within a decade. After a definitive return to Spain where he established himself in Barcelona, López wove an intricate web of business and social connections. He solidified his social position through the marriage of his daughter Isabel to Eusebi Güell, thus joining forces with an analogous *indiano* family. Together, López and Joan Güell advocated for Manzanedo and Zulueta's Liga Nacional. (López was granted the title of Marqués de Comillas in 1878 from a grateful Alfonso XII.) Financially, his numerous enterprises were at the core of the Catalan haute-bourgeoisie (Rodrigo y Alharilla, "Casa de comercio," 251). Moreover, his financial and political interests were closely intertwined with state politics: his Compañía Transatlántica shipping line transported thousands of emigrants to the Americas as well as troops to the Antilles during the Ten Years' War. López was also involved in the foundation of the Banco Hispano Colonial that funded the imperialist wars, and none other than Antonio Cánovas de Castillo assisted López with procuring the Philippine tobacco monopoly.

The Marqués de Comillas drew together not only the crème de la crème of finance and politics, but also many leading names in art, literature, and architecture. López's association with Barcelona's industrial renaissance was matched by his patronage of its cultural rebirth, in the person of Jacint Verdaguer, Antonio López's personal chaplain and employee of the Compañía Transatlántica. While aboard López's ship, the *Guipúzcoa*, traveling between Cuba and Spain, Verdaguer wrote the epic *L'Atlàntida* that, significantly, characterized *indianos* not as uncouth nouveau riche, but instead as the noble heirs of Columbus and Spain's glorious early modern empire. Verdaguer dedicated the work to the new *marqués* who, in turn, backed its publication in 1878. Seizing the representative power of Christopher Columbus (see Schmidt-Nowara, *Conquest*), López fashioned his image around that of the foundational transatlantic subject, much as many other *indianos* would do.

Having firmly established his social, political, and financial status in Cuba and Barcelona, López completed the *indiano* arc, returning to the village of his birth to construct a monument to himself and his personal success. His scheme exceeded the comparatively modest *casonas* of other *indianos* to comprise nothing less than the rebuilding of an entire village. Sazatornil aptly defines the *marqués*'s project as an "*escenificación*" (574, 584)—a wholesale staging of his power and influence on the scale more commonly associated with the monarchs of the early modern period than with capitalists. Cultivating excellence in architecture, sculpture, and pictorial art, López staged his *indiano* story in Comillas in much less diluted terms than in Barcelona, his habitual town of residence, where, in spite of his notable opulence, the artistic legacy of his money is associated primarily with his son-in-law, Eusebi Güell.

López constructed the *modernista* complex of Comillas with the talents of various Catalan architects and sculptors, including Joan Martorell, Josep Llimona, Agapito Valmitjana, Joan Roig i Soler, Navarro de Villena, and Antonio Gaudí. The actual number of buildings and monuments constructed by López and those of his circle was considerable, and they can be visited by following the eleven suggested stops on the Ruta Modernista prepared by the Comillas Tourist Office. This Ruta Modernista includes the exquisite "El Capricho" designed by Gaudí (see Figure 5), the neogothic Sobrellano palace, the modernist cemetery, and Pontifical University. Unofficially, the hamlet bears the traces of a feudal existence under the largesse of the López family interests, while the main bar in town, Filipinas, in the shadow of the palace, is a reliquary of the Compañía Transatlántica. The tour interlocks with Barcelona's route of the same name, highlighting several of the same architects. "Comillas fue la sede del modernismo catalán exportado." ("Ruta del Modernismo," Comillas Tourist Office; Comillas was the headquarters of an exported Catalan modernism.) The focus of the tour is on the beauty of the buildings and monuments as well as gratitude

Figure 5. "El Capricho" (Antonio Gaudí). Comillas, Cantabria. Original photograph by Lisa Surwillo.

toward Comillas. The entire town is a cult to its benefactor, López, and his modernization of it in terms of architectural beauty and infrastructure. The tour of the village rightly emphasizes the Comillas family's gifts of wealth and beauty.

In contrast, the *marqués*'s *negrero* past is less understood. The local Tourist Office explains that the topic is taboo at present, while conceding that it may be of interest at a later date: "[Eso] se debate en Barcelona, pero aquí no. Bueno, por el momento no, quién sabe si en el futuro. . . ." (That is discussed in Barcelona, but not here. Well, at least not now, who knows if it will be in the future. . . .)[18] Indeed, for a small village dependent upon tourism, the *indiano* continues to provide the townspeople's daily bread. However, this question divides the town more than first appears. Two guides among the team at the Sobrellano palace do explain the initial source of the López fortune during the tour in the museum hall, through discussion of a poster of the Compañía Transatlántica highlighting Fernando Poo. These guides connect the village of Comillas to Africa and America by explaining the structure of a slave trade that funded the benefactor's other enterprises. The historical accuracy of these comments is less interesting than the fact that this set of guides stated that they believe that most *indiano* money introduced into Cantabria came from illegal activities and that "hay que contar lo que hizo López" (what López did must be told). But they concede that the majority of palace guides consider such a narrative as "heresy." Among the tourists, according to these guides, it is primarily visitors from Cádiz and Barcelona who have a notion of the place of slavery in nineteenth-century colonialism and the narrative of the triumphant *indiano*, a distinction that demonstrates the unevenness of oblivion across Spain.

Santoña

The hometown of one of the greatest nineteenth-century *indiano* fortunes, Santoña, Cantabria (thirty miles from Santander), does not possess a major modernist mansion and is not on an established *ruta del indiano*. Juan Manuel de Manzanedo (Noja 1803–Madrid 1883) accumulated a fortune of fifty million *reales* in Cuba between 1823 and 1845 through predatory lending, slave trading, and other import-export businesses. With this initial capital, Manzanedo invested widely and became a pivotal figure in the national economy and banking systems, with a hand in both the Banco Hispano Colonial (along with Antonio Lopez, Ramón de Herrera, and Julián Zulueta) and the French Rothchilds (Sazatornil, 556).[19] His Liga Nacional worked aggressively to maintain the colonial status quo and stymie any attempts at fiscal or administrative reforms.[20] Known unofficially as the "representante general en Madrid de los negreros de Cuba,"[21] he founded the Círculo Hispano-Ultramarino (with eighty-seven provincial chapters throughout the Peninsula) with the express intent of overturning the Moret Law, ceasing commercial reform in the islands, and preventing the abolition of slavery:

> Basing themselves in Havana and Madrid and allying themselves with important figures from the Spanish military and political élite, such as General Francisco Serrano y Domínguez, the colonial interests effectively rallied supporters—landowners, merchants, manufacturers and *indianos*—from throughout the Peninsula to petition the Spanish government and to take to the street in support of slavery. (Schmidt-Nowara, "La España ultramarina," 200)

Manzanedo also made significant donations to the war effort in Africa in 1859–60, loaned the crown two million *reales* (interest free), and sent his own private army of 106 men and officers. At his death, he was the wealthiest man in Spain. Bahamonde and Cayuela compare the mythic rise of Manzanedo through the slave trade to the scale of vice and greed characterizing Baroja's *negreros*: "Si Manzanedo no es el piloto de altura que describe Baroja en su novela del mismo título, atribuyéndole el nombre y los apellidos del marqués, sí es al menos el personaje en la sombra que aporta su dinero a este tipo de operaciones." (204; If Manzanedo is not the *piloto de altura* that Baroja describes in his novel, giving him the *marqués*'s name, he is certainly at the very least the character in the shadow who lent his money to this type of scheme.)

Manzanedo was among the fiercest members of the opposition throughout the Democratic Sexenium (1868–74) and an equally fierce supporter of the Bourbon Restoration. He was pivotal in obtaining the recognition of Alfonso XII as legitimate pretender to the throne by the Carlist General Cabrera in the Acta de Paris (Sazatornil, 565) and was rewarded with a dukedom and the rank of *grande* by Alfonso XII within days of the king's coronation on March 22, 1875. Manzanedo's political and financial influence was matched by his social clout: the inauguration of his Madrid palace and his wife's pediatric foundation—the Niño Jesús Hospital—were gala events that attracted the presence of the royal family.

In Santoña, Manzanedo carefully constructed a monument to himself and laid the foundation for the cult of personality around his characterization as *indiano*, a profile still celebrated in the town today by a grateful citizenry whose ancestors experienced real material improvement in their lives through his beneficent works. The Santoña tourist office, housed in his palace, introduces its most famous *indiano* on a placard as an "indiano en Cuba desde su adolescencia y enriquecido en la isla con el comercio" (an *indiano* in Cuba since his adolescence and made wealthy in the island through the trade). The truncated phrase leaves the exact nature of the "comercio" unspecified, yet the truth is evoked in its obvious syntactical absence. The phrasing of the sign itself is part of an *escenificación* that represents historical events from overseas in such ways as to simultaneously reveal and occlude the American past. But the secret is not as silenced as in Comillas: Manzanedo is a local hero, but one situated squarely in the past. In the words of Francisco Javier López Marcano, the Consejero de Cultura, Turismo y Deporte del Gobierno de Cantabria:

> Juan Manuel Manzanedo y González es un claro referente de una generación surgida a principios del siglo XIX que muestra la inquietud, el esfuerzo y la generosidad de un grupo de ciudadanos de Cantabria que por circunstancias, se vieron abocados a emigrar a tierras lejanas y dejaron su impronta emprendedora. . . . Estos pioneros son ejemplo de arrojo y valentía, y fueron los primeros en tender puentes con las nuevas tierras y culturas, que ayudaron a conformar una de las comunidades más importantes y pujantes de la actualidad, la hispanoparlante. (5)
>
> (Juan Manuel Manzanedo y González is a clear reference point for a generation that came of age at the beginning of the nineteenth century that shows the concern, determination and generosity of a group of citizens from Cantabria who, because of circumstances, were forced to emigrate to distant lands where they left their entrepreneurial mark. . . . These pioneers are an example of boldness and courage and were the first to build bridges with these new lands and cultures that helped shape one of the most important and thriving communities of today, the Spanish-speaking world.)

The politician's statement is a clear example of Hispanism, but not one pitched as a continuation of the first American conquest; rather, he refers to a relationship with, surprisingly, "new lands," a designation that discounts the grand imperial age of the sixteenth and seventeenth centuries. Indeed, the version presented by López Marcano addresses Spain and its role in the Americas as both a Hispanist and a frontier story, appealing to a neoliberal mentality, hostile to the ideals of a so-called nanny state and celebratory of self-made men. While the frontier story is the quintessential

American romantic tale, pitting man against nature in a supposedly empty land, this American narrative of the frontier also shapes the *indiano* story as told in Santoña. Here, individuals (single men, presumably without the support of families or institutions) both created themselves through opportunities overseas and were created in the Americas—the dual actions comprised in the phrase "hacer las Américas." Thus the recent rediscovery of Manzanedo writes a new myth of the relations between Cuba and Spain as one based solely on hard work while it is only a half-secret that Manzanedo was a trader.

Garaña de Pría

In contrast to the treatment of López and Manzanedo as hometown heroes who rebuilt their native villages, Ramón Argüelles's birthplace takes visitors down a radically different historical path. The palace that Ramón Argüelles ordered to be built in 1881–82 in his village of birth, Garaña de Pría, is currently the site of a campground (see Figure 6). The Hotel Palacio Garaña is at the heart of the property but the present owner, Pablo Amieva, speaks of its grandeur with disdain and scorns the

Figure 6. Hotel Palacio Garaña, Garaña de Pría, Asturias. Original photograph by Lisa Surwillo.

marqués as an exploiter of both the slaves in Cuba and the local peasant population in Asturias. Visitors to the Palacio de Garaña are informed that Ramón Argüelles Alonso immediately entered the slave trade upon his arrival in Cuba and that, subsequently, he invested in the railroads.[22] His vast earnings allowed him to found the Almacén de Regla warehouses, own shares in the conservative newspaper *El Diario de la Marina*, and serve on the board of the Banco Español. By means of the Argüelles Brothers bank, in many cases, Argüelles controlled the sugar and tobacco growers' mortgages on their lands, as well as their harvest, animals, slaves, and machinery. In his one person, Argüelles controlled nearly every aspect of the slave economy, from the import of smuggled slaves to the export of slave-made sugar (see Buergo on this). He was a slave trader who, like financiers throughout the century, did not hesitate to bring the plantation system to the brink of financial ruin. Whereas Galdós feared that the imperialist influence of the *indianos* would destroy Spain, Argüelles was an *indiano* who garnered so much power that he endangered the viability of the state's imperial system. For example, he held municipal bonds up to $3,000,000 secured by mortgages of various public works, including canals, aqueducts, markets (including the Tacón Market), and the revenues from slaughterhouses. His role as creditor to the city of Havana was sufficiently vast as to place him in direct negotiations with the US government at the end of the Spanish-American War.[23]

The visit to the palace introduces some of this historical information about its founder, but more importantly, the palace itself embodies the *indiano* story: on a basic level, it was constructed with American wood. Moreover, based on his assessment of the craftsmanship of this structure as opposed to others built during the same years, Pablo Amieva believes that the Afro-Cubans that the *marqués* was known to have brought from Cuba built the mansion. The walls of the palace may well be the silent traces of an Afro-Cuban presence in Spain and, for those versed in the craft of carpentry, provide a means to study their contribution to modern Spanish architectural culture and resignify the site as an echo of the lived reality of coloniality in Spain. These unnamed and unacknowledged craftsmen are the historical counterpoint to the "negros y negras" who serve Olvido Páez in *La Regenta* (chapter XII) and move silently in the shadow of the *indiano* household.

In sum, Comillas is a local hero in a town with little to gain in exploring the slave trade; Manzanedo is a hero in a town equally indebted to its *indiano*, but because it is not part of a *ruta* dedicated to the *indianos*, the possibilities of recovering Manzanedo's story are strikingly different and there is less shame about his slave-trading past. In contrast, a visit to the Palacio de Garaña aggressively combats the hero myth of the slave trader and, in the palace turned campground where the cult of luxury and social ascent are not pursued, visitors are encouraged to reject received views regarding the nineteenth-century empire.

Malleza

Somao and Colombres may boast the most photographed *indiano* homes, and Llanes the highest cinematographic profile, but it is within the Parish of Salas (population six thousand) where one finds the most coherent tourist products of the *ruta*, even as its narrative is among the least triumphal. To walk-ins, the staff of the regional tourist office suggests Malleza as an *indiano* destination and lodging within the town of Salas at the Hotel Soto, an urban "Antigua Casa de Indianos" from 1896. The Hotel Soto, in turn, reproduces a map of the local Ruta de los Indianos in the interior pages of its pamphlet, inscribing itself into the itinerary. The *indiano* tourist product and cultural narrative are similarly tightly woven throughout the parish, with various constituent businesses reaffirming this larger story of the Comarca's identity as *indiana*.[24] The local government also promotes nine walking and driving routes (in addition to the Camino de Santiago) in the region: three of these are dedicated to the *indiano* legacy, and two are self-guided tours of Malleza, "La pequeña Habana" (Little Havana).[25]

According to the Salas Tourist Office, the wide range of offerings in such a small area can be explained by the steadily growing interest in *indianos* among both Spaniards and South Americans (especially from Cuba and Uruguay) who visit Salas in search of their family "origins." Elena Rodríguez Fernández, sommelier and head of the dining room at Al Son del Indiano in Malleza, estimates that 20 percent of the restaurant's clientele stems specifically from an unflagging interest in *indiano* tourism during the past eighteen years (that is, roughly since the quincentenary of 1492 and the revival of imperialist celebrations), and she credits promotion by the regional government of Malleza and the *indiano* route for its success.

The elaborate map of the *concejo* of Salas (including Salas, Mallecina, Malleza, and Cornellana) includes a lengthy section on "Arquitectura de Indianos" that summarizes the *indiano* story and profiles the parish of Malleza: "en la que se llega hacer popular el dicho 'cuando Cuba se acatarra, Malleza estornudaba.' Aquí se encuentran ejemplos de este tipo de arquitectura, con cierta preferencia por el estilo asturiano—Las Palmeras, Casa Panchón, Casa Cima, Casa de Don Vicente, Villa Alicia . . . —y si bien cada una cuenta una historia particular" (where the saying "When Cuba catches a cold, Malleza sneezes" became popular. Here we find examples of this type of architecture with a certain preference for Asturian styles in Las Palmeras, Casa Panchón, Casa Cima, Casa de Don Vicente, Villa Alicia . . . and each house tells its own story). The concerted effort among various government offices and local businesses draws visitors down a small and sinuous rural road to this town of less than one hundred people. Despite its remote location, Malleza has the most mature *indiano* route in Asturias, and commercial and regional marketing complement its unified narrative and clearly defined tourist product. The retention and promotion of the village's identity as "La Pequeña Habana" is not only sentimental but also a catalyst for economic development. The *indiano* route in the village of Malleza centers around the gourmet restaurant Al Son del Indiano, owned by Paulino Lorences and led by Chef Luis Rubio Quintana. As host of Al Son del Indiano, Lorences presents himself as the living archive of hundreds of personal stories of Mallezan *indianos*, passed down through oral histories, and he makes himself available to entertain visitors with these stories, facilitate walking tours, and, when possible, organize individual visits of the town's privately owned *indiano* mansions. While the *indianos* here did build architecturally spectacular *casonas*, as highlighted on the Salas Tourist Office flyers, Paulino Lorences's suggested *ruta* is just as likely to include a visit to the Masonic church or an oxidized bicycle—left, as local legend has it, by an *indiano* who has yet to return to fetch it (a poignant memorial to those who met hardship in the Americas)—as it is to include a succession of small palaces. In these ways, the material realities that prompted emigration to Cuba are communicated on a human level, and thus the story of the return is balanced with a recognition of the difficulty of departure. The discourse of triumph or conquest is tempered with discussion of transatlantic solidarity and freemason brotherhood, exempt from Spanish nationalistic discourse. Markedly, this version of the *indiano* story depicts Malleza as having acquired an "American" identity, an inversion of the Hispanist narrative found elsewhere that foregrounds the émigrés' role in imprinting "Spanishness" on the (former) colonies.

The building that houses the Al Son del Indiano restaurant is in a vernacular Asturian style but was initially built in the late nineteenth century with American money. Much as at the Archivo de Indianos, the three dining rooms are organized according to the various phases of the *indiano* experience: preparation, arrival, and return. Artifacts donated by members of the Malleza *indiano* community present local knowledge of emigrants' lives at sea, in Cuba, and upon their return. Here the silence that pervades Comillas gives way to details about the wide range of activities undertaken by Mallezans in Cuba: some held modest jobs in hospital cafeterias or on the telephone lines, while others were powerful bankers, held the monopoly on cement in Cuba, or ran the Cuban lottery. At the same time, photographs of Afro-Cuban laborers in tobacco fields are displayed on the walls of the restaurant alongside those of reporters for the *Diario de la Marina* (the fiercely pro-imperial conservative Cuban daily and investment scheme for many wealthy Spaniards in Cuba).[26] The ambiguity invites the visitor to come to her own conclusions as to the conditions in which the *indianos* of this town were able to create wealth.

Here, the story that frames the triumphs, successes, and fortunes brought "home" to improve the lives of poor Spaniards in small towns is that of a Spanish state unwilling or unable to do so. These *americanos* went to Cuba not to civilize the colony, but to modernize and civilize outlying areas of the metropolis. Through its story of personal, parochial, and family relationships, Malleza eschews a grand, state-based, epic Spanish imperialism; instead, the narrative retold by residents emphasizes the hardships of nineteenth-century Asturias, its rapid population growth,[27] and a sense of abandonment by the government in Madrid. The tale of self-sufficiency in the face of dismissal by the traditional powers of nineteenth-century Spain has less to do with the Americas per se than it does with a story of resistance to a traditional power structure and a centralized government, and it is collective rather than individual, transnational rather than nationalist. Cuba is cast as a stage where this nineteenth-century struggle was displaced and is, in turn, represented as success in its *escenificación* in Spain today.[28]

Loureiro has rightly argued that Spanish America is a ghost in Spanish nationalist discourse ("Spanish Nationalism"); however, regional stories such as that of Malleza place Cuba at the heart of its identity, not as a specter but as a contemporary reality. The rhetoric of the imperial family is reinterpreted yet again in Malleza, where it is discussed in terms of a transatlantic Masonic kinship. Neither the states of Spain and Cuba nor the empires of Spain and the United States figure in this story of transoceanic migrations. Indeed, 1898 is not even mentioned. One tourist pamphlet from Malleza explains that the region's decline did not take place when control of Cuba changed hands: "Hasta el año 1936, el capital cubano era el impulsor de la economía local." ("Historia de Malleza"; Until 1936, Cuban capital was the motor of the local economy.) The flow of emigrants and Cuban remittances continued until the beginning of the "años negros," when the civil war that brought Franco to power "ruined" the Comarca (according to Malleza's residents). The forces that the *indianos* had fled in the nineteenth century definitively won in 1939 and closed off opportunities for change. If other *rutas* favor state-based nationalist stories, Malleza's model is closer to Fernando Ortiz's theory of transculturation. By discarding the equation of society with nation, Malleza's transnational perspective acknowledges the migrant's incorporation into multiple labor markets and societies and sense of multiple belongings, but it also acknowledges the transatlantic junctures that result in the town of migrants' departure when it, too, becomes a space for forging new relationships of value, culture, and economics with distant locations.

Salas is a left-leaning region,[29] and their *indiano* story replicates their antistate version of history. Mallezans remember their *indianos* as forward-thinking Masons who remained so in the face of the 1941 Ley de Represión de la Masonería y del Comunismo (Law for the Suppression of Freemasonry and Communism). The townspeople proclaim a kinship with (pre- and postrevolution) Havana, and several have traveled to Cuba to share clothes, money, and basic supplies; they reference a sense of duty to help those who live in Cuba, which gave Malleza the economic stability it has today. These townspeople cast the relationship as one of supranational brotherhood with Cubans, that is, not imperial but rather personal and local.

Conclusion

The interpretive challenges of framing the transatlantic gaze in the postimperial age are not new. Nearly a century ago, a young Rafael Sánchez Mazas evoked, through literary nostalgia, the potential of the *indiano* palace as a scene for staging overseas stories, secrets, and anxieties. Like Galdós before him, Sánchez Mazas contemplated the differences between *indianos* and *negreros* through literature. In "Sonetos de un verano antiguo" (Sonnets from a summer past), a set of poems published in 1919, but reflecting upon a period of plenitude before 1898, the poet contrasts the perceptions of overseas success through the structure of the *casona indiana*, as the site where the imperial and the domestic converge. In

"Bordan las hijas del indiano" (The *indiano*'s daughters embroider) and "Las ventanas de casa del negrero" (The windows of the *negrero*'s house), Sánchez Mazas anthropomorphizes the *casona indiana* as the Atlantic adventurer's public face. In "Ventanas," the eyes of the "casa del negrero" gaze upon ships navigating westward on the Cantabrian sea and long for a son to resume maritime adventure:

> Ventanas que hace tiempo ven la playa
> entre los tristes pinos de un pinar,
> y en las tardes muy claras ven pasar
> los vapores que salen de Vizcaya.
> Tienen soñado, de mirar la raya
> del horizonte, un sueño de Ultramar,
> y hace años esperando están que vaya
> un hijo de la casa a navegar. (50)

> (Windows that have long looked upon the beach
> between the sad pines of a pine grove,
> and in the crisp afternoons they watch pass by
> the steamships leaving Vizcaya.
> They have dreamed, from gazing upon the edge
> of the horizon, an Overseas dream,
> and for years they have hoped for
> a son from the house to go sailing.)

The "raya" of the "horizonte" stresses the overseas dream in a striking enjambment. Moreover, the rhyme between "vaya" and "raya" emphasizes the distancing from the peninsular shore and the limits of land-based knowledge of what happens at sea. Indeed, the mansion's enthusiasm is tempered by the presentiment of impending doom. In spite of the *negrero*'s evident success (of which the house is the most visible testament), his home has witnessed shipwreck—*naufragios* is the final word of the poem. Shipwreck is a long-standing image of disaster and the hubris of empire; in this poem, it is the *negrero* himself and the Atlantic activities associated with him that have shipwrecked. The houses and their memories remain as the last remnants of a Hispanic world that has disappeared, where *negreros* were glorified and rules were made to be broken.

In contrast to the anxiety over a new generation that was to resume imperial adventures in the western seas, in "Bordan las hijas," Sánchez Mazas reveals the imperial at the very heart of the feminine, domestic sphere. Once the empire comes home and has been reintegrated through the forces of domesticity, the overseas adventurer (who may or may not have been a *negrero*) becomes, simply, an *indiano*. It is this domesticity (so often gendered feminine) and the ability of Spain to be at home with empire that transforms the *indiano* and initiates a violent erasure of the colonial while molding it into the language of nostalgia. In the poem, the emigrant is present only through his offspring; indeed, his daughters embody the success of his return. These women represent the domestication of the *indiano* and his spoils from the Atlantic in a way that underscores the place of *home* in both the return and the imperial gaze. Pushing the concept of domesticity to its limits, the *casona* without a family in "Ventanas" vocalizes a wish for a son to depart on the high seas. In the poem without women, the emigrant remains explicitly a *negrero*, without the mask of domesticity.

In the first quatrain of "Bordan las hijas," the two daughters undertake the most mundane of tasks for women of the idle class: sitting in the glow of the dining room on a summer evening, they embroider traditional floral designs. "Es prima noche. Bordan las hermanas." (VI; Dusk has settled. The sisters embroider.) However, even as they hold the needle and thread, the archetypical accessories of the home, their labors are related linguistically to the overseas origins of their luxurious surroundings. "Bordar," the act of adorning fabrics, phonetically and conceptually evokes numerous aspects of life on the high seas, in particular "borda" (the mainsail of a galley ship) and "bordada" (both "embroidered" and a navigation route). Shadows of their father's trade haunt their present beautification of the home. Truth, desire, and history are products of perspective: as the poem progresses, the frame of the speaker's gaze slowly shifts from the interior of the *casa* to the seas. The women who actively "bordan" in the first stanza are depicted in the passive tense by the second; meanwhile, the frame of the scene literally scopes out to comprise a maritime view, for the turn of the final tercet reveals that the poem in fact voices the observations of a sailor at sea who gazes upon the *indiano*'s daughters through a spyglass.

Both poems pivot on the perspective from the liminal space between ship and shore: when looking out upon the world, the house analyzes oceanic events with the eyes of a slave trader; when contemplated admiringly from afar by a sailor at sea, the house radiates a golden light of *indiano* wealth rewarded with tranquil domesticity, a similar safe space of "home" explored by Galdós in *El amigo Manso*. The actions that take place within the poems transpire through glass of various types, the relationship between domestic and colonial spaces is conditioned by the crisscrossing of gazes between the Peninsula and the sea. By pairing the two poems (in *Blanco y Negro* they appear side by side below a three-quarter-page illustration of the embroidering women, one of whom gazes directly at the reader of *Blanco y Negro* who then, in turn, assumes the viewpoint of the sailor), Sánchez Mazas emphasizes the dual character of the *casona*, and a dense nostalgia underscores that among the nineteenth-century Spain's *indiano-negreros*, even the most domestic of activities were inseparable from the imperial.

In his 1980 essay on "imperial hangovers" Martin Blinkhorn declared that "when Franco died, post-imperial nostalgia was interred with him" (23). Unfortunately, the claim was somewhat premature. For as Juan Aranzadi has written, neoimperial overtones characterized Spain during the years of the José María Aznar government. The conservative Partido Popular consciously invoked and performed aspects of the Hapsburg era; in terms of popular historiography, the Aznar years witnessed not only a revision of recent history, but

> la promoción mediática de numerosas biografías apologéticas de los monarcas responsables de la pasada grandeza imperial de España, la reivindicación de la Reconquista y de la larga lucha de "España contra el Islam' como antecedente de la cruzada de Bush contra el terrorismo islamista y, sobre todo, el énfasis patriótico en la antigüedad de España y en su inmemorial unidad. (168)

> (The promotion by the media of numerous sympathetic biographies of the monarchs responsible for Spain's former imperial grandeur, the vindication of the Reconquest and the long fight of "Spain against Islam" as the forerunner to Bush's crusade against Islamist terror and, especially, the patriotic emphasis on Spain's ancient creation and unity.)

A similar type of nostalgia for imperial grandeur informs the neocolonial tone of the *rutas del indiano*, but is filtered through local stories and a focus on *home* and the desire to return to the *patria chica* in the Iberian Peninsula. Yet like the twenty-first-century state itself, the local municipalities find the source of their modernization in their American roots. In other words, Blinkhorn was clearly both optimistic and short-sighted; nevertheless, a crucial break did take place at Franco's death. The current celebratory imperialist story is not simply pressed into the frame of the nation as had certainly been done during the governments of Primo de Rivera and Franco, but rather is emerging through very local and sometimes a-national perspectives. Aspects of the "Spanish" empire are individual and regional—when not municipal—and often promote a collective identity that may appear to have little to do with the Spanish state in the eyes of its practitioners. Today imperial nostalgia is screened through neoliberal and often antistate values. But the imperial nostalgia embracing the nineteenth-century cannot be fully disarticulated from an appreciation of Spain's American roots and an engagement with the nationalistic stereotype of Spain's "destiny" as empire.

§5 Family Ties and Narrative Confessions in Catalonia

As opposed to the idolatry he enjoys in Cantabria, Antonio López has a much less secure place in Catalonia, in spite of his crucial role in the development of Catalan finance. Indeed, the city of Barcelona has begun to revise visual and cartographic monuments to the first Marquis of Comillas, precisely because of the origins of his fortune in slavery. At the same time, the closest members of his coterie remain in the public's favor. His personal chaplain, Jacint Verdaguer, is revered as the founder of the modern Catalan literary canon, and his son-in-law Eusebi Güell remains glorified for having patronized Gaudí (currently undergoing canonization for sainthood), the architect who created the landscape of the modernist city with this same money. In April 2010, the avenue formerly named "Marqués de Comillas" in the Montjuïc area of the city was renamed for a man whose ideals and politics starkly opposed those of the *indiano* who had preceded him by a generation. Now called "Francesc Ferrer i Guàrdia," the avenue commemorates the anarchist and education activist falsely accused and condemned to death for his supposed participation in the "Tragic Week" of 1909.[1] Some Cantabrian commentators dismissed the move as antagonistic and motivated by anti-Spain, or Catalan-nationalist, sentiments.[2] But such provocations contribute little to understanding exactly how and why some segments of Barcelona have chosen to address or suppress its colonialist past. Informed attention on the part of the city's population to the past embedded in urban topography, the intersection of historiography with national as well as local legends, and a more distant and critical perspective on the legacy of Spain all uniquely position Barcelona to refashion its urban image as not only a European city but one that embraces its colonialist past. Politics play a crucial role in the current debate over the limits of historical memory, but the anti-Catalan discourse emerging from conservative sectors of Cantabria fails to capture the larger issues at stake.

On October 6, 2010, six months after the inauguration of the new Ferrer i Guàrdia, the labor unions CCOO (Confederación Sindical de Comisiones Obreras) and UGT en Catalunya (Unión general de trabajadores) sent a formal request to Jordi Hereu, then mayor of Barcelona, urging the removal of the statue of Antonio López from the plaza bearing his name (previously called San Sebastián) on the Passeig de Colom, near the newly renovated harbor. They also called for a new designation for the square, a change that would eliminate all traces of López from public monuments. Joan Carles Gallego, secretary general of the CCOO de Catalunya, and Josep M. Àlvarez, secretary general de UGT de Catalunya, grounded their request on the identity of the city of Barcelona as a haven for workers' rights. "Una ciutat digna" (a city with dignity) and "un model de ciutat" (a model city), Barcelona is not only the birthplace of the UGT but has been historically associated with workers' resistance to oppression—most famously during the Tragic Week. Barcelona, they argue, must be a city "que fomenti els valors del treball digne i amb drets" (that promotes the values of dignified labor and work with rights) and must not celebrate a figure who "féu la seva fortuna mitjançant l'esclavatge" (made his fortune through slavery) or "reconèixer la tasca d'aquells que van denigrar l'esser humà i el varen tractar com a mercadería" (acknowledge the deeds of those who denigrated human beings and treated them as commodities) (see Gallego and Álvarez). The union leaders do not explore the contours of the relationship of Barcelona's economic growth with its colonialist past; their immediate objective is the renunciation of the public veneration of a key member of Spain's slavocracy in the present. However, the proposed removal of a physical and visual commemoration of the slave trader, without an explanation of the complexities and impact of transatlantic imperialism on Catalan finance and society, threatens to marginalize the issues of race, violence, and domination intricately related to the growth of industrial Barcelona and its labor class, in order to privilege a particular political narrative of the modern city. As thousands of nineteenth-century artisans (if not actual laborers) attested in handwritten petitions to the central government against the proposed abolition of slavery in Puerto Rico, the health of Catalan industry was dependent on the protected markets of the slave-society colonies.[3] Abolition, it was understood, would have jeopardized the islands' subjection to the imperial regime and destroyed a profitable space of exchange in which the colonies were guaranteed markets for Spanish goods. That is, the modern city that cultivated the admirable and "proud" working class (itself subjected to deprivations and exploitations, to be sure) was inextricable from the condition of the Caribbean slaves as slaves. Today, Comillas is certainly not a hero to be revered, nor can his labor be seen as "digna"; nevertheless, he represents the nexus between two interdependent labor markets and the impossibility of divorcing Catalonia from the Atlantic.

In the past, Comillas's statue has been erected and taken down in accordance with the rise and fall of his public appreciation, notably disappearing in 1936, only to return in 1939 (Eaude, 72). The latest controversy over Comillas's name and image is not an isolated event, but rather the result of a larger reconceptualization of origins. Academic work has recovered an understanding of the complex commercial relationship between Cuba and Catalonia during the nineteenth century.[4] Popular interest in the same transatlantic connections is perhaps even more extensive. As Martín Rodrigo y Alharilla has shown, since about 1989, the press coverage in newspapers, Sunday inserts, and magazines for the general public have dedicated significant attention to the impact of *indianos* (and American slavery) on Catalan society (*Indians a Catalunya*, 11). Álex Bosch finds the marked Catalan interest in Cuba rooted in a desire to recover a lost, shared history with another province of the nineteenth-century crown. Literature humanizes this historical past, transforming information into sentiment and affective narratives (63). Indeed, in recent years there has been somewhat of a cottage industry producing literature and films that explore the place of Catalan imperialism and Afro-Cuban slave labor in the constitution of modern Catalonia. Galina Bakhtiarova has defined two trends within this corpus of Catalan music, film, and literature from the last decade of the twentieth century.[5] First, the figure of the *indiano* or *americano* has lost his heroic aura and acquires a morally ambiguous valence, a consequence of the works' frank assessment of the role of slavery and slave trading in the creation of nineteenth-century wealth that, in turn, transformed Catalonia into the most economically and industrially developed area in the Iberian Peninsula. Second, Barcelona is celebrated as the de facto metropolis to the Antillean colonies. The representation of the nineteenth-century Spanish empire as a fundamentally Catalan enterprise in these works situates Catalonia within the "imperial club"; that is, it appears as an equal in historical geopolitical terms to other European states, thus supporting present claims to statehood (Bahktiarova, 39).

Goytisolo and an Inconvenient Past

Juan Goytisolo pioneered the recovery and reconciliation of family ties to the Cuban slave era in *Señas de identidad* (1966), *Juan sin tierra* (1975), and his autobiography, *Coto vedado* (1985). These works constitute something more than a denunciation of the past. Akin to what James D. Fernández has written about apostrophic autobiographies of the nineteenth century, these texts "attempt to distinguish the autobiographical account from other erroneous contemporary accounts (or the author's preconversion account), by pretending to free the autobiographer from the contingencies of his contemporary moment, and the limited, fallible world- and self-view which that moment offers" ("A Life," 125). In *Coto vedado*, Goytisolo writes of learning as a child to read the story of nineteenth-century empire as his family's story. Theirs was a tale of architectural beauty in Barcelona, adventures of patriotic *voluntarios*, and of Cuba as a magical lost paradise that obscured the realities of Spanish control over the island. Their truth, however, was a façade:

> El mito familiar, escrupulosamente alimentado por mi padre, se esfumó para siempre tras la cruda verdad de un universo de desmán y pillaje, desafueros revestidos de piedad, abusos y tropelías inconfesables. Una tenaz, soterrada impresión de culpa, residuo sin duda de la difunta moral católica, se sumó a mi ya aguda conciencia de la iniquidad social española e índole irremediablemente parasitaria, decadente e inane del mundo al que pertenecía. (11)

> (The family myth, scrupulously nourished by my father, went up in smoke forever in light of the raw truth of a universe of theft and pillage, crimes dressed up as charity, and inconfessable abuses. A tenacious, deep impression of guilt, undoubtedly a residue of my defunct Catholic morals, joined my already sharpened consciousness of Spain's social inequality and the incorrigibly parasitic, decadent and inane nature of the world to which I belonged.)

A century before Goytisolo wrote *Coto vedado*, leading men of finance and industry openly protested against reforms in the Antilles, including moves toward abolition. Agustín Goytisolo and Antonio Goytisolo—the author's great-grandfather and grandfather—joined 2,674 other "Propietarios, fabricantes, navieros, comerciantes, industriales" (Proprietors, Manufacturers, Shipbuilders, Businessmen, Industrialists) from Barcelona in the largest single petition in Spain against colonial reforms.[6] They voiced their opposition to colonial reforms in Puerto Rico, arguing that, because it had the most to lose, Catalonia had the greatest right to influence imperial policies in the Antilles. The legislation of abolition—which would bring independence to the islands, they reasoned—was equivalent to Madrid's abandonment of Catalan fiscal health. Without the slave economies of Puerto Rico and Cuba and their captive markets, Catalan "campos se convertirian en yermos, sus fábricas se cerrarian, sus barcos se podririan en los puertos" (fields would become barren, her factories would close, her ships would rot in the ports). Writing to the central government, they claimed that Catalonia

> que tantos sacrificios ha hecho en pró de las posesiones Ultramarinas contribuyendo á su fomento, ilustracion y riqueza, tiene derecho á que se atiendan sus ruegos, á que se fije la atención en la justicia de sus reclamaciones. . . . ¿Quien consumiria, Exmo Sõr, lo que Cataluña produce, si las Antillas dejaran de ser españolas? ¿á dónde irian nuestros vinos, nuestros aceites, los productos todos de nuestra agricultura y de nuestra industria? ¿qué otros mercados tienen? Y nuestra marina ¿en que se ocuparia, impotente para competir con la de otras naciones y sin mas vida que la que le dá el trasporte [*sic*] de los productos nacionales á aquellos mercados . . . ?
>
> (that has made so many sacrifices in favor of the overseas possessions, contributing to their development, education and wealth, has the right to have its pleas addressed, to have attention focused on the justice of its claims. . . . Who would consume, your Excellency, what Catalonia produces if the Antilles cease to be Spanish? Where would our wines go, our oils, all of the products of our agriculture and of our industry? What other markets do they have? And our navy, what would it deal with, powerless to compete with the other nations and lifeless if not for the transportation of national products to those markets . . . ?)

But in postwar Spain, the centrality of slavocracy to Spanish industry and culture, so eloquently narrated by Galdós and widely known by his public, had become invisible to a young Juan Goytisolo. In the aforementioned works, the narrator explores the process by which this discovery of the Atlantic shaped his understanding of Spanish historiography. The vitality of contemporary historical myths hinges upon an ethical characterization of the colonialist project as grand adventure, much as Chimista does for Baroja. In all three novels by Goytisolo, discourse of the archive and the seeming assurances of its materiality counter the appeal of an inherited fantasy that had rejected the human and documentary traces of its origins. In *Juan sin tierra*, the narrator's consultation of documents detailing his great-grandfather's slave-owning properties contextualizes history in a material past that destroys both family and national myths. Casilda

Mendiola, his great-grandfather's slave, becomes the author's muse and progenitor of a life at odds with the bourgeois mentality of his grandfather and great-grandfather:

> Casilda Mendiola
> grito de dolor
> fuente secreta del proceso liberador
> de tu pluma
> razón oculta de tu desvío moral y artístico, social, religioso, sexual
> (*Juan sin tierra*, 298)
>
> (Casilda Mendiola
> cry of pain
> secret source of the liberating process of your pen
> hidden reason for your ethical artistic social religious and sexual deviation)
> (English translation: *Juan the Landless*, 147)

Brad Epps writes that in *Juan sin tierra* the narrative direction is the expiation of guilt resulting from "the mistreatment of a slave woman in colonial Cuba by a Spanish landowner" (*Significant*, 137). The Cuban connection ties the narrator of *Juan sin tierra* to that of *Señas de identidad* and implicates the narrator's sexual morality to that of the slave (137). The text that the narrator of *Juan sin tierra* writes in response to the documents from the slave woman constitutes a "site of reversal and a rectification, a redemptive rewriting that would make good the writing that precedes it" (Epps, "Thievish," 169). In all three novels Goytisolo "makes a case" for a new reading of the past, using documents to counter memory and opting for the written and the judicial, over the familial and the religious, as well as their ramifications in an inquisitorial state.

James D. Fernández posits that in undertaking such a rejection of his grandfather and great-grandfather's activities, Goytisolo ridicules origins and desacralizes paternity (see "La novela"), while Gonzalo Navajas reads Goytisolo as incapable of compassion and contemptuous of his family. Brad Epps underscores that as the author grapples with the concept of authenticity, he necessarily moves away from his bourgeois origins ("Thievish," 164). As Michael Ugarte has written, the intertexts of discovered objects and documents, in particular a letter from the mistress of one of his ancestors, create the narrator's identity in *Señas* (65). Goytisolo's narrator in *Señas* writes:

> Tus esfuerzos de reconstitución y de síntesis tropezaban con un grave obstáculo. Merced a los documentos y pruebas atesorados en las carpetas podías

desempolvar de tu memoria sucesos e incidentes que tiempo atrás hubieras dado por perdidos y que rescatados del olvido por medio de aquellos permitían iluminar no sólo tu biografía sino también facetas oscuras y reveladoras de la vida en España (juntamente personales y colectivos, públicos y privados, conjugando de modo armonioso la búsqueda interior y el testimonio objetivo, la comprensión íntima de ti mismo y el desenvolvimiento de la conciencia civil en los Reinos Taifas). (*Señas*, 165)

(Your efforts at reconstruction and synthesis had run up against a serious obstacle. Thanks to the documents and proofs stored away in the folders, you were able to dust off in your memory happenings and incidents that in the past you might have considered lost and which, once rescued from forgetfulness by these means, were able to shed light not only on your own biography, but also on certain obscure and revealing facets of life in Spain [the personal and the collective, the public and the private, joined together harmoniously both the inner search and the outside evidence, the intimate understanding of yourself and the growth of civic awareness in the Taifa kingdoms].) (English translation: *Marks of Identity*, 133)

After the archive has destroyed the credibility of private histories, the autobiographical subject's exploration of family lines also puts into question the moral values of domestic stories. His struggle over the contradictory oral and written histories about home and empire triggers the methodological assessment of how secrets from a distant "elsewhere" become part of a history of private, urban life, and consequently, how a national history of domestic (peninsular) life incorporates half-hidden activities undertaken overseas into its narratives.

The confessional mode is integral to autobiography, but Goytisolo confesses from beyond the limits of the community, outside Spain and without an explicit intention to reincorporate himself into his original society. In doing so, Goytisolo undermines the right of that same Spanish society to judge him. Rather than appeal for reconciliation and forgiveness on his family's behalf, while physically and spiritually in exile, he liberates himself from the community responsible for cultivating the *indiano*'s heroic identity. Moreover, he implicates his readers in his self-discovery and prompts them not to absolve his or his family's sins, as in a standard confessional, but rather to judge the values of the community in which they had been committed with impunity.

Confession is at the heart of not only autobiography but also a particular system of governance, the confessional state. Peter Brooks reminds us that the police interrogations central to the Western justice system since the age of romanticism, like confessional literature, are Catholic in origin. Both were born of the 1215 Lateran Council that mandated annual confession and established the Inquisition (15); Brooks notes that the Inquisition, the Reign of Terror and the Stalinist show trials constitute a partial list of what the uncontrolled demand for generalized confession can lead to (163). Franco's dictatorship, buttressed by summary arrests, torture, and confessions without accusations, is another such instance. Goytisolo's divulgation of the transgressions of his paternal family line partakes of this generalized, compulsory confession. But whereas a textbook confession entails an adherence to orthodoxy, Goytisolo undermines the logic of orthodoxy as he tells "all," including secrets that are not convenient to remember. Goytisolo, like his hero Blanco White, attacked the confessional state as a political system for Spain, and his recourse to confession in literary terms bears reconsideration. Through his confession Goytisolo succeeds in reviving the past to his Spanish readership, for such literature often prompts a "counter-confession in which the reader admits to complicity" (*Brooks*, 28). Subsequent Catalan writers have written such corresponding confessions.

As confessional autobiography, *Coto vedado* expanded upon the expiation of guilt developed in two earlier novels, *Señas de identidad* (1966) and *Juan sin tierra* (1975). The latter is a surrealist rejection of the narrator's family's past, reconstructed through a pastiche of documents, letters, and memories of photographs that offer glimmers of insight into their fantastical memories of Cuba. The narrator takes on wildly varying subject positions—from slaves to slave catchers—and skirts direct engagement with history by resorting to the constantly shifting perspective of an eternal outsider battling a societal desire to forget. As Brad Epps has argued, the "fragmented narrator—here as elsewhere sharing certain signs of identity with the author—is haunted by the 'sins' of the fathers (racism, paternalism, colonialism, and economic exploitation) and is conditioned, even at his most extravagant, by a system of guilt, debt, and morality" (*Significant*, 5). The title recalls the nom de plume of Blanco White in some letters published in *El Español*, where he battled the censorship of the Cádiz regency in order to analyze—and sometimes support—the independence movement in the Americas (see Goytisolo's edition of Blanco White's texts on the Americas). Blanco White signed his anti-slave-trade letters in *El Español* as "Juan Sintierra," and as is well known, Goytisolo found a predecessor in Blanco White as an equivalent "heterodox," traitor to Spain, self-banished Spaniard, and intellectual. Angel Loureiro has examined the centrality of Goytisolo's identification with and recovery of his predecessor to the authorial project:

> By vindicating such figures as Blanco White, whom the official culture consigned to an interested oblivion, and by identifying with him to the point of seeing himself as a reincarnation of the self-exiled Spanish priest; by portraying him as a victim of intolerance and orthodoxy—actually by misrepresenting him, and Goytisolo is aware of that misrepresentation—Goytisolo is rescuing from oblivion an alternative nation while simultaneously, in identifying himself with Blanco White, he finds confirmation of the appropriateness of his self-construction. (*Ethics*, 125)

It would make sense to end this book with the second "Juan sin tierra" who also wrote of slavery, Spain, and its legacy of imperial nightmares. However, since Goytisolo published his confessional novels, there has been a return to the issue of slavers in recent literature from Catalonia. Much as flashback and multiple narrative voices harshly juxtapose past and present in *Señas de identidad* and *Juan sin tierra*, Goytisolo's reading of the past anticipated the New Imperial History that, as Antoinette Burton has written, "challenge[s] the dichotomies of 'home' and 'away' that underwrite national and imperial histories" (11). In *Señas*, center (the family home in Catalonia) and periphery (plantations in Cienfuegos, Cuba) must be read together in order to understand the place of the Goytisolo family and the creation of the autobiographical self in Spain.[7] In other words, Goytisolo did not simply reject family myth; rather, he forged a new manner of narrating imperial history from the heart of a home. His autobiography initiated a subgenre of domestic novels that examine Catalonia's *negrero* past and its influence on the later evolution of Barcelona, Catalonia, and Spain.

Literary Confessions After Goytisolo

The three novels discussed here, by Carme Riera, Xavi Casino, and Rafael Escolà Tarrida, explicitly tie the origins of modern Barcelona to its slaving past. The genre of the historical novel allows its readers to return temporarily to the moment when the questions were first posed regarding how Catalonia's relationship to the colonies was to be constituted in the modern nation. But if the literary confession reveals what is shocking, unexpectedly, these three do not reveal anything new. Moreover, rather than indict Barcelona society, as Goytisolo does, they instead emphasize the act of confession—the contrition, penance, and absolution for moral sins. Confessional acts—even false confessions—in recent Catalan novels demonstrate a desire for absolution and the consequent forgetting of these crimes, so inconveniently recovered by Goytisolo in *Señas de identidad, Coto vedado*, and *Juan sin tierra*. The novels manifest the tension between the desire to demonstrate inclusion among the European metropoli, along the lines of what Bakhtiarova has identified, and a wish for absolution. In Riera, this desire for absolution stems from a sense of shame that itself is a result of a critical awareness of the past, much as in Goytisolo. In the case of Escolà Tarrida, a postcolonial awareness underscores the particularity of the Catalan case, as opposed to that of Spain, still refusing to see Cuba as more than a disastrous loss. Casino examines the porous character of the Catalan nation in a move that discards the nineteenth-century essentialist conceptualizations of a nation while dramatizing a culture's deportation of memories of nonautochthonous foundational elements.[8]

As Jordi Maluquer de Motes wrote in 1974, "Habitualment es destaca l'estreta vinculació que existí entre la pèrdua dels residus colonials de Cuba i Puerto Rico i la capitalizació del nacionalisme català com a arma de classe per part de la burguesia." (85; The tight link is regularly noted between the loss of the remaining colonies of Cuba and Puerto Rico and the investment in Catalan nationalism as an arm of class consolidation by the bourgeoisie.) Dominic Keown has discussed the character of this postimperial nationalism as one attuned to the interests of the wealthy: "The industrial bourgeoisie, alarmed by Spain's loss of the last American colonies . . . would lend its weight to the expression of a fully fledged nationalist agenda in the philosophy of Prat de la Riba (1870–1917) and his party of wealth-creators, the *Lliga Regionalista* (Regionalist League), formed in 1901" (18). The business class "decided to play the nationalist card in an attempt to gain greater socio-political control [and] underwrote the creation of the *Lliga*, which was to implement a policy founded on a greater respect in all ambits for Catalonia and its heritage of difference" (21).

But the political implications of the Antilles on Catalonia was multifaceted. Ucelay-Da Cal emphasizes that ties with Cuba played a decisive role in the development of the modern Catalan nation, beyond economics, that did not necessarily translate into a desire for emancipation. However, the loss of the American empire did prompt a reconsideration of the nature of political association, federations, and organizations. Moreover, the Cuban situation shaped opinions on self-determination in the Catalan, as well as the Canary Island, Basque, and Galician realms (69). In other words, the colonies made the metropolis in ways that were not immediately evident in the economic arrangement.

Following Goytisolo's scathing depiction of the bourgoisie and a recognition of the link between a particular formulation of Catalan identity and colonialism, Riera and Casino, in particular, examine not simply the boundaries of Barcelona or the Catalan nation, but also the backstory to the latter's reformulation and the establishment of the Catalan character as the hardworking bourgeois ideal. The three novels discussed here unsettle present definitions of the Catalan nation and nationalism by historicizing them in the nineteenth-century, when financing and, in many cases, culture (for example, in the case of Güell) originated not in the modernist Western fantasy of the bonded European nation (Burton, 6), but in the colonies. Moreover, they turn to the first half of the nineteenth century, a period less known than that of the Battalions of Catalan *voluntarios* and pro-colonial fund-raising that punctuated the pro-Spain response to the Ten Years' War (1868–78). But all three writers permit a fuller understanding of modernity/coloniality as interdependent terms beyond economics by exploring the period when Catalonia was deeply invested in the Spanish empire (Maluquer de Motes, 115–16); with a global understanding of history comes a reconceptualization of what is at stake in a given national identity.

More than a decade after the publication of Goytisolo's *Coto vedado*, Carme Riera wrote of the Cuban legacy in European families from a sharply distinct position. Her novel depicts the creation of family secrets in the Caribbean, their conversion into popular legend in Mallorca, and social dynamics in Catalan-speaking lands more broadly, while reprising the traditional formula of the imperial family. Like Goytisolo, Riera reads transatlantic history as it percolates through domestic spaces. However, rather than explore textuality in order to shatter a myth, Riera's fiction celebrates the place of mystery and lore in family narratives while explicitly calling for a reconsideration of global (both free and coerced) migrations that would lead to a more compassionate response to recent immigration to Spain, especially in the Spanish translation of the novel. For Riera, knowledge of the past is not conceptualized as an absolute truth, but rather a means of reconciling past transgressions with the present reconfigurations of the Iberian community. Framed as a transactional text, written to pay a debt to her grandmother, the author confesses a fictional family past—it is important to note that Riera's ancestors were colonialists in Cuba, although not exactly in the ways narrated in the novel—and challenges her contemporaries to change their own treatment of immigrants. Penance requires recognition of the porous nature of Catalan (and Spanish) culture, both past and present, rather than confirming it as the product of nations sealed off at their borders. However, there is no suggestion of absolution in her version of postcolonial consciousness, for in her depiction there can be no resolution.

Cap al cel obert (2000, Catalan original; 2001, Spanish translation) is a family story constructed around silence, oblivion, and the fluid contours of identity. The novel is a sequel to *Dins el darrer blau* and completes the family tale of Isabel Tarongi, burned at the stake in Mallorca in 1691 as a crypto-Jew at the end of the first novel. In *Cap al cel obert*, Riera sets Tarongi's descendants in nineteenth-century Cuba, where race is once again an organizing principle of society, but the concept of blood purity now shares power with an understanding of biological race based on phenotype: the logic of Atlantic slavery and the colonial regime. Folletinesque subplots of marriage, epistolary love, and mistaken identities abound in the first chapters of the book, setting up the themes of salvation and redemption at the conclusion. The protagonist, a newly arrived "xueta" from Mallorca, María Fortesa, marries a distant, older relative who shares her secret ethnic past. José Joaquín Fortalesa is a landowner and slave trafficker with vast influence in the Havana circles where conspiracies and secret alliances have the potential to transform the political and racial identity of the island. In spite of her husband's political and economic position, María is vulnerable to the machinations of her adult stepchildren, and consequently her place in the family and Cuban society is never secure. In the final chapters of the novel, María is deemed a Cuban nationalist, found guilty of participating in a separatist plot, and sentenced to death. Racial (anti-Jewish) motives exacerbate her characterization as a scapegoat for the island's political instability, and María is fated to repeat her ancestor's demise in a public execution. However, in preemancipatory fantasy, María escapes and is immortalized in popular legends that become part of family lore.

In *Cap al cel obert*, Riera domesticates the foreign, colonial theme of nineteenth-century slavery and the slave trade by building upon historical truths and allusions to an established literary world. Even though most of the novel takes place in Cuba and Mallorca, its insular tale is clearly a Spanish and in particular, Catalan story, with multiple allusions to the intricate ties between Catalonia and Cuba—including the possibility of a coordinated uprising against their common enemy, the Spanish state (325).

Cuba is the secret, seldom acknowledged, fiber of Catalan identity much as Jewishness is alternately hidden, revealed, forgotten, venerated, and punished by the novels' Creole characters. That is, for all of the novel's superficial exoticism, Riera depicts peninsular society to be profoundly unthinkable without its islands. Traversing morality and politics, past and present, America and Europe, *Cap al cel obert* depicts Spain's place in the Atlantic world as secured through its possessions in the Mediterranean and Caribbean seas whose connections bypass Madrid.

The intraimperial dependencies woven into the plot are articulated by María's adult stepson, Gabriel, who emphasizes that Barcelona's very structure elides any meaningful demarcations between the two provinces, with Cuba all but built into the capital. With a twenty-first-century sensitivity to the semantics of urban topography, Gabriel describes the city's main thoroughfares, which flow to the sea, as veritable ligaments drawing Barcelona and its economic colony together. "Des de la mar, s'arriba a Cuba, d'on prové la riquesa que podrà transformar el futur de la ciutat i de la comarca sencera." (209; One arrives to Cuba by sea, the source of the wealth capable of transforming Barcelona's future and that of the entire region.) But the regions united by economic interests are divided by competing patriotic discourses. That is, while Gabriel's uncle speaks of Catalan nationalism in wholly European terms, overlooking the impact that the Cuban situation had on Catalan ideas on autonomy (see Ucelay-Da Cal), the Creole nephew rejects this concept of Catalonia as a discrete and bounded entity. Gabriel's response to his uncle's seemingly solid and logical recitation of Catalan nationalism challenges the claim of authenticity at the core of a certain type of nationalism. While the Creole playboy Gabriel is anything but a subaltern (and the novel as a whole is decidedly about "White" culture), his perspective will resonate with a twenty-first-century readership aware that, as Frantz Fanon stated, "Europe is literally the creation of the Third World," but often all too eager to forget this complication.

Division, or an attempted demarcation, structures the novel. Riera's story develops centrifugally from the space of domestic, oral storytelling toward the written historical novel to conclude with critical observations on contemporary economic and demographic history. The progression allows for myth to flourish within the flawed historical imagination. The novel's open ending suggests that imperial Spain's interisland debts have yet to be resolved in any objective way, but global histories are ultimately personal. In a final "note" included only in the Spanish translation of the novel, Riera writes, "Con *Por el cielo y más allá* intento pagar una deuda con mi abuela y con la isla de Cuba, a la que tantos mallorquines emigraron hasta bien entrado el siglo XX." (With [this novel] I intend to pay a debt to my grandmother and to the island of Cuba where many Mallorcans emigrated until well into the twentieth century.) By wrapping her message in sentiment and aesthetics of the familial and domestic, built upon the possibly faulty ("quizás un poco trastornada por los años y las penas" [*Cielo*, 449; perhaps a bit upset by years and sorrows]) and decidedly historically inaccurate memory of her great-grandmother, Riera folds the past into the present and balances "truths" with storytelling as a way to approach a senseless past. Memory and "desmemoria" require regular correctives, and the fantasy of literature connects the personal and the documental to the lived present of the reader.

Individual stories of emigration and empire are inextricable from Spain's past and present economic and geopolitical stature: as Rosalía Cornejo Parriego has rightly noted, Riera's novel underscores the fact that Catalonia's participation in the colonial project in Cuba guaranteed its own modernization (8). In her Spanish "note," Riera insists on the role of fiction, in particular, in acknowledging the place of slave labor in the creation of today's wealthy Basque Country and Catalonia. Her argument alludes to Eric Williams's thesis (105) on industrialization's debts to slavery in order to advocate for imaginative writing in the reconceptualization of the role of the past in the present. However, she surpasses other writers' identification of the colonial roots at the heart of the metropolis and inverts traditional Atlantic positions. Within a global system whose constituent elements are in a fundamentally unstable relationship, Riera suggests that present immigrants have the right to make their fortunes in Spain and thus perhaps launch their homelands into the realm of the First World, as contemporary iterations of the migrant *indianos*:

> No hace tanto que fuimos emigrantes y también negreros. La Cataluña "rica i plena" y el industrializado País Vasco, por ejemplo, se levantaron, en gran parte, con capital proveniente de los ingenios esclavistas, y aunque no nos guste, quizá el hecho de reconocerlo nos permitiría ser más generosos y tolerantes con los inmigrantes, con cuantos son diferentes o, simplemente, no piensan lo mismo que nosotros. (452)

> (Not so long ago we were migrants and also slavers. The Catalonia "rica i plena" and the industrialized Basque Country, for example, rose, to a large extent, with capital from the sugar mills worked by slaves, and although we

might not like it, perhaps the act of recognizing it would allow us to be more generous and tolerant with immigrants, with those who are different, or simply, those that do not think like us.)

Thus, in spite of the marginality of the Afro-Cuban characters to the plot of the novel, the final pages recenter Africa within the contemporary Atlantic story. Riera thus closes the Spanish version of her novel by effectively inscribing contemporary immigrants into a transgenerational family tale. As Catalonia and the Basque Country made their wealth through African immigrants' ancestors, Basques and Catalans are called upon to tolerate the pursuit of wealth in the Peninsula undertaken by Black Africans and Latin Americans today. Riera suggests parallels between Spaniards and Africans in a way that recalls Blanco White's description of Spanish suffering during the Napoleonic invasion as experientially instructive in understanding the families broken by the slave trade in Africa.

The novel is important not only for its recasting of the nation-state vis-à-vis the slave trade, but also because Riera humanizes the crime of the slave trade, an aspect of the novel that underscores the stakes of what it means to view the nation in terms of the history of this monstrous trade. The plot and characterization of the novel also explore the nature of human traffic, the crime at the heart of the Atlantic empire. In opposition to the perspectives offered by male (anti)heroes of maritime novels, here we learn about the slave trade through the female protagonist, María Fortesa/Fortalesa. The novel follows her moral evolution as she acclimates to a life of comforts originating in human traffic and among race-based oppressive measures. María's amazement at the luxury and beauty that profits from the slave trade can buy is followed by acquiescence to their charms. "Mai no li haguera passat pel cap que tota aquella riquesa que l'envoltava procedís, en gran part, del negoci de carn humana. . . . Aviat s'adonà també que la inversió en els esclaus constituïa una de les parts més importants del capital dels Fortalesa." (*Cap al cel obert*, 177; It had never crossed her mind that all of the wealth that surrounded her derived, in great part, from the commerce in human flesh. . . . But she quickly ended up accepting that this investment constituted one of the most solid parts of the Fortalesas' holdings.) Her sincere surprise quickly fades, and she becomes a permissive participant in the slave system. María's ethical brutalization is part of colonization. Notably, the desensitization to violence is both state-sponsored and domestic, but moral lassitude is not gendered. Save the sanctified Father Claret, the sensibilities of all Spaniards (including abolitionists and Republicans) are utterly transformed through the experience of the massive benefits and easy luxury of state-sponsored slavery. But the narration of María's realization that beauty is the issue of slavery models an intellectual process for the reader who today both admires the modernist aesthetics or fiscal strength of Barcelona and recognizes the city's debts to the slave system. As British scholar Michael Eaude recently wrote:

> The money made from the sweat of slaves was converted into beautiful houses, parks and chapels. Güell's name became identified with great art, like Maecenas in Ancient Rome or the Medicis in Florence. The money's origins were forgotten, but spare a thought, as you gaze on Gaudí's wonderful buildings, for the Africans who died to create Barcelona's booming tourism industry. (75)

In *Cap al cel obert*, Havana captures European attention: it is the port and domain of the *negreros* and the site of the Spanish empire's open secrets. However, in a gothic subplot, slavery's true horrors are discovered in the countryside. The estate of Morena Clara, owned by the mysterious David Parker/Tomeu Moner, provides the setting for the novel's most provocative depictions of human trafficking and its race and gender-based logic. Morena Clara has neither agriculture nor Black slaves; rather, Parker breeds and raises lily-white bodies for a global sex trade. In an island obsessed with the racial composition of its population and the *blanqueamiento* of the island, Parker's position as "criador de blanques i de blancs, especialitzat a millorar la nostra raça" (190; breeder of White women and White men, specializing in improving our race) hints at the imperial roots of eugenics. But this "*negrero-blanquero*" also signals the lasting consequences of the normalization of slavery.

Race is a constant preoccupation in the novel as landowners attempt to navigate between political allegiances and labor demands. "Whiten and whiten again"—Saco's famous motto and recipe for liberation from Spanish governance—echoes through the plantation owners' closed-door meetings, even as their perceived need for African laborers undermines projects for Cuban independence contingent upon a sizeable white(ned) Creole population (*Cap al cel obert*, 200). Parker takes nineteenth-century imperial policies of slavery as civilization and strategic whitening to extremes: "emblanquinar" is precisely what Parker does at Morena Clara. His careful breeding of a finely tuned White labor force underscores both the role of race in nineteenth-century empire and the way an obsession with Black and mulatta bodies in Cuba fetishized Whiteness in the contemporary European sex trade.

David Parker is a composite of the most monstrous aspects of the Atlantic trade, with strong echoes of Pedro Blanco in his characterization: "Fill bastard d'un noble qui mai no l'havia volgut reconèixer, duia el llinatge de la mare, Moner, i nomia Tomeu. Molt jove s'havia embarcat amb Pedro Blanco, de qui havia après l'ofici de capità corsair." (*Cap al cel obert*, 162; Illegitimate child of a nobleman who refused to recognize him, he used his mother's surname, Moner, and was called Tomeu. While still quite young, he embarked with Pedro Blanco who taught him the profession of corsair.) He supposedly started his career as a Mallorcan corsair, then acquired British citizenship, large holdings in Brazil, and a plantation in Cuba. After making his fortune in Dahomey from the trade in Black African slaves, he turned to producing educated, refined young White women and men for the sex market throughout the world, across the Atlantic and the Pacific.[9]

Much as moral opposition to slavery was often gendered in nineteenth-century sentimental literature, Riera confronts her female characters with the dilemmas of trafficking. Angela Fortalesa, who, as a slave trader's daughter, is fully implicated in Cuban slavocracy, unexpectedly unmasks David Parker and is disconcerted by the naked truth behind the veneer of refinement performed by traffickers (154). Whereas in other Spanish works, such as Baroja's maritime novels, slave traders carry multiple valences, Angela sees David Parker as purely evil, even as he remains aesthetically seductive; although Angela is repelled by the diabolical truth of Parker's trafficking, she is nevertheless tempted to remain in his luxurious domain. "En lloc de sortir de pressa s'entretingué a guardir d'aquella dolça llangor" (157; Instead of hurrying to leave, she took her time enjoying the sweet languor) that the private spaces of Parker's home offered, and she "havia de fer esforços per anar de pressa i mantenir-se ferma en la decisió de marxar de seguida, en lloc de caure en la temptació de deixar-se envair per aquell benestar" (158; had to make an effort to move quickly and remain firm in her decision to leave as soon as she finished dressing and not give in to the temptation of letting herself be filled with the house's pleasures). Angela's loss of innocence echoes that of María Fortesa and structurally reproduces the constant tension between indignation and lassitude that contributed to the dual moralities in the colonies. Indeed, once back in the fold of the racial logic of her father's home, Angela does not question the transatlantic slave trade of Blacks or Cuban slave labor.

Modern concepts of race developed hand in hand with Atlantic slavery but by reracing the trade, Riera defamiliarizes slavery and imagines what Whiteness would mean if it were bred and traded and then introduced into a preexisting gendered market. When Blackness and the stereotypes of subservience associated with it are removed from the equivalence between *negro* and *esclavo*, what remain are trafficking, sexual abuse, and the empty rhetoric of enslavement as a means to civilize the oppressed. Indeed, Parker's slaves are among the most civilized people on the island, given their "educació exquisida, amb coneixements d'idiomes, música, dansa o cant, segons el grau d'interès o de capacitat de cada criatura. Excuso dir-li que totes han estat perfectament nostrades en les arts de l'amor." (154; polished education, with knowledge of languages, music, dancing or singing, according to the degree of interest or ability of each creature. Needless to say, all the women have been perfectly trained in the arts of love.) They are, however, no less desperate for freedom.

Riera's plot is not entirely a theoretical supposition. The nineteenth century witnessed a surge in the trafficking of White women for the global sex trade. Indeed, the international smuggling of women in and out of Spain was invoked to strengthen arguments for the abolition of slavery, and the two trades were seen as nearly coterminous. Rafael María de Labra first founded the Sociedad Abolicionista in 1865 to outlaw Black slavery in the Antilles; he then founded the Sociedad para la Abolición de la Prostitución Legal o Tolerada in 1883 to outlaw what he argued was legal slavery of White women within Spain itself (P. Fernández, 233). Riera nestles the trade in White women within Atlantic slavery for a contemporary readership accustomed to seeing prostitution but desensitized to its place within the history of human trafficking. The comparison between unfree sex workers and race-based colonial slavery is not new, but Riera's attention to the trafficker who facilitates the commerce changes the focus from the commodity to the middleman who negotiates the larger structures of race, gender, and economics behind these trades, whether imperial or not. That is, *Cap al cel obert* illustrates the practices of human trafficking central to nineteenth-century empire in terms that remain firmly entrenched on the streets of major cities and byways of small towns in Spain, where today they are encountered by Spaniards on nearly a daily basis. One of the more troubling realities of contemporary Spain finds the origin of its logic in the *negrero*. Any imperial nostalgia that the novel might initially provoke is stopped short with a contratemporal vision of Spain today as hosting a reincarnation of the worst of its colonial Antillean past.

Indeed, the neoimperialist nostalgia in the service of nationalism that Bakhtiarova identifies in Catalan works from the late twentieth century has largely disappeared in more recent literature. Nearly a decade after the film *Havanera 1820* unmasked the hardworking Catalan *americano* as a ruthless colonialist, Xavi Casino's first novel, *Tren de venganza* (2010), reconsiders the consequences of colonial transgressions for nineteenth-century Barcelona, ponders the paradoxes of modernity, and revels in both the marvels and the crimes of America. Unlike the other works examined here, in *Tren de venganza* there is no immediate family member confessing past crimes; rather, modern Barcelona itself is collectively prompted to come to terms with its own story as a modern industrial city, heir to *negrero* money. The book plots the idea that Catalan industrialization and its cultural modernity were due not simply to ingenuity, but rather part of a set of systemic transformations that took place around the Atlantic. As Peter Hulme has written, "The principal motifs and tropes of . . . European cultural tradition, far from being self-generated, were the product of constant, intricate, but mostly unacknowledged traffic with the non-European world" (cited in Burton, 3).

Set in the rapidly industrializing Catalan capital of 1848, *Tren de venganza* narrates the creation of Spain's first rail line, between Barcelona and Mataró, the hometown of a wealthy *indiano*. Casino imagines a city resistant to the modernization and industrialization promised by *indianos*, who struggle to win over the populace to their economic agenda. The basic facts are indisputable: colonial capital had a documented influence on Catalan industrialization.[10] But in the novel, antiprogress is portrayed, anachronistically, as anti-*negrero*, and the actual complexities of the transatlantic relationship are simplified. Nogués, head of the largest stagecoach company in the region, summarizes the anti-*indiano* position in language that combines nineteenth- and twenty-first-century ideologies: "Quienes como yo hemos trabajado duro para ser alguien en esta ciudad estamos hartos de esos 'americanos' que se fueron siendo unos don nadie y unos muertos de hambre y pretenden darnos lecciones y apoderarse de nuestros negocios con su dinero de negreros." (56; Those of us who have worked hard to be somebody in this city are fed up with these "Americans" who left as a bunch of starving nobodies and now want to teach us a lesson and take over our businesses with their *negrero* money.) Some sectors of the city express unease toward the construction of the railroad because of its English origin and Cuban usage—a veritable invasion of foreign invention and customs. An ideology of isolation, self-reliance, and the liberal faith in a self-made man (and society) is punctuated by sabotage: workers have been harmed and materials damaged, apparently by Catalans resistant to *indiano* innovations. The novel follows the narrator's investigation into the identity of the perpetrator of the assaults on progress. Rubén Cardona is a former police detective expelled from the force in 1843 for various political reasons, including abolitionism (*Tren*, 23) and his participation in the uprising against the "Ayacucho" Espartero (and the imperialism he represented) on December 3, 1842. His blunt observations throughout the novel on Spain's continued active role in the transatlantic slave trade exhibit bitterness toward the hypocritical society in which he lives, even as he, too, profits from the fruits of the trade. Like María Fortesa in *Cap al cel obert*, Casino's characters ultimately bend to the gains proffered by the *negreros*. However, it remains unclear if their initial reluctance is a result of moral rectitude or xenophobia.

The patron of the railroad, Tomás Boada, is an assemblage of stock characterizations of literary *indianos*. Although he is a stand-in for the historical Miquel Biada, Casino's Boada could just as easily represent Joan Güell or any number of analogous *indianos* whose material impact on the daily life of the city is still manifest today. An ardent royalist with a face permanently "tostado por el sol de ultramar" (*Tren*, 7), he associates with other powerful slave-trading *indianos* like Josep Xifré. Boada explains life in the Americas according to the prevailing logic of the first half of the century: "En mis primeros años en América trafiqué con esclavos; era una manera rápida y segura de ganar dinero. Y le diré algo: la vida en América es muy dura. Cuesta salir adelante, crear progreso. Sin esclavos, la economía de las colonias no existiría. Es simple, no habría mano de obra. . . . Por eso es necesario llevar negros de África." (24; In my first years in America I trafficked in slaves; it was a quick and reliable way of earning money. And I will tell you something: life in America is hard. It takes a lot to get ahead, create progress. Without slaves, the economy of the colonies would not exist. It is simple, there would be no labor. . . . That is why it is necessary to take Blacks from Africa.) The detective Cardona nevertheless perceives profound doubts behind this royalist Mason's recitation of nineteenth-century commonplaces and detects his unease over the moral cost of progress: "Estaba claro que en el interior de aquel hombre yacía una contradicción tremenda. Se decía liberal, pero defendía la vulneración de la libertad." (24; It was clear that inside that man there lay a tremendous contradiction. He called himself a liberal, but he defended the infringement of liberty.) Boada, and with him Spain's first railroad, becomes a synecdoche of the contradictions of the second imperial age, when slave labor underwrote Spain's political liberalization.

Damage to the train line derails Boada's simultaneous attempts to create a perpetual monument to himself and perform an act of contrition. Rather than build a charitable institution, the fictional *indiano* explains the modernization of Catalonia as a work of penance for crimes in America, confessing that in America, "hice algunas cosas de las que no me siento demasiado orgulloso. Lo único que me mueve en este momento de mi vida es dejar algo que merezca la pena y por lo que pueda ser recordado." (11; I did some things I do not feel too proud of. The only thing that drives me in this moment of my life is to leave something behind that is worthwhile and for which I can be remembered.) Boada, and the Barcelona that those of his cohort built, carried a heavy weight "que le costaba reconocer y le contradecía consigo mismo" (25; that was difficult to recognize and was at odds with who he was). How can Boada—or Barcelona itself—resolve all of these aspects of its past in its present?

A great deal of the novel is dedicated to exploring the motives, both economic and ideological, behind the attempts to derail the line. Sabotage is the most physical opposition to industrialization and the dehumanization of labor but presupposes the politicization of the working class (otherwise not present in the novel). Ideologically, the "vengeance" against the train in the novel is markedly different from, for example, the historic protests against mechanized looms that were mounted by textile workers in Barcelona in 1855. Principal characters voice their concerns over the relationship between industrializing Barcelona and the dehumanized labor—namely, slavery—that funds the growing city, but the working class does not articulate this worry.

The plot arrives at resolution when Cardona discovers that the motor of revenge was ignited during independence wars in Venezuela, when Masons on opposing sides violated the vows of fraternity and equality. (These wars—as well as the role of Masonic Lodges—all but condemned to oblivion today, shaped Barcelona history and its understanding of its previous relationship with the Americas.)[11] Cardona neutralizes Boada's adversary and memories of colonial crimes disappear with him; Boada's train departs and Catalonia continues on its path to industrial and financial preeminence. However, the novel continues after the crime has been solved and concludes not in Barcelona, but at the "House of Slaves" on the Island of Gorée, a worldwide symbol for the atrocities of human exploitation and a contemporary pilgrimage destination of the African diaspora. Madú,

Boada's onetime slave, uses a legacy from his master to travel here aboard a vessel that we are led to suspect was a slave ship, in order to die a free man in Africa. Whereas Boada had returned to Mataró to make penance for his sins as a slave trader, Madú's return to his port of departure in liberty is, according to Cardona, "su particular venganza contra la esclavitud" (167; his particular revenge against slavery). But there is more to this second denouement than the parallel returns of Boada and Madú: Barcelona is recast as an integral port on the triangular slave route. The novel reconnects Africa and Catalonia even as it dramatizes the process of oblivion of that connection.

The sentimental reunion of the Afro-Cuban with Africa in the dungeon of the "Slave Castle" is narratively ambiguous. A circle is closed, but reconciliation is also exiled. In other words, Casino queries whether there is a place for a memory of the slave trade and contributions of Africans to society in Barcelona. Or should the Afro-Cuban chapter of Catalan history, too, be "returned" to Africa and deposited at the Island of Gorée, in a contemporary version of American repatriation schemes of the nineteenth century? The place of the African slave in Europe in the eighteenth century was as a fashion accessory, a "beast in the boudoir" for women; in the nineteenth century, he became a sign of cultural and economic standing based on American wealth, cast in racial and imperial terms, and was attached to men. But such visibility of origins soon provoked discomfort, an early twentieth-century sentiment that Casino writes back into mid-nineteenth-century Barcelona. Upon Boada's death, the new head of the railroad firm explicitly refuses to keep Francisco/Madú at his side as a useful intelligent manager, retorting, "esto puede que les guste a los *americanos* pero no a mí" (100; maybe the *indianos* like having them around, but I don't). His industrial city has no place for Africans and thus begins to turn its back on the nonautochthonous elements in its colonial past. In the twenty-first century imagining of nineteenth-century Barcelona, the African and the racialized imperial wealth he embodied are written offshore. Casino's novel shows how a willingly forgetful society came to require the meditations on Europe, humanity, and profit offered by someone like Sartre, who wrote in the preface to Fanon's *The Wretched on the Earth*:

> You know well enough that we are exploiters. . . . This was not without excellent results, as witness our palaces, our cathedrals, and our great industrial cities. . . . Crammed with riches, Europe accorded the human status *de jure* to its inhabitants. With us, to be a man is to be an accomplice of colonialism,

> since all of us without exception have profited by colonial exploitation. . . . The European has only been able to become a man through creating slaves and monsters. (25–26)

In a similar way the novel begins to question the firm distinctions among Barcelona, Gorée, Venezuela, and Havana. Casino retells the story not simply of Catalan industrialization, but rather of how ways of telling that story have elided its extranational aspect.

Dinero negro, by Rafael Escolà Tarrida, published in November 2010, is one of the latest of the *negrero* books to appear in Catalonia. It follows the rise of two men, Roque Francisco Llopart and Pelegrí Guasch Galí, in the period between, roughly, the Congress of Vienna (1815) and the Escalera Conspiracy (1844). Llopart is a rich Catalan Creole plantation owner in Cuba who attempts to resolve his conflicting interests in slave trading, material improvements in the lives of his slaves, commerce with the United States, and cultural ties with Catalonia. In contrast, Guasch is a sailor who rose from the lowest of jobs in the Barcelona *drassanes* to the rank of captain in the merchant marines. Both men ultimately embrace abolitionism, but en route, each negotiates numerous contradictory realities of the Spanish empire during the first half of the nineteenth century, in particular, on the high seas. The novel is loosely structured as a bildungsroman, although here society too slowly learns to change its moral position. Stylistically, *Dinero negro* is classic maritime literature, having much in common with Baroja's series, *Mar*. Masterful deployment of technical language, analysis of nautical maps, detailed descriptions of shipbuilding, and dramatic maneuvering on the high seas grant the author significant authority. Transatlantic, Pacific, and Mediterranean trades—both licit and contraband—are linked with the Carlist Wars and disentailment of church lands in the Iberian Peninsula, the Escalera Conspiracy, the poet Plácido, *santería*, railroad construction on both sides of the Atlantic, and the repressive regimes of Captains General in both Catalonia and Cuba. Decidedly global, Escolà Tarrida's novel draws into a single narrative frame events as seemingly disparate as Leopoldo O'Donnell's brutal execution of revolutionary suspects in Matanzas, Miguel Tacón's overt corruption in Havana, Van Halen's bombing of Barcelona, and the 1842 violent repression of the city's *junta revolucionària* (whose elected leaders included prominent *indianos* like Xifré and Güell and future president of the republic, Laureano Figuerola) (see Balmes, 169). In sum, Escolà effectively writes a new fictional imperial history for Spain.

In Escolà's dramatic world characters' survival depends upon the economic ties between the Antilles and Barcelona. *Dinero negro* interrogates the cultural evolution of a society that, paradoxically, embodied European ideals as a consequence of its Caribbean roots and questions how Catalonia, both then and now, might decide when slave profits cease to be *dinero negro* and are instead incorporated into the story of Catalan industrialization. The humble Pelegrí Guasch articulates reformist sentiments among those for whom the press was out of reach. Famous antitrade figures from Catalonia such as Antonio María Claret or José Verdaguer put ideology into practice, but Escolà presents the ethical question of the trade at ground level, where it was embedded in employment decisions of the laboring class of Barcelona: Should one knowingly build or sail a slave ship? The novel brings us back to the recent petitions by the trade unions regarding "labor's" attitudes toward slavery and the Comillas statue. Even as the novel articulates the impossibility of a definitive break between the two nations and assumes the place of nineteenth-century novels that remained unwritten by imagined voices never heard, it ultimately attempts to close the conversation on the Afro-Catalan-Antillean triangle.

Escolà's brief condensation of forty years of transatlantic history into three hundred pages is marred with errors in chronology that suggest the imprecision of memory.[12] However, the author makes no pretense of historical scholarship; his stated objective is to unravel the story of his ancestors (Llopart and Gil—here renamed Bru, significantly, the name of Comillas's wife) and their financial position in Barcelona, from a perspective that is not accusatory, shameful, or defensive.[13] In the novel's afterword, Escolà responds to the interpretive space opened by the unnamed Goytisolo, reflecting, "Nos ha tocado vivir una época en la que todavía algunas personas se avergüenzan de sus antecesores. Creo que es un error. Es sano que nos avergoncemos de algunos hechos u omisiones propios, pero no de lo que cometieron nuestros antepasados. Respecto a ellos, tenemos que saber el qué y el porqué para sacar conclusiones y aprender a mejorar el futuro." (310; We live in a time in which some people are still ashamed of their predecessors. I think it is a mistake. It is healthy to be ashamed of certain of our own deeds or omissions, but not of what our ancestors did. As far as they are concerned, we have to know the "what and why" of their actions in order to draw conclusions and learn how to improve the future.) In spite of the author's claims at objectivity and liberation from a recent culture of contrition, the book clearly aims to absolve the Bru clan from responsibility for a sumptuous life lived at the expense of *bozales* and enslaved Afro-Cubans.

The novel concludes with a description of the construction of the modernist Sant Pau hospital in Barcelona, supposedly the final depository of the Gil family fortunes from Cuban slavery, shipping, and Parisian banking. Escolà suggests that the social benefits that the family's laundered slave money has granted to the population of Barcelona, by means of the hospital, symbolically erase its original sin and thus resolve the problems inherent in *dinero negro*. "El dinero negro fue donado . . . para . . . la construcción de aquella gran obra social: un hospital de Barcelona amplio y moderno." (297; The slave money was donated . . . for . . . the construction of that great social work: a large and modern hospital in Barcelona.) In a flourish of aesthetics and grammar, "negro" money is transformed into a "moderno" hospital. The publisher's marketing "blurb" condenses the hyperbolic optimism regarding absolution implicit in the denouement of the novel: "Gran parte del dinero ganado gracias al trabajo y el sufrimiento de los esclavos negros revertirá en magníficas obras sociales en Barcelona." (The bulk of the money earned through the work and suffering of Black slaves will revert in magnificent social works in Barcelona.)[14] "Gran parte" functions rhetorically here much as it does in Riera's "nota." However, where she opens a connection with a Catalonia "rica i plena," Escolà's link between slave-created wealth and social work is both historically imprecise and a social attempt to offer narrative closure to a tale of Catalan modernity (and *modernisme*) that has otherwise escaped a logical plotline. Escolà grants an absolution to the entire society not by reasoning that slavery civilized the Africans—as his nineteenth-century counterparts would have done—but by claiming that slavery civilized Barcelona and made it a more human place in ways still felt today.

The author's performance of sincerity is yet one more of the multiple literary interpretations of the place of slave money in Barcelona's past and present cultural, economic, and political life. Yet, the family tale of slavery and absolution is somewhat fantastical: Maluquer de Motes notes that although the historical Roc Francesc Llopert initially had trafficked slaves, he soon decided to remake himself and became prestigious as a moneylender in Cuba (109). That is, the Llopert family was part of the *negrero* economy, but not the traffickers of the novel. Likewise, the historical Gil family's direct involvement in the slave trade was minimal. Martín Rodrigo y Alharilla has documented that within Pedro Gil Babot's expansive import/export enterprise, piracy and the slave trade were only occasional occurrences (*La familia Gil*, 16, 26). The novel evidences a desire to confess participation in one of the worst colonial crimes and an emotional investment in a story in which a colonialist sensitivity and the expression of a deep guilt are more important than documentable facts. The elaboration of the *negrero* within one's own family demonstrates the attraction of the monstrous and the appeal of the horror of the slave-trader story to a larger narrative of original sin and redemption within a national framework. Escolà's largely fictional family tale moves the genre of Catalan family slave-trade stories to the historical position of a postimperial recovery of foundational crimes, self-forgiveness, and resolution ahead of other slave-based empires such as France, England, or the Netherlands (not to mention Spain).

Escolà has not had the last word: in March 2013, Jordi Tomàs published *El mar dels traïdors*, another novel that explores the role of Catalan *indianos* in the transatlantic slave trade, but set in the late nineteenth century. The novel presents the fictional diary and correspondence of a young doctor, Antoni, aboard the slave ship *Verge de Montserrat* and his conflicting economic and humanistic concerns over the health and well-being of the enslaved during the Middle Passage. Tomàs places no blame for the former age on contemporary society, although he is unforgiving of the past. Historical novels continue to present the overall facts about modernity and coloniality as if they were new information, but the real dramatic tension originates from the questions of resolution.

The confessional act (even when false) in recent Catalan novels demonstrates a desire for absolution and the consequent forgetting of these crimes, so inconveniently recovered by Goytisolo in *Señas de identidad*, *Coto vedado*, and *Juan sin tierra*. Indeed, in spite of general similarities, a single, national framework for the contemporary retellings of the *indiano* story across Spain is unthinkable, primarily because Asturias, Cantabria, and Catalonia do not have equivalent relationships with the Spanish state. In spite of the differences between, for example, Malleza and Comillas, both are deeply engaged politically and emotionally in the concept of "Spain." In contrast, Catalonia is at a sufficient distance from its historically integrationist economics to reassess its relationship with the nineteenth-century imperial state. Recent novels discussed here bring imperial history "home," even as this transatlantic perspective unsettles traditional definitions of Catalonia as an autonomous and autochthonous space. As observed in 1866, "Cataluña a impulso de los capitales ultramarinos, ha visto moverse sus máquinas, hermosearse sus poblaciones, regarse sus antes áridas llanuras, formarse sobre su azulado cielo esa aureola de fama y de renombre que la coloca a la cabeza del movimiento moderno en España." (Qtd. in Maluquer de Motes, "La burguesia," 112; Catalonia, driven by overseas capital, has seen her machines move, its people beautified, her previously arid plains irrigated, the shaping over its bluish sky of that aureole of fame and renown that places her at the head of the modern movement in Spain.)[15] The debt of the colonizer's culture to Cuba is recovered in light of postcolonialism in these Catalan novels that seek confession specifically in a historiographic mode.

The historical novel itself is particular to this endeavor. When Baroja's maritime novels narrated the process of forgetting in a discursive mode that was already dated and quaint, his narrator underscored, with some irony, the futility of literature's attempts to halt the oblivion produced by the passage of time. In contrast, the Catalan novels discussed here demonstrate a nineteenth-century realist belief in the ability of literature to educate and reshape a reader's understanding of the nation and his or her own place within it.

Conclusion
The Negrero *Resurfaces*

Until fairly recently the "odious trade" and its legacies have been conspicuously absent from public memory in the European countries that pioneered the Atlantic slave trade. In the past few decades, around the Atlantic rim, the African diaspora has instigated the reconsideration of the transatlantic slave trade and its legacies, leading to incipient acknowledgments in Europe. For example, pressed by Caribbean immigrants, the Dutch government has expressed its "remorse" over the transatlantic slave trade, while the French National Assembly declared the Atlantic slave trade a crime against humanity in 1998 following a march through Paris by forty thousand descendants of slaves.[1] In 2006 President Jacques Chirac named Édouard Glissant to establish a new cultural center devoted to the history of the trade. These actions prompted similar questions in Spain. In 2007, Mariano Barón Crespo, former president of the European Parliament, urged Spain to recognize its role in the slave trade, on the occasion of the slave trade's two-hundredth anniversary:

> El presidente Chirac, en nombre de Francia, y el *premier* Tony Blair, en nombre de Gran Bretaña, han pedido solemnemente perdón en nombre de la memoria histórica. En España no se ha producido todavía una reflexión crítica de fondo sobre este genocidio, a pesar del papel central que jugó nuestro país tanto en el establecimiento de la esclavitud ultramarina como en la resistencia a acabar con ella.
>
> (President Chirac, on behalf of France, and Prime Minister Tony Blair, on behalf of Great Britain, have solemnly asked for forgiveness in the name of historical memory. In Spain there has not yet been an in-depth critical reflection about this genocide, in spite of the central role our country played both in the establishment of slavery overseas and in the resistance to end it.)

On May 6, 2009, the Spanish Parliament considered a proposal by the right-wing Partido Popular to change the names of all streets in Spain that bear the names of known slave traders. The bill was ultimately withdrawn,[2] over concerns that such a move might make some (White) citizens uncomfortable.[3] Subsequently, in response to demands by the Black, African, and African descendent communities in the Peninsula, the Spanish Parliament held an unprecedented discussion of the colonial slave trade and the contributions of Black Europeans, past and present, to Spanish society. On February 17, 2010, a bipartisan commission acknowledged the role of Spain in the transatlantic slave trade as a crime against humanity and recognized the importance of the Black community in Spain. Aside from this and a few recent statements from within the halls of government, however, the traces of the slaving past in peninsular life have been, by and large, swept aside in a variation on the *pacto de silencio* that has set the tone for contemporary Spain's relationship to the past.

In conjunction with official recognition of the slave trade, Bristol, Amsterdam, and various regions in France have reinscribed their local stories into the global history of the nineteenth-century trade, highlighting locations that were implicated in human traffic and demonstrating how this "Caribbean" history is in fact deeply embedded in Continental life. As Saidiya Hartman wrote a decade ago, roots tourists (who voyage primarily to Africa) "could just as easily travel to Portugal or visit the Vatican" (Hartman, 764), and the requisite tourist infrastructure has begun to exist at various historical nodes in the trafficking network in Europe. In contrast, the *rutas del indiano* in Asturias and Cantabria attend to a different demographic and commemorate those who crossed the Atlantic at least twice, rather than those who were forced through the Middle Passage. The Dutch scholar of global memories of the slave trade, Gert Oostinde, has argued that countries like Spain do not officially remember the slave trade primarily because it has little to gain by engaging in an emotionally uncomfortable and potentially economically costly dialogue (58). In other words, until very recently there has been little incentive to restore the slave trade to public memory. Precisely because Spain lost the Caribbean colonies, it has not needed to take them into account, in the way that, for example, France has.[4] Nor could Spain hope to celebrate a centenary or bicentenary of beneficent abolition as Britain has done. In these ways and others, Spain's relationship to history (and historiography) differs markedly from that of its European neighbors.

As Josep Fradera has noted, Spanish intellectual life in the twentieth century developed without dialogue with its former colonies and within an "aggressive Spanish patriotic offensive" that sealed it off from challenges to the glorification of medieval Christian Spain and the Conquest of the Americas as the foundation of Spanish greatness (Schmidt-Nowara, "After 'Spain,'" 160). Ruth MacKay affirms that "the Franco era was not only repressive; it was an incubator for intellectual mediocrity" (199), and the general public's attitude toward the past, not to mention its framing narratives, was distorted by an inability to exercise critical skepticism (199–206). Today history is open for reinterpretation, as the *negrero* is again a focal point in debates over Spain's past and present place in the Atlantic world and its claims (cultural, economic, and political) over Africa and the Americas. In the nineteenth century Blanco White and Galdós wrote in the spaces connecting politics and literature; I intend here to connect the nineteenth-century efforts of Blanco White and Galdós with reinvigorated and updated journalistic and artistic works of recent years. The visual artist Iván Larra Plaza deflects realist expectations in a discursive mode that does not explicitly retell the story of the past. Across his collections, Larra Plaza draws past and present together and depicts the same *negrero* mentality that had so unsettled Galdós during the Restoration, underscoring its pervasiveness in the market mentality in Spain during its most recent economic boom. The actual nineteenth-century *negreros* have disappeared, but their geopolitical and financial lessons continue to inform the global capitalism in which Spanish neoimperialism reappeared in the late twentieth and early twentieth-first centuries.

In Madrid—a city no less implicated in nineteenth-century slavocracy than Barcelona, but generally more reluctant to adopt a postcolonial perspective—the past has begun to be interpreted through the contemporary effects of globalization and the millennial wave of African immigrants to Spain. In particular, the engravings and xylographs of Iván Larra Plaza since 2000 have interrogated the spaces and processes of human cargos from the slave age to the present in visual terms, transforming historiographic silences into absences. Throughout his oeuvre, Larra Plaza renders visible a cultural ignorance of racialized global economics, with Spain decidedly decentered in the relationships among Black/White/Brown and metropolis/colony. In earlier collections such as "Spanish Black Fashion Project" or "Niger_Nigra_Nigris," Black bodies are constantly in motion, projected, consumed, and fractured. However, in Larra Plaza's most incisive work, human cargo is only imagined. In "Cross-Docking" and

"Partial Loss," the artist explores the creation of value through transit and the erasure of the human. "Cross-Docking," a collection of sixteen xylographs (prints from wood engravings), depicts various transportation structures (carts, lifts, cargo holds, ships) employed in the creation of profit through "handling," a process whereby the chaos of organized movement erases a product's origins in labor and materials. The stark black-and-white engravings and xylographs of black ink on wood are devoid of any trace of the human. All items or people that enter these structures are reclassified according to a matrix of volume, weight, and value. Larra thus inverts, in visual language, one of the fundamental questions of liberalism, in Harriet Beecher Stowe's terms: At what point does a (hu) man become a thing?

Several xylographs in the series are entitled "continente"—a word that, in Spanish, lies in a semantic field among containers (such as shipping boxes), conventional geographic delineations born of European global expansion (such as "Africa" and "Europe"), and containment. The word alludes to the migration of people who depart one land mass in shipping containers, traverse the seas—where identities and values are open for renegotiation—and arrive in another land, where they often encounter attempts to "contain" the sexual, economic, or cultural impact of their migrant bodies. Across the larger collection, Larra tells a story wherein the apparatus of twenty-first-century shipping inherits the practices of the vessels of the most infamous trade of the nineteenth century. Alongside these images of carts, cranks, and pulleys are three containers explicitly constructed for human cargo: *Barco negrero I* (2000) (see Figure 7); *Barco negrero II* (2003) (see Figure 8); and *Migración* (2003) (see Figure 9). *Barco negrero VIII* (2003) complements the series. The three *barco negrero* pieces might seem to represent relics of a distant past, but the inclusion of the fourth ship in *Migración* within the "Cross-Docking" framework communicates continuity in shipping and containment practices that connect the age of the transatlantic slave trade with contemporary migrations of laborers and the importation of the products of outsourced labor into Europe.

Barco negrero I and its variation, *Barco negrero VIII* (not reproduced here), represent a desiccated hull of a slave ship, suspended in time and place. Stripped of mast, decks, and planks, the beached slave ship is laid out like the vertebrae of a decapitated and dissected sentient animal, or according to the destruction of slave ships ordered in the nineteenth-century Anglo-Spanish treaties. The partially dismantled ship is sliced into eight

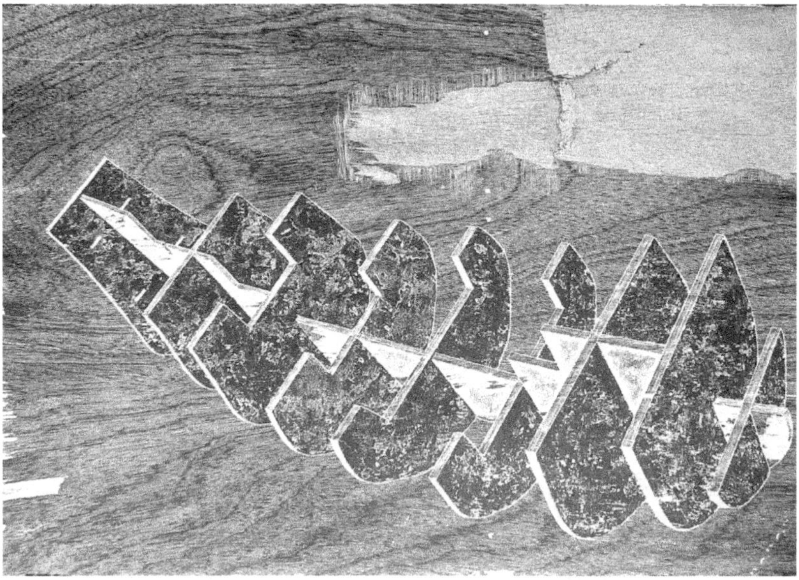

Figure 7. Iván Larra Plaza, *Barco negrero I* (2000, wood engraving, 70cm × 100cm). © 2013 Artists Rights Society (ARS), New York / VEGAP, Madrid. Reprinted with permission.

Figure 8. Iván Larra Plaza, *Barco negrero II* (2003, xylograph, 70cm × 100cm). © 2013 Artists Rights Society (ARS), New York / VEGAP, Madrid. Reprinted with permission.

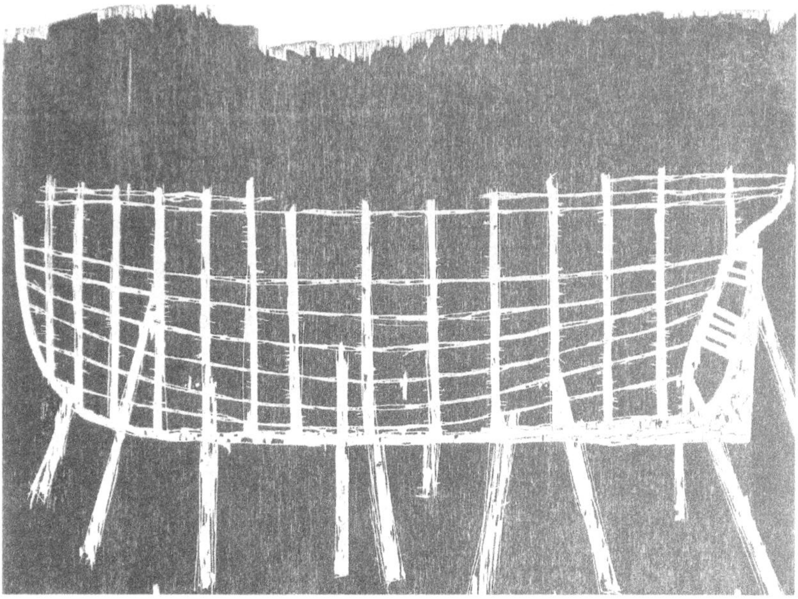

Figure 9. Iván Larra Plaza, *Migración* (2003, xylograph, 76cm × 110cm). © 2013 Artists Rights Society (ARS), New York / VEGAP, Madrid. Reprinted with permission.

discrete segments. One might suppose that it has simply fallen into disuse as times have changed, but *Barco negrero II* and *Migración* depict slave ships still under construction, ready to replace it. The complementary image, *Migración*, depicts a cutaway of the hull of a ship broadside, still at the shipyard, as yet out of water. The skeleton view of the ship's stem, keel, and future masts are in place although the beams have yet to be installed. This ship in gestation visually recalls the grids and links undergirding other shipping structures in "Cross-Dockings," such as the cage in *Contenedor III*, and it serves as a tie between the slave ships and other modern vehicles for cargo in transit. Larra's abandoned ships invite us to consider which aspects of a former global power's history can be silenced and "contained" within a current understanding of the place of violence in global capitalism.

Whereas *Barco negrero* and *Barco negrero VIII* depict a dismembered ship from an unusual angle, *Barco negrero II* represents a beautiful sinuous vessel under construction. Still in the building dock and not yet completely hewn from the wood plank from which the xylograph emerges, this nascent *barco negrero* has no slaves aboard. Whether a ship can be called a *negrero* without slaves present was a crucial question in the nineteenth century and remains so today. Larra's work invites us to examine the entrails of the *barco negrero*: Is there something essential about a slave ship, or a slaver that destines one for crime? Whereas Blanco White argued in essentialist romantic terms that all *negreros* are "cruel e insensible por naturaleza" (cruel and insensitive by nature), while none is "compasivo y humano por naturaleza" (*Bosquexo*, 58–59; compassionate and humane by nature), the equipment clause of the Anglo-Spanish treaty of 1835 attempted to define slave ships by materials that evidenced intent (such as chains, shackles, or extra food stores) while recognizing the near impossibility of determining which ship or sailor might be a slaver. In contrast, *Barco negrero*, *Barco negrero II*, and *Barco negrero VIII* are slavers simply because Larra Plaza has designated them as such.

Thematically, Larra Plaza's four ships are variations on the foundational abolitionist engraving of the modern era: "Description of a Slave Ship," published in 1789 by the London-based Society for Effecting the Abolition of the Slave Trade (see Figure 10). Marcus Wood considers the iconic depiction of the *Brookes* to be "the most famous, widely produced and widely adapted image representing slave conditions on the middle passage ever made" (17). He credits the massive success of the eighteenth-century print to the "conjunction of technical engraving with the depiction of a mass of black human flesh . . . a superb semiotic shock tactic" (27). Highly effective at representing the dehumanized packaging of African slaves as cargo, allotted infrahuman spaces, the engraving nonetheless reified the dehumanization by inviting viewers to see the Africans as, precisely, subjugated chattel.

The "Description" is, in fact, a series of cross-sections, overviews, and front and side views of the *Brookes*'s slave decks that slice and peel away the veneers of legal cargo limits in order to reveal the inhuman conditions at the heart of the slave system. It was created within an abolitionist propaganda project that prioritized a consideration of slaves as utterly helpless victims (Wood, 18) and, in turn, elicited a particular type of guilt on the part of Europeans in which the terrorized and vulnerable slaves, nearly childlike, suffered under their paternalistic gaze. The slave ship *Brookes* also entered early Spanish abolitionism as a visual preface to Blanco White's *Bosquexo* (that is, he inserted it after the title page). Although Blanco White called upon its pathos in his text, his arguments carved a different path, for he depicted African families as analogous to Spanish families, broken, as both were, by foreign invaders.

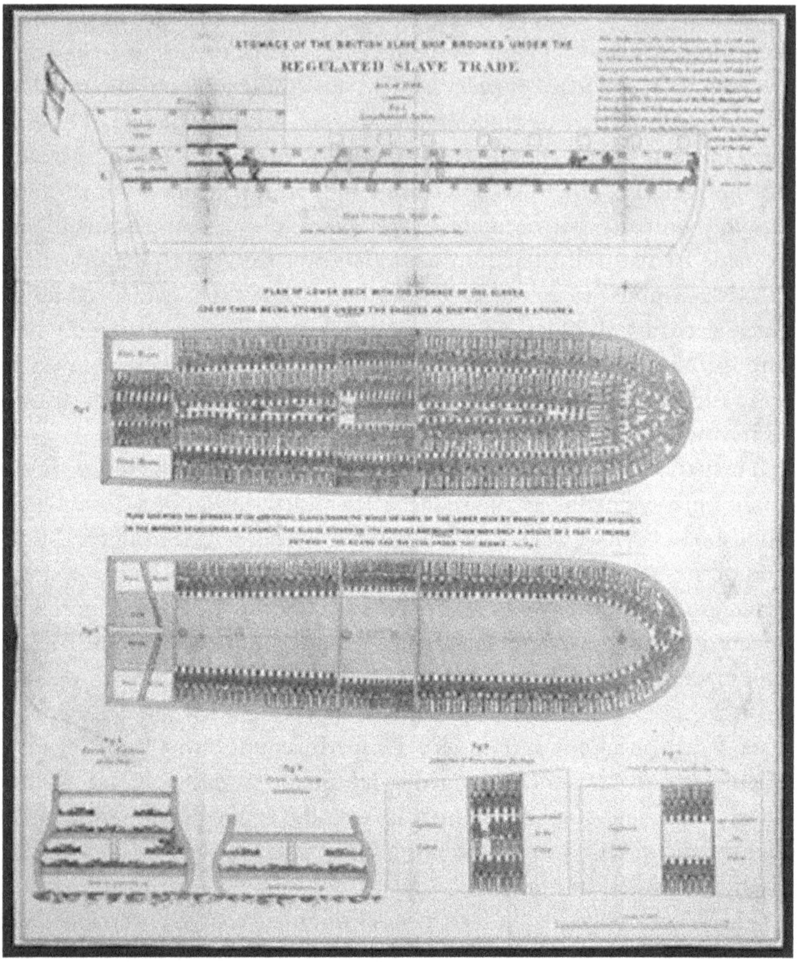

Figure 10. Stowage of the British slave ship *Brookes* under the Regulated Slave Trade Act of 1788. "An American Time Capsule: Three Centuries of Broadsides and Other Printed Ephemera," Piece 1 of 1. Library of Congress, n. p., n. d.

Iván Larra Plaza engages this icon of the Middle Passage but departs from both the original and Blanco White's engagement with it. He quotes the "Description" in *Barco negrero II* in his precise representations of the techniques in naval architecture and focus on the beauty of form, yet he refuses a representation of the enslaved as passive victims. Indeed, he does not represent them at all. Larra Plaza thus breaks with traditional abolitionist and humanitarian art, in which an implied European observer contemplates African tragedies. Here, the artist undermines this privileged voyeuristic position: now, we (European or not) see nothing. A cultivated inability to see the enslaved as subjects has given way to images in which we cannot see them at all and they risk disappearing from contemporary public consciousness altogether. Encompassing both past and present, Larra Plaza first captures historical gazes by representing a slave ship ready for cargo: this—not people, even as dehumanized, passive victims—is what nineteenth-century Spain saw. The human absence is significant: in Sibylle Fischer's analysis of nineteenth-century Caribbean antislavery literature, the salient characteristic is representation of those involved in the slave trade as "barbaric monsters," while what remained absent was "anonymity of a human being whose existence within the world of the master was reduced to the calculations of capital spent, economic output, longevity, reproductive possibilities and replacement costs" (17). Both Baroja's ironic depiction of profit-hungry Embil and Larra Plaza's empty slave ships are so effective precisely because they underscore the dehumanization and financial calculations at the heart of the system.

As the historical reluctance to see (and cease) the trade in human terms continues, "Cross-Docking" and "Partial Loss" present the materials of a Spain still involved in similar crimes. If ignorance is a "willed blindness" (Wood, 7), Larra Plaza represents contemporary Spain's refusal to see both its past and present role in trafficking human chattel in his empty slave ships. For Marcus Rediker, writing about public awareness of the slave trade and its legacy in contemporary race and class in the Anglo-American world, "the slaver is a ghost ship sailing on the edges of modern consciousness" (13). *Migración* and *Barco negrero II* caution viewers not to be fooled by the beached and scrapped slavers of the past: their replacements have already emerged.

Contemporary media has made explicit and widely diffused the ideas that Iván Larra Plaza suggests in his haunting images. Early in 2000, a brief note on the front page of the Sunday Supplement to *El País* described a new immigration phenomenon:

> Una marea de inmigrantes subsaharianos está llegando a Canarias desde las costas de Africa de la mano de una nueva clase de negreros: mafias con base en Marruecos, Mauritania, Cabo Verde y Guinea, en las que participan patrones de yate europeos, cobran verdaderas fortunas para los recursos de unos hombres y mujeres que huyen de la miseria extrema. En lo que va de año, más de mil han sido interceptados por los servicios de vigilancia, tres veces más que en el mismo período de 1999. Los que consiguen entrar son contratados como peones por constructores faltos de mano de obra o deben recurrir a la prostitución o al tráfico de drogas para subsistir. La mayoría proceden [*sic*] de tierras tan lejanas como Nigeria, Sierra Leona y Ghana. ("Los nuevos negreros," 1)

> (A tide of sub-Saharan immigrants is arriving in the Canary Islands from the Coast of Africa via the workings of a new class of *negreros*: mafias based in Morocco, Mauritania, Cape Verde, and Guinea who, in collaboration with European yacht owners, charge veritable fortunes given the resources of men and women fleeing extreme poverty. Thus far this year, border guards have intercepted more than one thousand immigrants, three times more than during the same period in 1999. Those who do succeed in entering are hired to work as day laborers by construction firms short on labor, or they turn to prostitution or drug dealing in order to survive. The majority comes from places as far away as Nigeria, Sierra Leone, and Ghana.)

In the first decade of the twenty-first century, *negreros* have reappeared, once again testing insular and peninsular Spain's economic, cultural, and racial policies by transporting sub-Saharans. The contemporary media of all ideological stripes (from the monarchist *ABC* to the progressive *Público*) consistently employ this term when discussing the new immigration, although the analysis that follows is based on articles published in *El País* (a centrist-leftist newspaper with the largest circulation in Spain). The nearly half-million daily readers of *El País* learn of past and present crimes simultaneously, for the articles emphasize a direct genealogy based on the *negreros*' profiteering and illegal debarkation of African men and women on Spanish national (or imperial) territory. The equivalent term "*négrier*" has not reappeared in France, nor are traffickers to England called "slave traders." This is an exclusively Spanish lexical phenomenon. As the Spanish paper explains, today's *negreros* work for international mafias "que han tomado el relevo de los negreros del siglo diecinueve" (Barbulo, "El buque," 24; who have taken over from the nineteenth-century slavers). Human trafficking has, of course, never disappeared, but *El País* implies that a very specific crime has been revived and, in doing so, engages horrors from the past to illustrate the gravity of the present. Indeed, these phantom ships are a microcosm of global crime little changed from Baroja's *buques negreros*. The *Kolossoka*, for example, was built in Lithuania, bore a Ukrainian flag, and was captured in Tenerife (Barbulo, "Cazado el negrero," 64). The story of its Senegalese and Russian owners recalls that of Antonio López: the 22 million peseta profit (about USD$110,000 in 2000) earned on an initial delivery of forty-five Senegalese men and women to Gran Canaria, served as an investment for subsequent emigration enterprises.

The former director of Spain's Centro Nacional de Inteligencia (within the Defense Ministry), Alberto Saiz, affirmed in 2007 that there were many boats off the coast of West Africa "de dudosa utilidad, pero no les puede llamar negreros, a menos que transporten personas" ("El CNI," 15; of questionable purpose, but that can't be called *negreros*, unless they transport people). The problem of how to arrest suspected slave ships devoid of human cargo is not new—British diplomats dispatched this difficulty with the equipment clause—but Saiz's observation is wholly modern. Nineteenth-century contraband *negreros* transported humans who, by definition, had been robbed of legal personhood, so, in fact, no slave ships then transported recognized "*personas*." (Indeed, the *Dictionary of the Real Academia Española* of both 1868 and 1989 defined a *negrero* as "personas ó cosas dedicadas á la trata de negros" [persons or things dedicated to the trade in *negros*]; the only persons on a nineteenth-century slave ship were the traders, while the enslaved were quite simply *negros*.) Nevertheless, exactly where the personhood of those transported today is to be found—either while aboard or on Spanish soil—is unclear.

In some corners, racially, economically, and culturally motivated fears have generated a discourse of "invasion" that shows little compassion for the immigrants; yet others present a more stereoscopic view, analyzing African-Spanish relations from several centuries simultaneously and contextualizing them within Spain's long tradition of forced oceanic transportation. Observations such as "la historia universal de la infamia está llena de barcos" (Atencia; the global history of infamy is full of boats) punctuate reports on current events that renegotiate the colonial past and revive imperialist structures in the transnational present. In a short but emotionally charged essay, journalist José Manuel Atencia outlines a long chain of African and Spanish suffering in the Atlantic, in which the present case is but the latest link. Following a well-trod path, he names Fray Bartolomé de las Casas as the source of an Atlantic commerce "del que participaban todos los grandes estados europeos y que abastecía con los denominados barcos negreros, en uno de los episodios mas vergonzantes de la historia de la humanidad" (in which all of the great European states participated and was stocked by the so-called *barcos negreros*, in one of the most shameful episodes of the history of humankind). He compares the sale of fifteen million Africans during the sixteenth to nineteenth centuries to the situations of both present-day immigrants and Spanish Civil War exiles cast adrift aboard the *Stanbrook* in 1939 in their common loss of state and personhood (Atencia). For a population still processing the atrocities of the twentieth century, the Franco era is one frame for understanding preceding and subsequent human tragedies.

Although the reintroduction of the terminology of *negrero* ships has resurfaced knowledge of the legal and illegal Atlantic trade of Spain's past, there are crucial differences between past and present. Between August 2006 and May 2007, seventeen thousand Africans entered Spain via *negreros*, while seven thousand were intercepted; in all of 2006, thirty-one thousand Africans entered the Canary Islands: these numbers are certainly comparable to the busiest years of the nineteenth-century trade.[5] But we must remember that these numbers were matched by migrations in the opposite direction; for example, thirty thousand Spaniards relocated to French Algeria in 1914 (Schubert, 45). Moreover, today's traffic is simultaneously intra-African, Atlantic, and global, as the colonial comes "home" to the metropolis and Spanish history folds back upon itself. A more apt comparison might be with the first sub-Saharan African slaves brought to Portugal in a systematic way in the 1440s by Prince Henry the Navigator, even though the transportation of African people to the Americas, and their subsequent conversion into colonial slaves who created the prosperity of modern Europe, is an effectively disturbing image. In addition, much as nineteenth-century *negreros* transported Chinese contract laborers (in a scheme promoted by Julián Zulueta, who was known as "*el principe de los negreros*") and Mexican Yucatecans to the Antilles, today's human cargo includes men and women from Pakistan and elsewhere beyond the Atlantic rim who may or may not be seen phenotypically as conventionally "Black" but are cast together as "*negros*" in terms of racialized labor, geopolitical imbalances of power, and juridical nonpersonhood.

The roles of the various actors in the oceanic transportation of laborers have changed substantially and, as much as the present is framed by the *negrero* past, the opposite is also true. For example, today the European Union (Frontex) assists Spain in patrolling and identifying potential *negrero* ships disguised as fishing vessels off the coasts of Senegal and Mauritania ("El CNI," 15). However, when the transatlantic trade was outlawed nearly two centuries ago, the British navy patrolled the African coast, interfering with the interests of Hispano-Antilleans and the Spanish crown: a simple analogy between past and present *negreros* could very easily whitewash the culpability of the nineteenth-century Spanish state and business interests. Indeed, in their coverage of contemporary immigration, the conservative *ABC* also uses the term "negreros" but emphasizes Spain's commitment to halting illegal traffic. For example, the cover story on February 13, 2007, on the repatriation of several hundred men attempting to enter Spain via a *buque negrero* reported a version of facts that emphasized the cost of the operation to the Spanish government. For, "después de que Madrid 'donara' [original emphasis] más de 600.000 euros, fletara varios aviones con policías y afrontase el coste de la repatriación, los casi 400 inmigrantes que se hacinaba en el carguero 'Marine 1' desembarcaron ayer en el puerto maruitano de Nadibú" (*ABC*, "Final de la pesadilla," 1; after Madrid "donated" more than six hundred thousand euros, chartered several police airplanes and faced the cost of repatriation, the nearly four hundred immigrants that were stacked in the cargo ship 'Marine 1' disembarked yesterday in the Mauritanian port of Nouadhibou). In this perspective, Madrid is the victim of global migrations (at the price of 1,500 euros per immigrant) while the men aboard are nothing more than cargo and an economic burden for the central government of Spain. Here *negreros* are the state's antagonist—in contrast to their historic allegiance with Isabelline and Restoration governments.

The resurrection of the *negrero* raises important questions about the way modernity and its most cherished precepts are reinterpreted by Spaniards in the context of current immigration trends. Is a twenty-first-century *buque negrero* actually a slave ship? There is no other term in nineteenth-century Spanish to describe such a vessel. If so, what is the agency of current immigrants contracted with *negreros*, who often pay exorbitant fees (20,000 French francs in 2001, about USD$3,000) for a one-way voyage from Dakar to Gran Canaria in infrahuman conditions? Who owns their personhood? Their labor? *Negrero* captains still make sizeable profits, but now the *negro* pays to traverse a portion of the Atlantic. While it may no longer be acceptable to say that one might "*travailler comme un nègre*" in France, as the former head of the House of Guerlain recently discovered,[6] the relationship among race, legal and illegal labor, and immigration remains unclear, and traditional linguistic frameworks fail both to fully reflect present realities and to challenge Eurocentric perspectives on human trafficking. *Negreros* from the sixteenth to nineteenth centuries nominally engaged with discourses of civilization and evangelization to justify their trade; contemporary immigration entrepreneurs capitalize on Africans' misery and their dreams of a European El Dorado. It is unlikely that African migrants searching for a better economic life see themselves as reincarnations of the enslaved nineteenth-century laborers sent to Cuba, in spite of the comparisons made by Spanish newspapers of their voyages with those of the past.

Perhaps the current immigration disaster created by the new *negreros* will succeed in causing all of Western Europe, but especially Spain, to consider the contemporary implications of its former imperial policies. *Negreros* are a point of entry into the racial politics, exploitation, and trafficking carried out in modern Spain during the nineteenth century under imperialist capitalism, in the name of "the nation," and tolerated by a liberal regime. The new immigration from both the former colonies and Africa in contemporary Iberian societies may well take the debate over the place of the *negrero*, his policies, and the nation he assisted in creating into uncharted waters. The voices of these new immigrants may question the stability of "Spain" as a meaningful concept in ways as yet unseen in the Peninsula.

Today's *negreros* are not the immediate heirs of the nineteenth century, but they are certainly villains of a similar story. Blanco White's distress at the decimation of Africa by Europeans who saw not culture, civilization, and families but merely cheap labor in the neighboring continent is sadly not outdated as *monstruos por oficio* returned to Africa nearly two centuries later to reinstate once-familiar practices, reconstruct temporary housing along the same coastal inlets, and renegotiate the price of personhood. The economic divide between the Global North and South has carved new Atlantic routes even as it has revived ancient trades.

Reference Matter

Notes

Introduction

1. For the earlier numbers, see Curtin, 25.

2. See Sala-Molins, *Le Code Noir* and *L'Afrique aux Amériques*.

3. "Tratado o acto de venta de una escuadra que cedió al rey de España el emperador de Rusia: firmado en Madrid el 11 de agosto de 1817." Article 6 states: "Su Majestad católica cede a su Majestad imperial la suma de cuatrocientas mil libras esterlinas, concedida a España por la Inglaterra a título de indemnización por la abolición del tráfico de negros; y para poder disponer de esta cantidad, su Majestad católica se obliga para con su Majestad imperial a concluir tan luego como fuere posible, el convenio propuesto por la Inglaterra y a insistir al ratificarle en que se entreguen doscientas mil libras esterlinas al hacerse el canje de las ratificaciones; y en cuanto al pago de las otras doscientas mil libras esterlinas se haga pasados que sean seis meses, término señalado para la conclusion del tráfico de negros" (Archivo Histórico Nacional, *Tratados*, 796).

4. Víctor Sánchez Sánchez has since addressed some of these issues specifically regarding music in "La habanera."

5. See the anonymous pamphlet *Verdaderas causas en que don Juan Álvarez y Mendizabal ha fundado su opinion para que en la isla de Cuba no rija la constitución política de la monarquía española*. The accusation came at the expulsion of the Ultramar representatives, a move that destroyed any pretense of equality within the Spanish nation for the Antilles.

6. See Ruth Hill's *Hierarchy, Commerce, and Fraud in Bourbon Spanish America* for an untangling of the terms of identity in eighteenth-century Americas, especially 7–11, for a discussion of the terms "empire," "colony," and "monarchy."

7. See David Murray's *Odious Commerce*, especially chapter 2, for a discussion of the relationship among Spain, slavers, and England in the years before Spain signed the 1817 treaty. In *Negreros catalanes y gaditanos en la trata cubana, 1827–1833*, Enrique Sosa Rodríguez examines the early years of the illegal trade.

8. While in Cuba, O'Donnell chose corruption over morality, as the fictive O'Donnell and Teresa Villaescusa both will do in the novel. Not only did he collect exorbitant bribes from each slave smuggled into Cuba, but also he was central to the Escalera slave rebellion suppression. As Duvon Corbitt reported, he repressed the slave uprisings of 1843 in Matanzas province "so vigorously that his name has become almost synonymous with cruelty in the minds of the later generations of Cubans" (538). O'Donnell was also responsible for the execution of Gabriel de la Concepción Valdés, the poet "Plácido." He was supported by Julián Zulueta and other wealthy White planters and *negreros* who cited his "infatigable celo y actividad el feliz resultado de salvarnos del abismo y de haber conservado pa. V.M. esta joya preciosa de su Corona" (qtd. in Corbitt, 540).

9. See Martí-López for a discussion of the importance of imported works and the domestication of foreign literature in the nineteenth century.

10. See Vila Vilar, 24; Cortés López, 29.

11. Blanco White was certainly not Spain's first abolitionist. Isidoro Antillón y Marzo's "Disertación sobre el origen de la esclavitud" broke open a conversation regarding how to free slaves, end the slave trade, and maintain the prosperity of Spanish colonies. André Pons underscores the difference between Isidoro Antillón and Blanco White's much more pragmatic arguments that did not criticize Antillean planters or their treatment of Africans of Afro-Hispanics already enslaved in the Americas. "Para valorar la originalidad de su postura, recordemos que en su *Disertación sobre el origen de la esclavitud de los Negros*, Antillón, conocido como uno de los primeros antiesclavistas de siglo, amigo de Blanco White, pedía la abolición de la esclavitud, como lo indica el título, posponiendo la cuestión de la trata, y aducía 'los derechos imprescriptibles del hombre' en la línea de la Revolución Francesa; su actitud, aunque atrevida y generosa, era algo utópica pues hacía poco caso de las realidades o de las mentalidades" (Pons, "Blanco White abolicionista II," 30).

12. Also published in Portuguese by Ellerton and Henderson in London in 1821 as *Bosquejo sobre o commercio em escravos; e reflexões sobre este trafico considerado moral, politica e cristãmente* (available in Goldsmiths' Kress library of economic literature database).

13. See Number VI (September 30, 1810) for a clarification of his position, in Goytisolo, *Blanco White*, 119–22). All quotes come from Juan Goytisolo, *Blanco White, El Español y la independencia de Hispanoamérica*.

14. Chapter 4, Article 22, effectively shut down any possibility of citizenship to Spanish or Spanish American men of African heritage. They could earn it only in cases of service to the nation or the demonstration of talent and conduct, so long as they were of legitimate birth, married, legally resident in Spanish lands, and exercised a profession using their own capital. "Art. 22. A los españoles que por cualquier línea son habidos y reputados por originarios del Africa, les queda abierta la puerta de la virtud y del merecimiento para ser

ciudadanos: en su consecuencia las Cortes concederán carta de ciudadano a los que hicieren servicios calificados a la Patria, o a los que se distingan por su talento, aplicación y conducta, con la condición de que sean hijos de legítimo matrimonio de padres ingenuos; de que estén casados con mujer ingenua, y avecindados en los dominios de las Españas, y de que ejerzan alguna profesión, oficio o industria útil con un capital propio" (Archivo Histórico Nacional, Constitución [1812]).

15. See Tamar Herzog, *Defining Nations*, 156–62, for a discussion of the debates that led to the inclusion of Spanish Creoles and Amerindians as Spanish citizens and the exclusion of Spaniards of African descent. Herzog's analysis is that "the inclusion of Spaniards and Indians and the exclusion of Africans was a compromise adopted to avoid a direct confrontation between European and American Spaniards, as well as between conservatives and liberals. It ensured that the bulk of Spanish citizens would still reside within the confines of the Old World" (162).

16. See Hannaford, *Race*, chapter 5, for a discussion of the link between monstrosity and race.

17. See Enriqueta Vila Vilar and Luisa Vila Vilar's excellent *Los abolicionistas españoles, siglo XIX*, for such an anthology that also includes the publications of the Spanish Abolitionist Society.

Chapter 1: Negro Tomás and the Trader

An earlier version of this chapter was published as "Representing the Slave Trader: *Haley* and the Slave Ship; or Spain's *Uncle Tom's Cabin*," *PMLA* 120, no. 3 (2005): 768–82.

1. See "Libros prohibidos por su santidad" which decreed on September 6, 1852: "Maria la spagnuola: storia contemporanea de madrid, composta da Venceslao Ayguals de Izco: prima versione italiana di F. Giuntini. *Decr. Eodem. prohib. Decr. Diei 6 septembris 1852. Italus interpres laudailiter se subjecit et opus reprobavit.*" For the prohibition of the entire trilogy in Cuba, see the reprinted letter from José Llector Castroverde to Demetrio Ayguals de Izco (brother and agent for Wenceslao), October 25, 1855. Reprinted in Ayguals de Izco, *Palacio*, 777.

2. An example of another Spanish play about redeemed slave traders is the *zarzuela* entitled *El capitán negrero* by Antonio García Gutiérrez and Emilio Arrieta in 1865.

3. I am grateful to Professor Josep M. Fradera for sending me a copy of this rare book.

4. For a masterful overview of the plot of the first two novels, see Sebold, 32–35.

5. "En las manifestaciones antiesclavistas de Ayguals, posteriores a 1851, aparece siempre el recuerdo de *Uncle Tom's Cabin*: Quizá haya en esas manifestaciones alguna realidad más candente en el pensamiento de un demócrata cuyas obras se expanden por Cuba" (Benítez, 113).

6. In comparison, a megahit such as Eugène Sue's *El judío errante* (Le juif

errant) had eleven editions in Spain between 1845 and 1871 (Palau y Dulcet, 286) and was published simultaneously in 1844 by three Madrid firms as well as one in both Cádiz and Barcelona (Martí-López, 37). Dumas's *El Conde de Montecristo* had four different translations in 1846 (Montesinos, 186).

7. Botrel's exact numbers for 1860: of a national population of 15,673,481, 24 percent, or 3,835,770 were literate. David Ringrose has pointed out the scarcity of reliable census data for the nineteenth century but has estimated the national population in 1857 at 15,454,000 (*Transportation*, 133) and that of Madrid in 1853 at 231,866 (*Madrid*, 27).

8. *La nación* (Madrid), October 12, 1852, 1.

9. Representative of this double-speak is the following notice from *La Época*, which reports that officially all is well in Cuba, yet hints at some unspeakable news item: "Por la via de los Estados-Unidos se han recibido noticias interesantes de la isla de Cuba, á que daremos publicidad luego que sean aprobadas por la censura. Seguia reinando la tranquilidad en aquellas leales provincias. La *Gaceta* nada dice hoy acerca de estas noticias." ("Boletín," October 24, 1852, 2; Via the United States there has been interesting news about Cuba, which we will publish as soon as it is approved by the censors. Tranquility reigns in those loyal provinces. The *Gaceta* [official publication of the government] has said nothing about this news today.) *La nación* reported that the *Diario de Cataluña* had published news from New York: "Hemos recibido la *Crónica de Nueva Yorck* [*sic*] del 24 del pasado y 2 de los corrientes. Por el estracto que damos á continuacion verán nuestros lectores qué concepto merecen á la sensata prensa Americana los rumores de una nueva intentona de los patrioteros contra nuestras Antillas. Por lo demás reina la mas completa paz en aquellas hermosas posesiones." News about possible filibuster invasions only appeared as commentary on American newspapers (from the *Mirror de Nueva-York*): "No dudamos que nuestro gobierno vigilará y tomará eficaces medidas para impedir que otra partida de muchachos engañados perezcan en otra espedicion de merodeo contra Cuba" (*La nación*, October 24, 1852, 1).

10. "En la choza del Tio Tomás," *La nación*, January 29, 1853, 2.

11. Manuscript note on title page of 1852 copy at Biblioteca Nacional in Madrid: "Presentado para los efectos de la ley de propiedad literaria en 17 de En de 1853" (Stowe, "La choza de Tom").

12. Hartzenbush links him to six different commercial ventures at midcentury, including *El iris* (1841), *El universo* (1852–53), and *Album pintoresco* (1852–53).

13. Alda Blanco, too, has analyzed the racial theories of late nineteenth-century Spain (several decades after the translation of *Uncle Tom's Cabin* was published) that dominated conversations at the Congreso Geográfico Hispano-Portugués-Americano in 1892. These described the Spanish race, itself a product of racial mixing, as particularly able to assimilate other races with which comes into contact (*Cultura y conciencia*, 122).

14. Leading this discussion were several members of the Del Monte literary

circle, mentioned above. See Luis's *Literary Bondage* for a discussion of the reformist position promoted by these writers.

15. The Spanish Dramatic Company "Luque" performed yet another adaptation of *Cabana* [sic] *de Tom o la esclavitud de los negros* at the Teatro California/California Theater in July 1874. Advertisement in *Figaro*, July 18, 1874; see Kanellos, 204.

16. Note that Bengalí conjugates all verbs in the imperative tense of the plural second person, the form that slaves, en masse, would have heard from their overseers, a linguistic characteristic that underscores his lack of individual identity.

17. See also *El mensajero*, "Teatros" column from April 5, 1853, for a similar assessment of the drama.

18. Similarly, *El Enano* of Madrid avoided any commentary on the content of the play, noting simply that "aunque de escaso mérito literario, déjó satisfechos á los espectadores por la buena ejecucion y por las decoraciones, que son de muy buen efecto" (April 5, 1853, 2).

19. Confirmed in *El Clamor Público*, "Crónica de teatros," on March 29, 1853, 4.

20. The queen mother's involvement in corruption at all levels, especially as regards the illegal slave trade has been amply documented. Bahamonde and Cayuela in *Hacer las Américas* studied the *duques*' Sociedad Comercial based on the deeds filed in the Archivo Histórico de Protocolos notariales de Madrid, no. 25,888. Also see Pérez de la Riva; La Verdad.

Chapter 2: The Colony in the Capital

1. See Maluquer de Motes; Fradera; and Schmidt-Nowara's *Empire and Antislavery*.

2. Caudet argues that *indianos* allow Galdós to push the limits of naturalism and the concept of "molde" (introduction to *El amigo Manso*, 99).

3. Sinnigen has identified a general disdain toward the colonies in Galdós, manifested, in part, in consistently condescending language casting Cuba as a feminine entity to be dominated by imperial and masculine reason (116). Of course, these gendered metaphors were widespread in the nineteenth century, and his general disdain notwithstanding, Galdós does question the validity of Spain's imperial logic.

4. Larra had noted the shifting terms of representations of power in the national arena during romanticism. His review of Dumas's *Anthony* comments on the move from the father/daughter struggle to that of matrimony (Kirkpatrick, 52–53). Galdós takes a similar model to its transatlantic limits half a century later. What Larra identifies as a class allegory becomes, in *El amigo Manso*, a contemplation of the potential limits to the nation.

5. Stephen Jacobson has written regarding the Union Liberal government in 1858 and its lasting legacy in nineteenth-century politics: "The rise of O'Donnell begs the question of whether Spain was governing the empire or the empire was

governing it. It is probable that Cuban plantation owners influenced metropolitan politics to a greater extent than any colonial lobby in any other European country at the time" (79).

6. See Schmidt-Nowara, *La España ultramarina*, 191–214, for a detailed analysis of the political force of this patriotic discourse.

7. Domingo Acebrón reviews the criticisms toward the Republicans in the Spanish Parliament during the war. For example, Senator Eduardo Benot chastised them for cowering in fear of the "empresarios de carne negra" (61).

8. See "Mujeres nacidas en las Antillas." The women refer to the condition of Afro-Hispanic slaves in the Antilles as "la mal llamada esclavitud," arguing through a convoluted moral logic that slavery, as it is understood in Europe, doesn't actually exist in the colonies.

9. The *voluntarios* not only opposed the abolition of slavery in Cuba, but plotted military action to ensure it. Domingo Acebrón cites the affirmation by "Ramón Herrera, Marqués de la Mortera [*sic*; she must mean Ramón Herrera y Gutiérrez, 3rd Conde de la Mortera] y jefe del 5° batallón de Voluntarios, de la pretensión de organizar una expedición de 5000 Voluntarios hacia Puerto Rico y obligar al General Primo de Rivera, a abandonar el país e instalar un gobierno dirigido por los negreros" (Domingo Acebrón, 80).

10. See chapters 5, 6, and 7 of *Mala hierba. La lucha por la vida II.*

11. Domestic violence entered the Spanish penal code a century later with the "LO 3/1989 de 21 de junio" and Article 425 of the Penal Code.

12. Historical White Creole women did agitate, of course, for independence. They included, for example, Emilia Casanova de Villaverde, who founded the Liga de las Hijas de Cuba in New York City in 1869. Women of all races fought in the Ten Years' War in Cuba: Mercedes de Varona and Mariana Grajales Cuello are just two of the better known of many such women who fought on the side of independence. I don't mean to discount their role in transatlantic negotiations, but rather I wish to point out that women's role in rebellion and political agitation did not become part of the gendered dynamics of empire—an omission that Galdós addresses as problematic for Spain. For a study of the place of gender in Cuban independence, see Prados-Torreira.

13. Ido del Sagrario appears in a total of eight novels and *episodios*, including *Tormento*, *Fortunata y Jacinta*, and *El doctor Centeno*. See Shoemaker.

14. John Sinnigen has also suggested Said's model for examining references to the Cuba, Mexico, and the Philippines in various novels in terms of the colonies' contribution to national culture (116).

15. Letter to *Clarín* dated May 5, 1885. Letters published by Dionisio Gamallo Fierro in *La voz de Asturias*, August 17 and 27, 1978.

16. The Marquis de Fúcar and his daughter, Pepa, have a central role in the earlier novel *La familia de León Roch* where his scandalous wealth is morally repulsive, but not so explicitly tied to the slave trade. The Marquise of San Salomó

describes him thus: "El Marqués de Fúcar, ese que los periódicos llamaban antes *el tratante en blancos* y ahora le llaman *egregio* porque se ha enriquecido adoquinando calles, haciendo ferrocarriles de muñecas, envenenando a España con su tabaco, que dicen es la hoja seca de los paseos, y, por último, prestando dinero al Tesoro durante la Guerra, al doscientos por ciento; un buen apunte, un gran señor de ahora, un dije del siglo, un noble haitiano, un engendro del parlamentarismo y de *contratismo* (Galdós, *La familia de León Roch*, 440). One can't help but wonder how much Galdós borrowed from the storied lives of Antonio López and Juan Manzano in this composite of imperial vices. Fúcar's even more despicable son-in-law (and friend of José María Manso), Federico Cimarra, accuses Fúcar of "trata a los españoles como a negros comprados o a blancos vendibles."

17. He is followed briefly by an unnamed man from Málaga and the Marqués de Flandes.

18. "Botín" is the Spanish term for "booty" resulting from the sack of a city.

19. Although this novel takes place several years after the end of the Cuban war, it is highly realistic in its depiction of anxieties over colonial banking schemes. Quiroz has uncovered that Antonio Cánovas del Castillo and his brother were involved in Cuban fiscal reforms that sparked wide criticisms of official favoritism toward the government contractors and debt-holders in a debate that lasted into the 1880s (101). See also García Mariño, qtd. in Quiroz, 101n140.

20. Representative of this position is *La cuestión de Cuba en 1884*.

21. Isidora Rufete, too, took money from Sánchez Botín to pay the debts of her lover, Joaquín Pez, who had none of José María's scruples in accepting it. In this universe of recurring characters, José María's apprehensions further damage Joaquín's character.

22. In "The Unfinished Anagnorisis," Eamonn Rodgers focuses on José María's reliability as a narrator: "simultaneously reliable and unreliable about the same things" (131). Rodgers explores how José María's moral perspectives change after his stroke—not simply because the final section is written by Ido del Sagrario (131). Rodgers has analyzed a moral anagnorisis of José María grounded in the deep irony that all of society assumes that he and Camila have had an affair when, in fact, her moral rectitude distracted him from his finances (133–34). Moreover, José María is forced to accept that he, not fate, is responsible for his choices. The ensuing stroke places him in the bestial position that he had envisioned for Constantino (137) but allows him to understand love and forgiveness beyond the bounds of conventional society. However, Rodgers finds José María's moral outrage and Eloísa's prostitution to pay his debts to be a marker of the incompleteness of his anagnorisis (139). I argue that rather than incomplete, the anagnorisis is multifaceted. José María is disgusted by Eloísa's traffic with Botín, as much for her role in the transaction as his own, and the horror of finding Botín—unspeakably discomforting from the first—as his savior. These transgressions do not occur in isolation.

Chapter 3: Baroja's Atlantic, Beyond Slavery

1. *El laberinto de las sirenas* narrates the adventures of an older Shanti Andía but takes place almost entirely in Italy and has but minor mention of the slave trade.

2. The crowns of Spain and England signed treaties in 1817 and 1835. The second added that ships outfitted for slaves, even if none were found aboard, were to be declared illegal slave ships.

3. Although the focus of this chapter is the Atlantic routes, Baroja's global maritime system illustrates the interconnectedness of the transatlantic routes (Antilles to Spain) with those to India, the Philippines, Africa, and China. The story of the slave trade, for example, is part of a larger history of human traffic encompassing both Africans and the trade in coolies, and Baroja's characters develop through their actions in various waterways (Cape of Good Hope, Bay of Biscay, South China Sea). The novels anticipate the important observations by Brad Epps regarding the risks of pushing the Pacific and African dimensions of the modern empire out of the frame, by privileging a strictly American-European dyad. See Epps, "Al sur y al este."

4. Although, as Luis Fernández Cifuentes has written, the cartographic character of the Generation of '98 is more complex than literary history has charted out for it.

5. The loss of the bulk of the empire at the independence of the American republics appears in the background of all three novels. For example, Ignacio Embil's father dies while serving in the Spanish navy in Peru (*Pilotos*, 77).

6. Of course, neither Baroja nor I suggest that Basque sailors were singlehandedly responsible for the nineteenth-century slave trade. Historians have documented the massive participation of American slave ships (see Murray), and within the *Mar* novels, Baroja's slavers include men of numerous European nations and both African and European heritage. However, the series' focus is the fading history of Basque sailors—in the slave trade and other commercial ventures in the Atlantic and Pacific Oceans.

7. For example, Ursula Lamb's research demonstrates that since the sixteenth century, there was concern over the number of foreigners aboard Spanish ships. As Peter Linebaugh and Marcus Rediker have written regarding the eighteenth century, the banding together of criminals ("banditti of all nations") across national, racial, and cultural lines was alarming to imperial governments (164). In this context, Baroja's emphasis on the survival of Basque maritime communities is somewhat unusual.

8. The absence of Basque from Martín Fernández Navarrete's 1831 multilingual *Diccionario*, a manual of sorts for facilitating communication at sea, is significant.

9. Juan de Aguirre pilots a slave ship that transports Africans to Brazil; the slavers did not favor one empire over another.

10. In spite of a rejection of English claims to humanitarianism in these novels, they are not anti-English. The criticisms are focused on the hypocrisy related to empire. For example, Embil remarks that "lo que hacían los ingleses constituía una trata hipócrita, oficial y disimulada" (*Pilotos*, 195). Embil also describes barbarous treatment of Blacks by the English in Jamaica (*Pilotos*, 227–28). Indeed, Alberich has argued that Baroja greatly admired English literature and that his concept of the action novel was inspired by English adventure novels (103).

11. While exiled from Spain by Fernando VII, in England the influential Spanish cartographer and cosmographer Felipe Bauzá collaborated with Alexander von Humboldt and Francis Beaufort. In a letter from May 22, 1829, Bauzá notes the transition between Spanish (*altura*) models of navigation and cartography and English reliance on multiple chronometers. "I must laugh . . . about the idea that they [the English] now have to fix every point on the globe with many chronometers, coming and going; it is not a bad idea, but it will not bring the exact result which they seek; Astronomical observation of some points with the spaces between them timed by chronometers coming and going, I believe to have an advantage over chronometric measurement by itself" (see Lamb, XVI–327, XVI–355n5; trans. by Lamb).

12. "Diario": "s.m. *Pil* Cuaderno de historia de toda la navegacion, incluso la cuenta por menor de los rumbos, distancias &c., en la misma forma que se practica en el de bitacora. V. *Cuaderno*. Todo oficial de Guerra, guardiamarina y piloto está por ordenanza obligado á llevar este diario, que presenta en el departamento á su arribo, si asi lo exigen sus superiores" (Fernández Navarrete, 223).

13. The detailed description of the Atlantic trade in *Pilotos* has its counterpoint in the attention to the Pacific coolie trade in part 6 of *Estrella*.

14. "Es lamentable que Embil hable más de sí mismo, y de su vida, y de sus proyectos, un poco vulgares, que de los planes y empresas llevados a cabo por su extraño camarada" (*Pilotos*, 75).

15. The English official who captures Embil multiple times attempting to cross the Atlantic with slaves refers to Embil's miserable fame with this expression.

16. Haydée Rivera also regards the slave ship as a microcosm of contemporary society, but she analyzes it as a criticism of flaws such as "la falsificación del ser humano" (131).

17. Schurz related that during his first interview with the Spanish minister of foreign affairs, Saturnino Calderón Collantes "seriously" and "sincerely" declared the "universally known fact about which there could be no reasonable dispute, that Spain was not only the most civilized, but also the most powerful country in Europe" (254).

18. Chimista's attitude of "sour grapes" toward the former American colonies is so blatantly conservative that it is risible. Because the republics are not available for him to exploit through corruption or even nominally licit means, he dis-

misses them entirely. The imperial family, to this "hero," is based on oppression. "'Esas repúblicas hispanoamericanas no marchan. Son catorce o quince hijas sosas que ha tenido España más allá del mar, que la han aniquilado y que no le van a dar ningún lustre.' Chimista iba a Filipinas a pasar una corta temporada, como representante de una sociedad formada para explotar la riqueza de aquel archipiélago" (*Estrella*, 151).

19. For example, see works by Sebastián Arbó, Emilio González López, and José Corrales Egea.

20. Domingo Yndurain is representative of this line of criticism that dismisses any ethical agenda in the novels: "Para Baroja la literatura ha perdido toda finalidad trascendente. Para él se trata sólo de pasar un buen rato" (360). Mary Lee Bretz reviews the various critical positions on Baroja's ideology. Among those who find him devoid of depth are Torrente Ballester and Max Aub with García Vicente and John Reid dissenting.

Chapter 4: Postimperial Detours and Retours

1. The routes are, from west to east: Castropol to Boal, Navia to Otur, Luarca to Cudillero, Somao to La Ferrería, Riberas de Pravia to Grado, Noreña to Cangas de Onís, Villaviciosa to Ribadesella, Pría to Llanes, and La Arquera to Alevia (Braña, 8–9).

2. A word about Spanish geography is in order. Although this chapter focuses on Asturias and Cantabria, the *indiano* phenomenon is not exclusive to those regions: Canary Islanders, Galicians, Basques, and Catalans were all immersed in the nineteenth-century migration to the Americas. The celebrated romantic dramatists José Zorrilla and Antonio García Gutiérrez both spent significant time in Mexico and Cuba, respectively. Many of the leading families of the nineteenth-century Catalan bourgeoisie were founded on Cuban fortunes drawing on the slave trade and the sugar economy. These included Joan Güell, Vidal Quadras, Josep Amell, Josep Canela, Josep Taltavull, Franisco Gumá, the Samà clan, and Josep Xifré (Rodrigo y Alharilla, "Con un pie," 360).

3. At various moments, massive colonization schemes were launched to populate strategic lands, such as Louisiana and Florida (Martínez Shaw, 236).

4. See articles in *La Joven Asturias*, May 14, 1865; *El Faro Asturiano*, May 7, 1856; and *El eco de Avilés*, January 20–27, 1867. All reproduced by Ojeda and San Miguel.

5. The state paid the passage, living expenses for one year, and "la exención de tributos" (qtd. in Ojeda and San Miguel, 20).

6. See Conlon, for a discussion of the *indiano* as literary character in a wide range of Spanish authors.

7. Pedro de Vargas sees the brother's new title as the icing on the cake for the newlyweds. "Para que todo les salga bien a estos enamorados esposos, resulta ahora, según cartas de la Habana, que el hermano de Pepita, cuyas tunanterías

recelábamos que afrentasen a la familia, casi o sin casi va a honrarla y a encumbrarla haciéndose personaje. En tanto tiempo como hacía que no sabíamos de él, ha aprovechado bien las coyunturas, y le ha soplado la suerte. Ha tenido nuevo empleo en las aduanas, ha comerciado luego en negros, ha quebrado después, que viene a ser para ciertos hombres de negocios como una buena poda para los árboles, la cual hace que retoñen con más brío, y hoy está tan boyante, que tiene resuelto ingresar en la primera aristocracia, titulando de marqués o de duque. Pepita se asusta y se escandaliza de esta improvisada fortuna, pero yo le digo que no sea tonta: si su hermano es y había de ser de todos modos un pillete, ¿no es mejor que lo sea con buena estrella?" (Valera, 349).

8. An especially large and exquisite example is the Parc Samà in Cambrils on the Catalan coast, with a variety of palms, chestnuts, and other plants from throughout the Americas.

9. See Mejías-López, especially page 18, for a discussion of Clarín's anxiety over Spanish American literary modernism.

10. As Tortella and Comín have written regarding the first half of the nineteenth century, the government, too, continued to rely on American money rather than cultivate new financial practices (181). Specifically, a necessary overhaul of the tax system—crucial to preventing royal bankruptcy and modernizing the banking system—was postponed for decades (until the Mon-Santillán reforms of 1845); as a result, this retained belief in the utility of traditional reliance on American wealth. "There can be no doubt that this traditional dependence on resources from America led finance ministers into a series of bad habits" (Tortella and Comín, 162).

11. Financial documentation is nonexistent. Unlike in, for example, California, there are no laws in Spain requiring banks or insurance companies to inform on the sources of wealth earned through slavery. See California's Slavery Era Insurance Registry; Law SB2119 requires all insurers operating in California to report their profits (or those of their predecessor companies) stemming from slavery or the slave trade.

12. "No todos los que fueron a América hicieron fortuna, pero sí muchos. Y todos los que la hicieron, eso sí, regresaron a su tierra con ella" ("Cantabria, tierra de indianos").

13. To give but one example: Cuban wealth funded the commercialization of Castilian wheat that was then sold to the fiercely protected markets of the Antilles. José Samà y Mota (of the Samà clan) and Carlos Sierra founded C Sierra y Cía in Santander in 1858 for this trade (Rodrigo y Alharilla, "Con un pie," 383).

14. See also Moreno Fraginals and Ely.

15. "J'appelle négrier, non-seulement le capitaine de navire qui vole, achète, enchaîne, encaque et vend des hommes noirs ou sang-mêlés, qui même les jette à la mer pour faire disparaître le corps de délit, mais encore tout individu qui, par une coopération directe ou indirecte, est complice de ces crimes. Ainsi, la

dénomination de négriers comprend les armateurs, affréteurs, actionnaires, commanditaires, assureurs, colon-planteurs, gérans, capitaines, contre-maîtres, et jusqu'au dernier des matelots, participant à ce trafic honteux" (Gregoire, 1).

16. Accessed as a handout from the Hotel Villa La Argentina where the original article was pasted into a new document without bibliographical information (and an incorrect date) with the title "La fundación Bellavista de los hermanos García Fernández, en Tucumán. Una historia ejemplar del esfuerzo español en América" [1954] (José Evaristo Casariego).

17. For example, consider the relationship between American money and the growth of the Spanish banking system, as studied by Rafael Anes.

18. Personal interview at Comillas Tourist Office, November 3, 2010.

19. See Martín Rodrigo y Alharilla, "El banco hispano-colonial y Cuba 1876–1898," where the historian untangles the business and political connections that founded this bank, whose primary purpose was to finance colonial wars.

20. For example during the First Republic, Overseas (Ultramar) Minister José Cristóbal Sorní decreed liberty for ten thousand slaves that did not appear in the official slave census, invoking the law of July 4, 1870 (Piqueras, 205).

21. Miguel Morayta, *Historia general de España* Madrid 1886–96, T. XIII, pp. 1131–33, cited Espada Burgos, 286n33.

22. "Cantabria, tierra de indianos," gestures toward a recognition of the nature colonial enterprises when speculating on why the *indianos* were so generous with their hometowns and entertains the idea that perhaps they were attempting to obtain a divine pardon "después de haber ganado el dinero en condiciones muy adversas—en ocasiones incluso con esclavos"; however, the unnamed author doesn't really explain who suffered adverse situations. The assertion thus is simultaneously negated.

23. US Congress House and Military Government of Cuba (1898–1902). *Annual Reports of the War Department for the Fiscal Year ended June 30, 1900. Report of the Lieutenant-General Commanding the Army*, in seven parts, pts. 2, 57, 101, and 102.

24. The region deftly promotes various distinct, but complementary cultures and equally emphasizes its *vaqueira* cattle-ranging and *indiano* heritages.

25. The two itineraries for Malleza can be accessed on the municipal website: http://www.ayto-salas.es/portal_localweb/RecursosWeb/DOCUMENTOS/2/0_295_1.pdf, and http://www.aytosalas.es/portal_localweb/p_20_contenedor1.jsp?seccion=s_fdes_d1_v1.jsp&codbusqueda=78&language=es&codResi=2&codMenuPN=91&codMenuSN=142&codMenuTN=147&codMenu=153&level=1.

The itinerary for *La ruta de los indianos* throughout the region is also available from the municipality: http://www.ayto-salas.es/portal_localweb/p_20_contenedor1.jsp?seccion=s_fdes_d1_v1.jsp&codbusqueda=81&language=es&codResi=2&codMenuPN=91&codMenuSN=142&codMenuTN=148&codMenu=156&level=1.

26. See Cervantes-Rodríguez, 255, for a discussion of the newspaper.

27. This concurs with academic explanations as well. See Ojeda and San Miguel.

28. See Cervantes-Rodríguez, 24, for an overview of transnational interpretations of immigration.

29. See http://www.facc.info/Contenido.aspx?Id=197&mn=2 for the voting records in Asturias broken down by region. Accessed January 7, 2011.

Chapter 5: Family Ties and Narrative Confessions in Catalonia

1. See *ABC*, "Barcelona cambia."

2. For example, a blogger for *El Diario Montanés* with the provocative *nom de blog* "Elmarques" responded that "El catalanismo cateto quiere borrar la huella de Antonio López."

3. Similar petitions were submitted by many groups including the Junta del Comercio y la industria de Málaga (Malaga Chamber of Commerce and Industry); Proprietors, Businessmen of Noya (Coruña); Ynstituto agrícola Catalan de San Ysidro (Catalan Agricultural Institute of Saint Isidro); Colegio de Abogados de Málaga (Bar Association of Málaga); Centro Monárquico liberal de Villanueva y Geltrú (Liberal Monarchical Center of Villanueva y Geltrú), the villages of Cazalla in the outskirts of Seville and Ampuero in Santander; and the Centro Hispano-ultramarino de Cádiz. See Archivo Histórico Nacional, Ultramar, leg. 3554, exp. 3, "Exposiciones contra las reformas en las Antillas."

4. Nearly thirty years ago, Josep Maria Fradera demonstrated the massive participation of Catalans in the nineteenth-century slave trade. See Fradera, "La participació" and *Catalunya i Ultramar*; and more recently, Rodrigo y Alharilla, "Con un pie."

5. Bakhtiarova focuses her analysis on the miniseries *Havanera 1820* (1993) by Antoni Verdaguer, the novels *En el mar de les Antilles* (1998) by Manel Alonso i Catalá, and *Habanera: El encuentro con un oculto pasado antillano* (1999) by Ángeles Dalmau.

6. Barcelona, December 5, 1872, AHN leg. 3554, exp. 3, n. 7. Güell appears on the tenth page of signatures, Agustín Goytisolo on the fifty-third, and Antonio Goytisolo on the sixty-ninth.

7. See Domínguez Búrdalo, for a study of the shifting significance of Cuba across Goytisolo's oeuvre.

8. My thanks to Carmen Sanjuán-Pastor for her insightful questions on these points.

9. Tomeu Moner's partner and ersatz sister Dorothy Parker (whose homonymity with the twentieth-century American poet is simply unfortunate) traffics the young merchandise around the globe to "serralls d'Orient, bordells luxosíssims de París, freqüentats per prínceps, datxes russes propietat dels tzars" (Riera, 155; Eastern seraglios, exquisite brothels in Paris, frequented by princes, Russian dachas, owned by the czars).

10. American money from sugar plantations bought contraband machines from England to bring the steam age to Barcelona. See Fradera, *Industria i mercat*; Gascon i Soler.

11. For a recent study of the Masons in the Antilles, see Arroyo.

12. For example, Capitán General Leopoldo O'Donnell is described as arriving in 1843 "cargado de títulos y condecoraciones como el de Grande de España, Duque de Tetuán" (Escolà Tarrida, 246). Both of these were granted after the 1860 Battle of Tetuán, long after his departure from Cuba.

13. *Dinero negro* was published within weeks of the study of the Serra-Gil family by the historian Martín Rodrigo y Alharilla.

14. See http://www.editorialjuventud.es/3820.html.

15. "Las Antillas," I, no. 1 (December 10, 1866), qtd. in Maluquer de Motes, 112.

Conclusion

1. See www.cm98.fr.

2. "Relativa al reconocimiento de la comunidad negra española. Presentada por el grupo parlamentario Popular en el congreso" (número de expediente 161/000944; *Boletín oficial de las Cortes Generales. Congreso de los diputados*, IX Legislatura, Serie D: General, 26 de febrero de 2010, num. 343; available at www.congreso.es).

3. A second resolution was approved at the same time. "Sobre memoria de la esclavitud, reconocimiento y apoyo a la comunidad negra, africana y de afrodescendientes en España. Presentada por el Grupo Parlamentario Socialista" (número de expediente 161/001273, *Boletín oficial de las Cortes Generales. Congreso de los diputados*, IX Legislatura, Serie D: General, 26 de febrero de 2010, num. 343; available at www.congreso.es).

4. See Reinhardt, for a study of Martiniquais demands for corrections to French history.

5. On these figures, see slavevoyages.org.

6. A summary of the response to Jean-Paul Guerlain's comments on France 2 on October 15, 2010—boycotts, demonstrations, and Internet responses—can be found at http://www.lexpress.fr/styles/mode-beaute/beaute/jean-paul-guerlain-fache-en-parlant-des-negres_928689.html.

Bibliography

"12 de enero de 1853." *El Heraldo* (Madrid). January 12, 1853, 1.

ABC. "Barcelona cambia la avenida Marqués de Comillas por Ferrer i Guàrdia." April 4, 2010. http://www.abc.es/20100414/catalunya-catalunya/barcelona-cambia-avenida-marques-20100414.html. Accessed January 20, 2014.

———. "Final de la pesadilla en el barco negrero." February 13, 2007. http://hemeroteca.abc.es/nav/Navigate.exe.hemeroteca/madrid/abc/2007/02/13/001.html. Accessed November 30, 2010.

Aguado, Laura. "Un palacio indiano en Cantabria." LaRazón.es. March 13, 2009. http://www.larazon.es/noticia/un-palacio-indiano-en-cantabria. *Accessed January 28, 2014.*

Al Son del Indiano. "Historia de Malleza." Single-sheet flyer, 2005.

Alas, Leopoldo. *La Regenta*. Ed. Gonzalo Sobejano, vol. 2, no. 110. Madrid: Castalia, 1981.

———. *La Regenta*. Trans. John Rutherford. London: Penguin, 1984.

Alberich, José. *Los ingleses y otros temas de Pío Baroja*. Madrid: Alfaguara, 1966.

Alcalá Galiano, Dionisio. *Cuba en 1858*. Madrid: Imprenta Beltrán y Viñas, 1859.

Aldecoa, Ignacio. "*Las inquietudes de Shanti Andía*." In *Baroja y su mundo*, vol. 1, 157–61. Madrid: Arión, 1962.

Almeida, Joselyn. "Blanco White and the Making of Anglo-Hispanic Romanticism." *European Romantic Review* 17, no. 4 (2006): 437–56.

Alonso Álvarez, Luis. "Comercio exterior y formación de capital financiero: El tráfico de negros hispano-cubano 1821–68." *Anuario de Estudios Americanos* 51, no. 2 (1994): 75–92.

Amores, Juan Bosco. *Cuba y España, 1868–1898: El final de un sueño*. Pamplona, Spain: Ediciones Universidad de Navarra, 1998.

Andrews, Naomi J. "Breaking the Ties: French Romantic Socialism and the Critique of Liberal Slave Emancipation." *The Journal of Modern History* 85, no. 3 (2013): 489–527.

———. "D'Eichthal and Urbain's *Lettres sur la race noire et la race blanche*: Race, Gender and Reconciliation after Slave Emancipation." *Nineteenth-Century French Studies* 39, nos. 3–4 (2011): 240–58.

Anes, Rafael. *Comerciantes-banqueros y banqueros en los orígenes de la banca regional asturiana.* PhD diss., Facultad de Ciencias Económicas, Universidad de Oviedo, 1985.

Aranzadi, Juan. "Historia y nacionalismos en España hoy." In *La Cultura de la Memoria*, ed. Ignacio Olmos and Nikky Keilholz-Rühle, 159–70. Frankfurt: Verveurt, 2009.

Arbó, Sebastián Juan. *Pío Baroja y su tiempo.* Barcelona: Planeta, 1964.

Archivo Histórico Nacional (Madrid). "Mujeres nacidas en las Antillas." Legajo 3554/3 N. 30.

Arenas, Nani. "Iconos de la prosperidad indiana." *El País.* August 14, 2004. http://elviajero.elpais.com/articulo/viajes/Iconos/%20prosperidad/indiana/elpviavia/20040814elpviavje_3/Tes. *Accessed November 29, 2010.*

Aristotle. "Physics." In *The Basic Works of Aristotle.* Ed. Richard McKeon, 218–397. New York: Random House, 1941.

———. "Politics." In *The Basic Works of Aristotle.* Ed. Richard McKeon, 1127–324. New York: Random House, 1941.

Arrieta, Emilio, and Antonio García Gutiérrez. *El capitán negrero.* Madrid: Administración Lírico-dramática, 1865.

Arroyo, Jossianna. *Writing Secrecy in Caribbean Freemasonry.* New York: Palgrave Macmillan, 2013.

Atencia, José Manuel. "El barco de los paria." *El País.* February 13, 2007. http://elpais.com/diario/2007/02/13/andalucia/1171322533_850215.html. Accessed December 15, 2013.

Ayguals de Izco, Wencesalo. "¡Escándalo!" *El Fandango.* December 15, 1845, 203.

———. *María la hija de un jornalero, historia-novela original.* Madrid: Imprenta de D. W. Ayguals de Izco, 1847.

———. *La marquesa de Bellaflor; ó, El niño de la inclusa. Historia-novela original.* Madrid: Imprenta de D. Wencesalao Ayguals de Izco, 1846–47.

———. *Palacio de los crimenes.* 3d ed. Madrid: n.p., 1869.

B*** "Biografia." In *La choza de Tomas*, ed. Mellado, iii–vii. N.p.: n.p., 1853.

———. "Mistress Enriqueta Beecher-Stowe, y su novela." *El Universo Pintoresco.* July 15, 1853, 1–2.

Bach, Raymond. "Recurring Characters in Modiano's Oeuvre." In *Paradigms of Memory: The Occupation and Other Hi/Stories in the Novels of Patrick Modiano*, ed. Martine Guyot-Bender and William VanderWolk, 165–79. New York: Peter Lang, 1998.

Bahamonde Magro, Ángel, and José Cayuela. *Hacer las Américas: Las elites coloniales españolas en el siglo XIX.* Madrid: Alianza Editorial, 1992.

Bakhtiarova, Galina. "Americanos, indianos, mulatas y otros: Cataluña y Cuba entre el deseo colonial y la nostalgia imperial." In *Memoria colonial e inmigración: La negritud en la España posfranquista*, ed. Rosalía Cornejo Parriego, 39–52. Barcelona: Edicions Bellaterra, 2007.

Bakhtin, Mikhail. *The Dialogic Imagination: Four Essays*. Ed. Michael Holquist; trans. Caryl Emerson and Michael Holquist. Austin: University of Texas Press, 1981.

Balmes, Jaume. "Espartero: Sucesos de Barcelona." In *La Sociedad: Revista religiosa, filosófica, política y literaria*, vol. 2, 145–212. Barcelona: A Brusi, 1843.

Barbulo, Tomás. "El buque 'negrero' zarpó de Dakar 15 días antes de llegar a Tenerife." *El País*. April 20, 2001. http://elpais.com/diario/2001/04/20/espana/987717616_850215.html. Accessed May 12, 2012.

———. "Cazado el negrero del 'Ashva'." *El Pais*. May 26, 2001. http://elpais.com/diario/2001/05/26/ultima/990828001_850215.html. Accessed October 8, 2010.

"Barcelona, contra el Marqués de Comillas." *El Diario Montañés*. October 18, 2010. http://blogs.eldiariomontanes.es/elmarquesdecomillas/. Accessed November 17, 2010.

Baroja, Pío. *La estrella del capitán Chimista*. Ed. Juan María Marín Martínez. Madrid: Anaya, 2003.

———. *Las inquietudes de Shanti Andía*. Ed. Julio Caro Baroja. Madrid: Caro Raggio/Cátedra, 2007.

———. *Mala hierba. La lucha por la vida II*. Ed. Juan María Marín Martínez. Madrid: Cátedra, 2010.

———. "El mar y el marino." In *Obras completas*, vol. 5, 785–87. Madrid: Nueva, 1948.

———. *Momentum catastrophicum*. Madrid: Caro Raggio, 1919.

———. *Los pilotos de altura*. Ed. Juan María Marín Martínez. Madrid: Anaya, 2002.

Barón Crespo, Mariano. "España ante la esclavitud" *El país*. March 27, 2007. elpais.com/diario/2007/03/27/opinion/1174946405_850215.html. Accessed December 28, 2013.

Benítez, Rubén. *Ideología del folletín español: Wenceslao Ayguals de Izco (1801–1873)*. Madrid: J. Porrúa, 1979.

Bergad, Laird W., Fe Iglesias García, and María del Carmen Barcia. *The Cuban Slave Market, 1790–1880*. New York: Cambridge University Press, 1995.

Bermúdez, Silvia. "Rocking the Boat: The Black Atlantic in Spanish Pop Music from the 1980s and the 90s." *Arizona Journal of Hispanic Cultural Studies* 5 (2001): 177–93.

Blanc y Navarro, Luis. *Romper cadenas*. Madrid: Imprenta de la Asociación del Arte de Imprimir, 1873.

Blanco, Alda. *Cultura y conciencia imperial en la España del siglo XIX*. Valencia, Spain: Publicaciones de la Universitat de València, 2012.

———. Introduction to *Lo prohibido*, by Benito Pérez Galdós, 5–34. Ed. Alda Blanco. Madrid: Akal Ediciones, 2006.

———. "Spain at the Crossroads: Imperial Nostalgia or Modern Colonialism?" *A Contra Corriente* 5, no. 1 (2007): 1–11.

Blanco White, Joseph. *Bosquexo del comercio en esclavos: y reflexiones sobre este tráfico considerado moral, política, y cristianamente*. London: Ellerton and Henderson, 1814.

Blinkhorn, Martin. "Spain: The 'Spanish Problem' and The Imperial Myth." *Journal of Contemporary History* 15, no. 1 (1980): 5–25.

Bly, Peter. "The Philosopher of History: *El amigo de Manso*." In *Galdós's Novel of the Historical Imagination: A Study of the Contemporary Novels*, 134–41. Liverpool, UK: Francis Cairns, 1986.

"Boletín del día." *La Época* (Madrid). October 24, 1852, 2.

"Boletín del día." *La Época* (Madrid). October 29, 1852, 1.

Bosch, Álex. "Cuba en la literatura catalana contemporánea." *Cuadernos Hispanoamericanos* 648 (2004): 63–71.

Botrel, Jean-François. "La novela por entregas: Unidad de creación y de consumo." In *Creación y público en la literatura española*, ed. Jean-François Botrel and Serge Salaün, vol. 5, 111–55. Madrid: Editorial Castalia, 1974.

Braña, Alejandro. *Asturias, tierra de indianos: Rutas para descubrir su legado*. Meres, Asturias, Spain: Ediciones Nuevedoce, 2010.

Bretz, Mary Lee. *La evolución novelística de Pío Baroja*. Madrid: Studia Humanitatis, 1979.

Britt Arredondo, Christopher. *Quixotism: The Imaginative Denial of Spain's Loss of Empire*. Albany: State University of New York Press, 2005.

Brooks, Peter. *Troubling Confessions: Speaking Guilt in Law and Literature*. Chicago: University of Chicago Press, 2000.

Buergo, Guillermo F. "La huella del indiano." *El Comercio*. April 11, 2010. http://www.elcomerciodigital.com/v/20100411/oriente/huella-indiano-20100411.html. Accessed October 1, 2010.

Burton, Antoinette. "Introduction: On the Inadequacy and the Indispensability of the Nation." In *After the Imperial Turn: Thinking with and Through the Nation*, 1–23. Durham, NC, and London: Duke University Press, 2003.

Cabrera, Mercedes, Antonio Elorza, Javier Valero, and Matilde Vázquez. "Datos para un estudio cuantitativo de la prensa diaria madrileña, 1850–1875." In *Prensa y sociedad en España*, ed. Manuel Tuñón de Lara, Antonio Elorza, and Manuel Pérez Ledesma, 47–148. Madrid: Cuadernos para el Diálogo, 1975.

California. *California's Slavery Era Insurance Registry SB2119*. August 2000. http://www.insurance.ca.gov/0100-consumers/0300-public-programs/0200-slavery-era-insur. Accessed on December 3, 2010.

"Cantabria, tierra de indianos." *El Diario Montañés*. May 16, 2010. www.eldiario

montanes.es/v/20100516/cantabria/cantabria-tierra-indianos-20100516.html. Accessed October 1, 2010.

Carsten, Janet, and Stephen High-Jones. Introduction to *About the House: Lévi-Strauss and Beyond*, 1–46. New York: Cambridge University Press, 1995.

Casanovas, Joan. *Bread, or Bullets!: Urban Labor and Spanish Colonialism in Cuba, 1850–1898*. Pittsburgh, PA: University of Pittsburgh Press, 1998.

C[asariego], J[osé] E[varisto]. "La fundación 'Bella Vista,' de los hermanos García Fernández, en Tucumán: Una historia ejemplar del esfuerzo español en América." *ABC* (Madrid). May 4, 1956.

Casino, Xavi. *Tren de venganza*. Barcelona: Roca Editorial de Libros, S. L., 2010.

Caudet, Francisco. Introduction to *El amigo Manso*, by Benito Pérez Galdós, 9–126. Madrid: Cátedra, 2001.

Cayuela Fernández, José G. *Bahía de Ultramar: España y Cuba en el siglo XIX. El control de las relaciones coloniales*. Madrid: Siglo Veintiuno Editores, 1993.

Cervantes-Rodríguez, Margarita. *International Migration in Cuba: Accumulation, Imperial Designs, and Transnational Social Fields*. University Park: Pennsylvania State University Press, 2011.

Cervantes, Miguel de Saavedra. *Don Quixote*. Trans. Edith Grossman. New York: HarperCollins, 2003.

———. *Don Quijote de la Mancha*. Ed. Francisco Rico. Barcelona: Crítica, 2001.

Césaire, Aimé. *Discourse on Colonialism*. Trans. Joan Pinkham. New York: Monthly Review Press, 1972.

Ciplijauskaité, Biruté. "Distancia como estilo en Pío Baroja." *Ínsula* 26 (1971): 1–10. Reprinted in *Modernismo y 98*, ed. José-Carlos Mainer, 355–61. Barcelona: Crítica, 1980.

Coffey, Mary. "Un curso de filosofía práctica: Galdós's Assessment of Spanish Colonial History." *Anales Galdosianos* 38–39 (2003–4): 49–67.

Cohen, Margaret. "Traveling Genres." *New Literary History* 34, no. 3 (2003): 481–99.

Concha, José de la. *Memorias sobre el estado político, gobierno y administración de la Isla de Cuba*. Madrid: J. Trujillo, 1853.

Conlon, Joy Margaret Ann. "Empire and Emigration: The Representation of the *indiano* in Nineteenth- and Twentieth-Century Spanish Literature." PhD diss., Department of Spanish and Portuguese, Stanford University, 2002.

Connerton, Paul. *How Modernity Forgets*. Cambridge: Cambridge University Press, 2009.

———. *How Societies Remember*. New York: Cambridge University Press, 1989.

Coopan, Vilashini. "Hauntologies of Form: Race, Genre, and the Literary World System." *Gramma: Journal of Theory and Criticism* 13 (2005): 71–86.

Cooper, Barbara T. "*Le Docteur noir*: A French Romantic Drama in Blackface." *French Forum* 28, no. 1 (2003): 77–90.

Corbitt, Duvon C. "A Petition for the Continuation of O'Donnell as Captain

General of Cuba." *The Hispanic American Historical Review* 16, no. 4 (1936): 537–43.

Cornejo Parriego, Rosalía. "*Por el cielo y más allá* de Carme Riera: Fluctuaciones y fijaciones raciales en un folletín colonialista." *Cincinnati Romance Review* 30 (2011): 3–16.

Corrales Egea, José. "De *La sensualidad pervertida* a *La estrella del Capitán Chimista*." In *Baroja y su mundo*, ed. Fernando Baeza, vol. 1, 183–206. Madrid: Arión, 1962.

"Correo Estrangero." *La nación* (Madrid). January 30, 1853, 2.

Cortes Constituyentes. *Diario de Sesiones de las Cortes Constituyentes*. June 17, 1870, 8914.

Cortés, José Miguel G. *Orden y caos: Un estudio cultural sobre lo monstruoso en las artes*. Barcelona: Editorial Anagrama, S. A., 1997.

Cortés López, José Luis. *La esclavitud negra en la España peninsular del siglo XVI*. Salamanca, Spain: Ediciones Universidad de Salamanca, 1989.

Corwin, Arthur F. *Spain and the Abolition of Slavery in Cuba, 1817–1886*. Austin: University of Texas Press, 1967.

"Crónica de teatros." *El Clamor Público*. March 29, 1853: 4.

La cuestión de Cuba en 1884. Madrid: Aurelio J. Alaria, 1885.

Curtin, Philip. *The Atlantic Slave Trade: A Census*. Madison: University of Wisconsin Press, 1969.

Delgado, Luisa Elena. "El lugar del salvaje (Galdós y la representación del indiano)." In *Homenaje a Alfonso Armas Ayala*, 303–13. Las Palmas de Gran Canaria, Spain: Cabildo, 2000.

Domingo Acebrón, María Dolores. *Los voluntarios y su papel contrarrevolucionario en la Guerra de los Diez Años en Cuba, 1868–1878: Les corps de volontaires et leur rôle contre-révolutionnaire dans la Guerre de Dix Ans à Cuba, 1868–1878*. Paris: L'Harmattan, 1996.

Domínguez Búrdalo, José. "Castradas señas de identidad: Cuba en la obra de Juan Goytisolo." *Arizona Journal for Hispanic Cultural Studies* 10, no. 1 (2006): 131–50.

Dormoy, Géraldine. "Jean-Paul Guerlain fâche en parlant des 'nègres.'" *L'express*. Style section, October 18, 2010. http://www.lexpress.fr/styles/mode-beaute/beaute/jean-paul-guerlain-fache-en-parlant-des-negres_928689.html. Accessed November 1, 2010.

Douglas, Adam. *The Beast Within*. New York: Avon Books, 1992.

Dumanoir, Philippe M., and Adolphe d'Ennery. *La case de l'oncle Tom: Drame en huit actes*. Paris: Michel Lévy Frères, 1853.

DuPont, Denise. *Realism as Resistance: Romanticism and Authorship in Galdós, Clarín and Baroja*. Lewisburg, PA: Bucknell University Press, 2006.

Eaude, Michael. *Catalonia: A Cultural History*. Oxford: Oxford University Press, 2007.

Editorial Juventud. *Dinero negro, Rafael Escolà*. http://www.editorialjuventud.es/3820.html. Accessed January 20, 2013.

"El Ayuntamiento estrena la señalización de la ruta Indiana." *El Comercio Digital*. April 12, 2006. http://www.elcomerciodigital.com/pg060412/prensa/noticias/Oriente/200604/12/GIJ-ORI-090.html. Accessed January 28, 2014.

"El CNI admite que vigila posibles barcos 'negreros.'" *El País*. October 26, 2007. http://elpais.com/diario/2007/10/26/espana/1193349602_850215.html. Accessed December 5, 2013.

Ely, Roland T. *Cuando reinaba su majestad el azúcar; Estudio histórico-sociológico de una tragedia latinoamericana: El monocultivo en Cuba, origen y evolución del proceso*. Buenos Aires: Editorial Sudamericana, 1963.

Epps, Bradley S. "Al sur y al este: la vertiente africana de los estudios transatlánticos postcoloniales." In *Estudios transatlánticos postcoloniales*, ed. Ileana Rodríguez and Josebe Martínez, vol. 1, 121–60. Mexico City: Anthropos-Universidad Autónoma Metropolitana, 2010.

———. *Significant Violence: Oppression and Resistance in the Narratives of Juan Goytisolo, 1970–1990*. Oxford: Oxford University Press, 1996.

———. "Thievish Subjectivity: Self-Writing in Jean Genet and Juan Goytisolo." *Revista de Estudios Hispánicos* 26 (1992): 163–81.

Escolà Tarrida, Rafael. *Dinero negro: Una historia de negreros catalanes*. Barcelona: Editorial Juventud, 2010.

Escriche, Joaquín. *Diccionario razonado de legislación y jurisprudencia*. Madrid: Imprenta de E. Cuesta, 1851.

Espada Burgos, Manuel. *Alfonso XII y los orígenes de la Restauración*. 2d ed. Madrid: CSIC, 1990.

Fanon, Frantz. *The Wretched on the Earth*. Trans. Constance Farrington. New York: Grove Press, 1968.

Federación Asturiana de Concejos. "Bases de Datos." http://www.facc.info/Contenido.aspx?Id=197&mn=2. Accessed on January 7, 2011.

Fernández, James D. "A Life of Reading, the Readings of a Life: Joseph Blanco White." *Revista de Estudios Hispánicos* 24, no. 2 (1990): 121–42.

———. "La novela familiar del autobiógrafo: Juan Goytisolo." *Anthropos* 125 (1991): 54–60.

Fernández, Pura. *Mujer pública y vida privada: Del arte eunuco a la novela lupanaria*. Rochester, NY: Tamesis, 2008.

Fernández Cifuentes, Luis. "Apasionadas simetrías: sobre la identidad del 98." *Anales de la literatura española* 22, no. 1 (1997): 103–30.

Fernández Navarrete, Martín. *Diccionario marítimo español*. Madrid: Imprenta Real, 1831.

Fischer, Sibylle. *Modernity Disavowed: Haiti and the Cultures of Slavery in the Age of Revolution*. Durham, NC: Duke University Press, 2004.

"Folletín. Revista de Teatros." *Diario Español* (Madrid). April 11, 1853, 1.

Foucault, Michel. *The History of Madness*. Ed. Jean Khalfa. Trans. Jonathan Murphy and Jean Khalfa. New York: Routledge, 2006.

Fradera, Josep Maria. *Colonias para después de un imperio*. Barcelona: Bellaterra, 2005.

———. *Indústria i mercat: Les bases comercials de la industria catalana moderna (1814–1845)*. Barcelona: Crítica, 1987.

———. "La participació catalana en el tràfic e'esclaus (1789–1845)." *Recerques* 16 (1984): 119–39.

———, et al. *Catalunya i Ultramar. Poder i negoci a les colonies espanyoles (1760–1914)*. Barcelona: Ambit Serveis Editorials, 1995.

Franco, José Luciano. *Comercio clandestino de esclavos*. Havana: Editorial de Ciencias Sociales, 1980.

"Gacetilla de la capital." *El Heraldo* (Madrid). March 29, 1853, 4.

Gallego, Joan Carles, and Josep M. Àlvarez, to Jordi Hereu, October 6, 2010. UGT Archive, Catalonia.

García Mariño, Francisco A. *Unos bonos sin abono: Injusticias sufridas por los suscritores al patriótico empréstito de 9 de agosto de 1872, colocado en la isla de Cuba en 31 de enero de 1873*. Madrid: Imp. Aurelio J. Alaria, 1881.

Gascon i Soler, Marc. "Les origines de l'industrie mécanique moderne en Catalogne: L'exemple de l'atelier de l'*indiano* Joan Domènech i Coll (1839–1867)." *Méditerranée* 106 (2006): 39–48.

Gies, David Thatcher. *The Theatre in Nineteenth-Century Spain*. New York: Cambridge University Press, 1994.

Gifra Adroher, Pere. "Ramón de Valladares, traductor y adaptador de *Uncle Tom's Cabin*." In *Traducción y traductores, del Romanticismo al Realismo*, ed. Francisco Lafarga and Luis Pegenaute, 217–29. New York: Peter Lang, 2006.

Gilman, Stephen. *Galdós and the Art of the European Novel, 1867–1887*. Princeton, NJ: Princeton University Press, 1981.

Gilmore, David D. *Monsters: Evil Beings, Mythical Beasts, and All Manner of Imaginary Terrors*. Philadelphia: University of Pennsylvania Press, 2003.

Gomáriz, José. "Francisco de Arango y Parreño: El discurso esclavista de la ilustración cubana." *Cuban Studies* 35 (2004): 45–61.

González López, Emilio. *El arte narrativo de Pío Baroja: Las trilogías*. New York: Las Américas, 1971.

Goode, Joshua Seth. *Impurity of Blood: Defining Race in Spain, 1870–1930*. Baton Rouge: Louisiana State University Press, 2009.

Goytisolo, Juan. *Blanco White, El Español y la independencia de Hispanoamérica: Con una selección de textos de José María Blanco White*. Madrid: Taurus, 2010.

———. *Coto vedado*. Barcelona: Seix Barral, 1985.

———. *Juan sin tierra*. Barcelona: Seix Barral, 1977.

———. *Juan the Landless*. Trans. Peter Bush. Champaign, IL: Dalkey Archive Press, 2009.

———. *Marks of Identity*. Trans. Gregory Rabassa. New York: Grove Press, 1969.

———. "Recuperación de una figura: José María Blanco White." In *Blanco White: El Español y la independencia de Hispanoamérica*, ed. Juan Goytisolo, 13–84. Madrid: Taurus, 2010.

———. *Señas de identidad*. Mexico City: J. M[ortiz], 1966.

Graham, Brian, and Michael Murray. "The Spiritual and the Profane: The Pilgrimage to Santiago de Compostela." *Cultural Geographies* 4, no. 4 (1997): 389–409.

Gregoire, Henri. *Des peines infamantes à infliger aux négriers*. Paris: Baudouin Frères, 1822.

Gullón, Germán. "La cultura finisecular española y el imperialismo: 1898 (Cuba, España y Norteamérica)." In *La Generación del 98 frente al nuevo fin de siglo*, ed. Jesús Torrecilla, 91–116. Amsterdam: Rodopi, 2000.

Gullón, Ricardo. *Galdós, novelista moderno*. Madrid: Gredos, 1966.

Havana. "Representación del Consulado de la Habana de 21 de octubre de 1818." In *Observaciones sobre la suerte de los negros del Afirca, considerados en su propia patria, y transplantados á las Antillas Españolas: Y reclamación contra el tratado celebrado con los ingleses el año de 1817*. Madrid: Imprenta del Universal, 1821.

Hall, Catherine, and Sonya Rose. "Introduction: Being at Home with the Empire." In *At Home with the Empire: Metropolitan Culture and the Imperial World*, ed. Catherine Hall and Sonya Rose, 1–31. New York: Cambridge University Press, 2006.

Hall, Stuart. "When Was 'the Post-Colonial'? Thinking at the Limit." *The Post-Colonial Question: Common Skies, Divided Horizons*, ed. Iain Chambers and Lidia Curti, 242–60. New York: Routledge, 1996.

Hannaford, Ivan. *Race: The History of an Idea in the West*. Washington, DC: Woodrow Wilson Center Press, 1996.

Hartman, Saidiya. "The Time of Slavery." *South Atlantic Quarterly* 101, no. 4 (2002): 757–77.

Hartzenbusch, Eugenio. *Apuntes para un catálogo de periódicos madrileños desde el año 1661 hasta 1870*. Madrid: Biblioteca Nacional, Oller y Ramos, D.L., 1993.

Herzog, Tamar. *Defining Nations: Immigrants and Citizens in Early Modern Spain and Spanish America*. New Haven, CT: Yale University Press, 2003.

Hill, Ruth. *Hierarchy, Commerce, and Fraud in Bourbon Spanish America: A Postal Inspector's Exposé*. Nashville, TN: Vanderbilt University Press, 2005.

Hulme, Peter. "Subversive Archipelagos: Colonial Discourse and the Break-Up of Continental Theory." *Dispositio* 14, nos. 36–38 (1989): 1–23.

Iarocci, Michael. *Properties of Modernity: Romantic Spain, Modern Europe, and the Legacies of Empire*. Nashville, TN: Vanderbilt University Press, 2006.

Jacobson, Stephen. "Imperial Ambitions in an Era of Decline: Micromilitarism and the Eclipse of the Spanish Empire, 1858–1923." In *Endless Empire: Spain's Retreat, Europe's Eclipse, and America's Decline*, ed. Alfred W. McCoy, Josep M.

Fradera, and Stephen Jacobson, 74–91. Madison: University of Wisconsin Press, 2012.

Jagoe, Catherine. *Ambiguous Angels: Gender in the Novels of Galdós*. Berkeley: University of California Press, 1994.

Jovellanos, Gaspar Melchor de. "Carta Sexta [a Ponz]. Agricultura y propiedades de Asturias." In *Obras publicadas e inéditas de Don Gaspar Melchor de Jovellanos*, ed. Cándido Nocedal, vol. 2, 290–94. Madrid: M. Rivadeneyra, 1859.

Kanellos, Nicolás. *A History of Hispanic Theatre in the United States: Origins to 1940*. Austin: University of Texas Press, 1990.

Kaplan, Cora. "Imagining Empire: History, Fantasy and Literature." In *At Home with the Empire: Metropolitan Culture and the Imperial World*, ed. Catherine Hall and Sonya Rose, 191–211. New York: Cambridge University Press, 2006.

Katzew, Ilona. *Casta Painting: Images of Race in Eighteenth-Century Mexico*. New Haven, CT: Yale University Press, 2004.

Keown, Dominic. "Contemporary Catalan Culture." In *A Companion to Catalan Culture*, ed. Dominic Keown, 13–40. Woodbridge, UK: Tamesis, 2011.

Kirkpatrick, Susan. *Las Románticas: Women Writers and Subjectivity in Spain, 1835–1850*. Berkeley: University of California Press, 1989.

Knight, Franklin W. "Origins of Wealth and the Sugar Revolution in Cuba, 1750–1850." *Hispanic American Historical Review* 57, no. 2 (1977): 231–53.

Kowaleski-Wallace, Elizabeth. *The British Slave Trade and Public Memory*. New York: Columbia University Press, 2006.

Kronik, John W. "Galdós and the Grotesque." *Anales Galdosianos, Anejo* (1978): 39–52.

Labanyi, Jo. *Gender and Modernization in the Spanish Realist Novel*. Oxford: Oxford University Press, 2000.

Lamb, Ursula. *Cosmographers and Pilots of the Spanish Maritime Empire*. London: Variorum, 1995.

Lanero, Juan José, and Secundino Villoria. "Primeras traducciones españolas de 'La cabaña del tío Tom.'" *Livius* 8 (1996): 99–119.

Larra, Luis M. "La poetisa." *El Universo Pintoresco* (Madrid). July 15, 1853, 2.

Larra Plaza, Iván. *Barco negrero*. 2000. Imprint on wooded fiber plate. Biblioteca Nacional de España, Madrid.

———. *Barco negrero II*. 2003. Xylograph. Private collection.

———. *Barco negrero VIII*. 2003. Xylopgrah on wood plate. Private collection.

———. *Cross-Docking*. 2004. 16 Xylographs. Galería Zambucho Ediciones, Madrid.

———. *Migración*. 2003. Xylograph. Private collection.

Levine, Alan. *Sensual Philosophy: Toleration, Skepticism, and Montaigne's Politics of the Self.* Lanham, MD: Lexington Books, 2001.

"Libros prohibidos por Su Santidad." *La Censura*. October 1853, n.p.

Linebaugh, Peter, and Marcus Rediker. *The Many-Headed Hydra: Sailors, Slaves,*

Commoners, and the Hidden History of the Revolutionary Atlantic. Boston: Beacon Press, 2000.

López-Baralt, Mercedes. *La gestación de Fortunata y Jacinta: Galdós y la novela como re-escritura*. Río Piedras, Puerto Rico: Ediciones Huracán, 1992.

López Marcano, Francisco Javier. "Prólogo." Preface to *Juan Manuel Manzanedo y González. Primer marqués de Manzanedo, primer duque de Santoña*, by Manuel Adolfo Muela, 1–20. Santander, Spain: Consejería de Cultura, Turismo y Deporte del Gobierno de Cantabria, 2005.

Loureiro, Angel. *The Ethics of Autobiography: Replacing the Subject in Modern Spain*. Nashville, TN: Vanderbilt University Press, 2000.

———. "Spanish Nationalism and the Ghost of Empire." *Journal of Spanish Cultural Studies* 4, no. 1 (2003): 65–76.

Lourens, Marlien. "Route Tourism: A Roadmap for Successful Destinations and Local Economic Development." *Development Southern Africa* 24, no. 3 (2007): 475–90.

Luis, William. *Literary Bondage: Slavery in Cuban Narrative*. Austin: University of Texas Press, 1990.

Luna, Ángel de, and Rafael Leopoldo Palomino. *Haley, ó, el traficante de negros: Drama en cuatro actos, en prosa*. Cádiz, Spain: Pantoja, 1853.

MacKay, Ruth. "History on the Line. The Good Fight and Good History: The Spanish Civil War." *History Workshop Journal* 70, no. 1 (2010): 199–206.

Maluquer de Motes, Jordi. "La burguesía catalana i l'esclavitud colonial: Modes de producció i pràctica política." *Recerques* 3 (1974): 83–116.

———. *Nación e inmigración: Los españoles en Cuba (ss. XIX y XX)*. Barcelona: Ediciones Júcar, 1992.

Martí-López, Elisa. *Borrowed Words: Translation, Imitation, and the Making of the Nineteenth-Century Novel in Spain*. Lewisburg, PA: Bucknell University Press, 2002.

Martin-Márquez, Susan. *Disorientations: Spanish Colonialism in Africa and the Performance of Identity*. New Haven, CT: Yale University Press, 2008.

Martinez, Jenny. *The Slave Trade and the Origins of International Human Rights Law*. New York: Oxford University Press, 2012.

Martínez Martín, Jesús A. *Historia de la edición en España, 1836–1936*. Madrid: Marcial Pons, 2002.

Martínez Shaw, Carlos. *La emigración española a América (1492–1824)*. Colombres, Spain: Fundación Archivo de Indianos, 1994.

Matthews, Christopher. "The Location of Archeology." In *Ethnographic Archaeologies: Reflections on Stakeholders and Archaeological Practices*, ed. Quetzil E. Castañeda and Christopher Matthews, 157–82. Lanham, MD: AltaMira, 2008.

McGovern, Timothy. *Galdós Beyond Realism: Reading and the Creation of Magical Worlds*. Newark, DE: Juan de la Cuesta, 2004.

Medina, F. Javier, and Jordi Tresserras. "Turismo enológico y rutas del vino en

Cataluña. Análisis de casos: D.O. Penedès, D.O. Priorat y D.O. Montsant." *Pasos* 6, no. 3 (2008): 493–509.

Mejías-López, Alejandro. "*Modernismo*'s Inverted Conquest and the Ruins of Imperial Nostalgia: Rethinking the Hispanic Atlantic in Contemporary Critical Discourse." *Arizona Journal of Hispanic Cultural Studies* 12 (2008): 1–23.

Mencos Valdés, Eduardo, and Anneli Bojstad. *Indianos: La gran aventura*. Madrid: Antonio Machado, 2004.

Menéndez y Pelayo, Marcelino. *Historia de los heterodoxos españoles*. 2 vols. Madrid: Homo Legens, 2011.

Meyer, Dorothea. "Tourism Routes and Gateways: Key Issues for the Development of Tourism Routes and Gateways and their Potential for Pro-Poor Tourism." Overseas Development Institute. April 2004. http://www.odi.org.uk. Accessed on November 8, 2010.

Mignolo, Walter. *Local Histories/Global Designs: Coloniality, Subaltern Knowledges, and Border Thinking*. Princeton, NJ: Princeton University Press, 2000.

Miller, Christopher L. *The French Atlantic Triangle: Literature and Culture of the Slave Trade*. Durham, NC: Duke University Press, 2008.

Montesinos, José. *Galdós*. 3 vols. Madrid: Editorial Castalia, 1968.

Moreno Fraginals, Manuel. *El ingenio*. Havana: Editorial de Ciencias Sociales, 1978.

Murphy, G. Martin, and André Pons. "Further Letters of Blanco White to Robert Southey." *BHS* 62, no. 4 (1985): 357–72.

Murray, David R. *Odious Commerce: Britain, Spain, and the Abolition of the Cuban Slave Trade*. New York: Cambridge University Press, 1980.

Naranjo Orovio, Consuelo, and Miguel Ángel Puig-Samper Mulero. "El legado hispano y la conciencia nacional en Cuba." *Revista de Indias* 50, no. 190 (1990): 789–808.

Navajas, Gonzalo. "Confession and Ethics in Juan Goytisolo's Fictive Autobiographies." *Letras Peninsulares* 3, nos. 2–3 (1990): 259–78.

Nerlich, Michael. *The Ideology of Adventure: Studies in Modern Consciousness, 1100–1750*. Trans. Ruth Crowley. Minneapolis: Minnesota University Press, 1987.

"Novedades." *Las novedades*. March 23, 1853, 1.

"Los nuevos negreros." *El País*. May 8, 2000, 1.

Oficina de Turismo de Comillas. "Ruta del modernismo: Comillas más que un capricho" (map). N.p.

O'Gavan, Juan Bernardo. *Observaciones sobre la suerte de los negros del Africa, considerados en su propia patria, y transplantados á las Antillas Españolas: Y reclamación contra el tratado celebrado con los ingleses el año de 1817*. Madrid: Imprenta del Universal, 1821.

Ojeda, Germán, and José Luis San Miguel. *Campesinos, Emigrantes, Indianos*. Salinas, Asturias, Spain: Ayalga, 1985.

Ojito, Mirta. "Family Vacations: In Old Asturias, a Legacy from the New World." *New York Times*. February 13, 2005, E8.

Oostinde, Gert. "The Slippery Paths of Commemoration and Heritage Tourism: The Netherlands, Ghana, and the Rediscovery of Atlantic Slavery." *New West Indian Guide* 79, nos. 1–2 (2005): 55–77.

Ortiz, Fernando. *Contrapunto cubano del tabaco y el azúcar: (advertencia de sus contrastes agrarios, económicos, históricos y sociales, su etnografía y su tranculturación)*. Ed. Enrico Mario Santí. Madrid: Cátedra, 2002.

Ott, Oliver. "Le personnage de l'indiano dans *La tierra de Alvargonzález*." *Cahiers du GRIAS* 11 (2004): 83–114.

Padrón, Ricardo. *The Spacious Word: Cartography, Literature, and Empire in Early Modern Spain*. Chicago: University of Chicago Press, 2004.

Pagden, Anthony. *Lords of All the World: Ideologies of Empire in Spain, Britain and France c.1500–c.1800*. New Haven, CT: Yale University Press, 1994.

Palau y Dulcet, Antonio. *Manual del librero hispanoamericano*. 2d ed., vol. 22, 1948–77. Barcelona: Editorial Palau Dulcet, 1990.

"Parte Política." *El Heraldo*. December 30, 1852, n.p.

"Parte Política. Ministerio de Estado." *El Heraldo*. February 22, 1853, 1–2.

Pérez Galdós, Benito. "Amadeo I." In *Obras Completas, Episodios Nacionales*, ed. Federico Carlos Sainz de Robles. 4 vols. Madrid: Aguilar, 1971.

———. *El amigo Manso*. Ed. Francisco Caudet. Madrid: Cátedra, 2001.

———. "Cánovas." In *Obras Completas, Episodios Nacionales*, ed. Federico Carlos Sainz de Robles. 4 vols. Madrid: Aguilar, 1971.

———. *La desheredada*. Ed. Enrique Miralles. Barcelona: Planeta, 1992.

———. *La familia de León Roch*. Ed. Íñigo Sánchez Llama. Madrid: Ediciones Catédra, 2003.

———. *O'Donnell*. Episodios Nacionales 4, vol. 5. Madrid: Hernando, 1909.

———. *Lo prohibido*. Ed. Alda Blanco. Madrid: Akal Ediciones, 2006.

Pérez de la Riva, Juan. "Riesgo y ventura de San Martín." *Revista de la Biblioteca Nacional José Martí* (1967): 51–58.

"El periodismo y la literatura en los Estados Unidos." *El Heraldo* (Madrid). January 16, 1853, 2.

Piqueras, José Antonio. "Censos *lato sensu*: La abolición de la esclavitud y el número de esclavos en Cuba." *Revista de Indias* 251 (2011): 193–230.

Pons, André. "Blanco White abolicionista: El Bosquexo del Comercio en esclavos, I-II." *Cuadernos Hispanoamericanos* 559–60 (1997): 29–38, 63–73.

———. "Bolívar y Blanco White." *Anuario de Estudios Americanos* 55, no. 2 (1998): 507–29.

Prados-Torreira, Teresa. *Mambisas: Rebel Women in Nineteenth Century Cuba*. Gainesville: University Press of Florida, 2005.

Prat de la Riba, Enric. "Cuba i Catalunya." December 3, 1897. In *Obra completa*,

ed. Albert Balcells and Josep M. Ainaud de Lasarte, vol. 1. Barcelona: Institut d'Estudis Catalans-Proa, 1998.
Principado de Asturias. *Concejo de Salas: Puerta de Occidente* (map). Cornellana, Spain: Consejería de Trabajo y Fomento de Empleo, 2001.
Quiroz, Alfonso W. "Implicit Costs of Empire: Bureaucratic Corruption in Nineteenth-Century Cuba." *Journal of Latin American Studies* 35, no. 3 (2003): 473–511.
Rauch, Basil. *American Interest in Cuba: 1848–1855*. New York: Columbia University Press, 1948.
Recorridos de Senderismo. "Paseo por Malleza." http://www.ayto-salas.es/portal_localweb/RecursosWeb/DOCUMENTOS/2/0_295_1.pdf. Accessed on January 3, 2011.
Rediker, Marcus. *The Slave Ship: A Human History*. New York: Viking, 2007.
Redondo, Agustín. "Burlas y veras: La Princesa Micomicona y Sancho negrero (I, 29)." *Edad de Oro* 15 (1996): 125–40.
Reinhardt, Catherine. *Claims to Memory: Beyond Slavery and Emancipation in the French Caribbean*. New York: Berghahn Books, 2006.
Resina, Joan Ramon. "*Pepita Jiménez*: del idilio a la Restauración." *BHS* 72 (1995): 175–93.
Richards, Jeffrey. Introduction to *Imperialism and Juvenile Literature*, 1–11. Manchester, UK: Manchester University Press, 1989.
Richards, Sandra. "What Is to Be Remembered? Tourism to Ghana's Castle-Dungeons." *Theatre Journal* 57, no. 4 (2005): 617–37.
Riera, Carme. *Cap al cel obert*. Barcelona: Ediciones Destino, 2000.
———. *Por el cielo y más allá*. Madrid: Alfaguara, 2001.
Ringrose, David R. *Madrid and the Spanish Economy, 1560–1850*. Berkeley and Los Angeles: University of California Press, 1983.
———. *Transportation and Economic Stagnation in Spain, 1750–1850*. Durham, NC: Duke University Press, 1970.
Ríos-Font, Wadda. "Forbidden Transactions: The Economic Realism of Benito Pérez Galdós's *Lo prohibido*." In *Studies in Honor of Vernon Chamberlin*, ed. Mark A. Harping, 165–87. Newark, DE: Juan de la Cuesta, 2011.
Rivera, Haydée. *Pío Baroja y las novelas del mar*. New York: Anaya, 1972.
Rodgers, Eamonn J. "The Unfinished Anagnorisis: The Illness and Death of José María Bueno de Guzmán in Galdós' *Lo prohibido*." In *Galdós' House of Fiction: Papers Given at the Birmingham Galdós Colloquium*, ed. Anthony Hedley Clarke, Eamonn J. Rodgers, and Kevin Mackenzie, 127–41. Llangrannog, UK: Dolphin Book Co., 1991.
Rodrigo y Alharilla, Martín. "El banco hispano-colonial y Cuba 1876–1898." *Illes i Imperis* 4 (2001): 49–70.
———. "La casa de comercio de los marqueses de Comillas (1844–1920): continuidad y cambio en el capitalismo español." In *Fortuna y negocios: formación*

y gestión de los grandes patrimonios (siglos XVI-XX), ed. Ricardo Robledo Hernández and Hilario Casado Alonso, 251–74. Valladolid, Spain: Universidad de Valladolid, 2002.

———. "Con un pie en Catalunya y otro en Cuba: la familia Samá, de Vilanova." In *Estudis històrics i documents dels arxius de protocols*, 359–98. *Barcelona: El Colegio, 1998.*

———. *La familia Gil. Empresarios catalanes en la Europa del siglo XIX*. Barcelona: Fundación Gas Natural, 2010.

———. *Indians a Catalunya: Capitals cubans en l'economia catalana*. Barcelona: Fundació Noguera, 2007.

Rogers, Paul Patrick. *The Spanish Drama Collection in the Oberlin College Library*. Oberlin, OH: Oberlin Printing, 1940.

Said, Edward W. *Culture and Imperialism*. New York: Alfred A. Knopf, 1993.

Sala-Molins, Louis. *L'Afrique aux Amériques: Le Code Noir espagnol*. Paris: Presses Universitaires de France, 1992.

———. *Le Code Noir, ou le Calvaire de Canaan*. Paris: Presses Universitaires de France, 1987.

Sánchez Aranda, José Javier, and Carlos Barrera. *Historia del periodismo español: Desde sus orígenes hasta 1975*. Pamplona, Spain: Ediciones Universidad de Navarra, 1992.

Sánchez Mazas, Rafael. "Sonetos de un verano antiguo." *Blanco y Negro*. November 30, 1919, 50.

Sánchez Sánchez, Víctor. "La habanera en la zarzuela española del siglo XIX: Idealización marinera de un mundo tropical." *Cuadernos de Música, Artes Visuales y Artes Escénicas* 3, no. 1 (2006–7): 4–26.

Santoña Oficina de Turismo. "Santoña forma parte de la nueva imagen de España en el Extranjero." *New Santoña* (2010): 16–17.

Sartre, Jean-Paul. Preface to *The Wretched on the Earth*, by Frantz Fanon, 7–31. New York: Grove Press, 1968.

Sazatornil Ruiz, Luis, ed. *Arte y mecenazgo indiano. Del Cantábrico al Caribe*. Gijón, Spain: Ediciones Trea-Fundación Carolina-MEC, 2007.

Schmidt-Nowara, Christopher. "After 'Spain': A Dialogue with Josep M. Fradera on Spanish Colonial Historiography." In *After the Imperial Turn: Thinking With and Through the Nation*, ed. Antoinette Burton, 157–69. Durham, NC: Duke University Press, 2003.

———. *The Conquest of History: Spanish Colonialism and National Histories in the Nineteenth Century*. Pittsburgh, PA: University of Pittsburgh Press, 2006.

———. *Empire and Antislavery: Spain, Cuba, and Puerto Rico, 1833–1874*. Pittsburgh, PA: University of Pittsburgh Press, 1999.

———. "'La España ultramarina': Colonialism and Nation-Building in Nineteenth-Century Spain." *European History Quarterly* 34, no. 2 (2004): 191–214.

Schubert, Adrian. *A Social History of Modern Spain*. London: Cambridge University Press, 1990.

Schulman, Ivan A. "The Portrait of the Slave: Ideology and Aesthetics in the Cuban Antislavery Novel." In *Comparative Perspectives on Slavery in New World Plantation Societies*, ed. Vera Rubin and Arthur Tuden, 356–67. New York: New York Academy of Sciences, 1977.

Schurz, Carl. *The Reminiscences of Carl Schurz*. Volume two. 1852-63. New York: The McClure Company, 1909.

Sebold, Russell. *En el principio del movimiento realista: Credo y novelística de Ayguals de Izco*. Madrid: Cátedra, 2007.

Shoemaker, W. H. "Galdós' Literary Creativity: D. José Ido del Sagrario." *Hispanic Review* 19, no. 3 (1951): 204–37.

Silverstein, Stephen Andrew. "The Jewish Slave Trader Trope in Abolitionist Discourses of the Caribbean, 1839–1882." PhD diss., Department of Spanish, University of Virginia, 2012.

Sinnigen, John H. "Cuba en Galdós: La función de las colonias en el discurso metropolitano." *Casa de las Américas* 212, no. 39 (1998): 115–21.

Smith, Norman R. "Portentous Births and the Monstrous Imagination in Renaissance Culture." In *Marvels, Monsters and Miracles: Studies in the Medieval and Early Modern Imagination*, ed. Timothy S. Jones and David A. Sprunger. Kalamazoo, MI: Medieval Institute Publications, 2002.

Sonesson, Birgit. *Catalanes en las Antillas: un estudio de casos*. Colombres, Spain: Fundación Archivo de Indianos, 1995.

Sosa Rodríguez, Enrique. *Negreros catalanes y gaditanos en la trata cubana, 1827–1833*. Havana: Fundación Fernando Ortiz, 1998.

Spain. *Constitución política de la monarquía española* (1812). In *Constituciones y códigos políticos españoles, 1808–1978*, ed. Julio Montero, 39–72. Barcelona: Ariel Practicum, 1998.

———. *Royal Order of 23 Apr. 1852 Article 8*. Cádiz, Spain: Archivo Histórico de la Provincia de Cádiz, 1852.

———. *Tratados, convenios y declaraciones de paz y comercio que han hecho con las potencias estranjeras los monarcas españoles de la casa de Borbon*. Ed. Alejandro del Cantillo. Madrid: Imprenta de Alegria y Charlain, 1843.

Stowe, Harriet Beecher. "La Cabaña del tío Tomás." *El Clamor Público* (Madrid), January 9, 1853.

———. "La Cabaña del Tío Tomás." *La Época* (Madrid). January 26, 1853.

———. "La cabaña del tío Tom." *La nación* (Madrid). January 20, 1853.

———. "La Cabaña del Tio Tomás." *Las Novedades* (Madrid). January 9, 1853.

———. *La Cabaña del Tío Tomás*. Barcelona: Imprenta de Antonio Brusi, 1853; Separata de Folletín del *Diario de Barcelona*.

———. *La cabaña del Tío Tomás*. Trans. *El Clamor Público*. Barcelona: Manuel Sauri, 1853.

———. *La cabaña del tío Tom*. Trans. A. A. Oribuela. Paris: Ignacio Boix, 1852.
———. *La cabaña del tío Tom*. Trans. A. A. Oribuela. Barcelona: Juan Olivares, 1853.
———. *La choza de Tomás*. Madrid and Paris: Francisco de Paula Mellado, 1853.
———. *La choza del negro Tomás*. Madrid: Imprenta de J. D. Marés, 1853.
———. *La choza del tío Tom*. Cádiz, Spain: Arjona, 1853.
———. *La choza de Tom*. Trans. Wencesalo Ayguals de Izco. Madrid: Ayguals de Izco Hermanos, 1852.
———. *La choza de Tom*. 2d ed. Trans. Wencesalo Ayguals de Izco. Madrid: Ayguals de Izco Hermanos, 1853.
———. *La choza del Tío Tom*. Trans. Peregrín García Cadena. Valencia: Imprenta de José Rius, 1853.
———. "La choza del tío Tom." Trans. José A. Matute. *Album Pintoresco* (Madrid). January 9, 1853.
———. *La choza de Tom*. Trans. J. P. Ruiz. Madrid: Est. Tip. De la Biblioteca Selecta, 1853.
"Teatros." *El Enano*. April 5, 1853, 2.
"Teatros." *El Heraldo*. April 2, 1853, 4.
Terry, Arthur. "*Lo prohibido*: Unreliable Narrator and Untruthful Narrative." In *Galdós Studies*, ed. John E. Varey, 62–89. London: Tamesis Books Limited, 1970.
Tomàs, Jordi. *El mar des traïdors*. Barcelona: Proa, 2013.
Tomich, Dale. "The Wealth of Empire: Francisco Arango y Parreño, Political Economy and the Second Slavery in Cuba." *Comparative Studies in Society and History* 45, no. 1 (2003): 4–28.
Torres Ramírez, Bibiano. *La Compañía Gaditana de Negros*. Sevilla: Escuela de Estudios Hispano-Americanos de Sevilla, 1973.
Tortella, Gabriel. "The Role of Banks and Government in Spanish Economic Development 1850–1935." In *The State, the Financial System, and Economic Modernization*, ed. Richard Eugene Sylla, Richard H. Tilly, and Gabriel Tortella Casares, 158–81. Cambridge: Cambridge University Press, 1999.
Tortella, Gabriel, and Francisco Comín. "Fiscal and Monetary Institutions in Spain (1600–1900)." In *Transferring Wealth and Power from the Old to the New World: Monetary and Fiscal Institutions in the 17th Through the 19th Century*, ed. Michael D. Bordo and Roberto Cortés-Conde, 140–86. New York: Cambridge University Press, 2001.
Trouillot, Michel-Rolph. *Silencing the Past: Power and the Production of History*. Boston: Beacon Press, 1995.
Turner, Harriet. "The Control of Confusion and Clarity in *El amigo Manso*." *Anales Galdosianos* XV (1980): 45–59.
Ucelay-Da Cal, Enric. *El imperialismo catalán: Prat de la Riba, Cambó, D'Ors y la conquista moral de España*. Barcelona: Edhasa, 2003.

Ugarte, Michael. *Trilogy of Treason: An Intertextual Study of Juan Goytisolo*. Columbia: University of Missouri Press, 1982.

United States War Department. *Annual Report of the Secretary of War*, vol. 1, pt. 4. Washington, DC: GPO, 1900.

Valera, Juan. *Pepita Jiménez*. Ed. Leonardo Romero. Madrid: Cátedra, 1989.

Valiña, Carmen V. "Dormir como un indiano" Público.es. September 22, 2010. http://www.publico.es/237164/dormir-como-un-indiano.

Valis, Noël. *Sacred Realism: Religion and the Imagination in Modern Spanish Narrative*. New Haven, CT: Yale University Press, 2010.

Valladares, Ramón de. *La cabaña de Tom ó la esclavitud de los negros*. 4th ed. Madrid: Sociedad de Autores Españoles, 1911.

V[allarino], B[altasar]. *El marinero africano, vida marítima del dia: Novela original*. Barcelona: Agustín Gaspar, 1844.

"Variedades." *El Clamor Público* (Madrid). January 13, 1853, 1.

La Verdad. *Cuestion negrera de la isla de Cuba por los editores y colaboradores de 'La Verdad'*. New York: Imprenta de *La verdad*, 1851.

Verdaderas causas en que don Juan Álvarez y Mendizábal ha fundado su opinión para que en la isla de Cuba no rija la constitución política de la monarquía española. Bourdeaux: n.p., 1837.

Vila Vilar, Enriqueta. *Hispanoamérica y el comercio de esclavos*. Sevilla: Escuela de Estudios Hispano-Americanos, 1977.

Vila Vilar, Enriqueta, and Luisa Vila Vilar, eds. "La abolición en España en el siglo XIX." Introduction to *Los abolicionistas españoles, siglo XIX*, 11–21. Madrid: Ediciones de Cultura Hispánica, 1996.

Villaverde, Cirilio. *Cecilia Valdés, o, La loma del Ángel*. Ed. Jean Lamore. Madrid: Cátedra, 1992.

Waters, Hazel. "Putting on 'Uncle Tom' on the Victorian Stage." *Race and Class* 42, no. 3 (2001): 29–48.

Whiston, James. "Change and Creativity in Galdós' Writing." In *New Galdós Studies: Essays in Memory of John Varey*, ed. Nicholas G. Round, 27–41. Rochester, NY: Tamesis, 2003.

———. "Ironía y psicología en *Lo prohibido* de Galdós." *Romance Quarterly* 37, no. 2 (1990): 199–208.

White, Joseph Blanco. *Bosquexo del comercio en esclavos: Y reflexiones sobre este tráfico considerado moral, política, y cristianamente*. London: Ellerton and Henderson, 1814.

Wilberforce, William. *A Letter on the Abolition of the Slave Trade; Addressed to the Freeholders and Other Inhabitants of Yorkshire*. London: Luke Hansard & Sons, 1807.

Willem, Linda M. "The Narrative Premise of Galdós's *Lo prohibido*." *Romance Quarterly* 38, no. 2 (1991): 189–96.

Williams, Claire. "Re-branding Paradise: São Tomé and Príncipe in Recent Portuguese Culture." Lecture presented at "Beyond Slavery in the Iberian Atlantic," second conference in the "Rethinking the Iberian Atlantic Series," Liverpool, September 15, 2007.

Williams, Eric Eustace. *Capitalism and Slavery*. Chapel Hill: University of North Carolina Press, 1994.

Wood, Marcus. *Blind Memory: Visual Representations of Slavery in England and America*. New York: Routledge, 2000.

Yndurain, Domingo. "Teoría de la novela en Baroja." *Cuadernos Hispanoamericanos* 233 (1969): 355–88.

Zorrilla, José. *Don Juan Tenorio*. Ed. David T. Gies. Madrid: Editorial Castalia, 1994.

Index

CPSIA information can be obtained
at www.ICGtesting.com
Printed in the USA
JSHW040007290220
4536JS00002B/2

9 781503 613645